CARDUS IN T

SCORE BOARD
80
NOT OUT

Cartoon by *PAPAS* presented to *Sir Neville Cardus on his 80th birthday*

CARDUS IN THE COVERS

Neville Cardus

Macdonald
Queen Anne Press

A QUEEN ANNE PRESS BOOK

© 1978 by Souvenir Press

First published in Great Britain in 1978 by Souvenir Press Ltd

First published in paperback in Great Britain in 1990 by
Queen Anne Press, a division of
Macdonald & Co (Publishers)
Orbit House
1 New Fetter Lane
London EC4A 1AR

A member of Maxwell Macmillan Pergamon Publishing
Corporation

Cover illustration and design: Deborah Holmes

British Library Cataloguing in Publication Data
Cardus, Neville, *1888–1975*
    Cardus in the covers.
    1. Cricket
    I. Title
    796.35′8

    ISBN 0–356–19048–X

Reproduced, printed and bound in Great Britain
by Richard Clay Ltd, Bungay, Suffolk

ACKNOWLEDGMENTS

The publishers are grateful to the editor of *The Guardian*, to Richards Press, to William Collins, to *Playfair Cricket Annual*, edited by Gordon Ross, and to Cassell & Co Ltd for their co-operation in assembling the articles in *Cardus in the Covers*. The publishers are particularly grateful to Margaret Hughes for her generous assistance in planning and compiling the book.

CONTENTS

THE CORONATION TESTS

INTRODUCTION

I CANNOT remember how I became interested in cricket. There were no games organized at the Board school which I attended more or less irregularly, morning and afternoon, from the age of eight to thirteen, when I joined the ranks of the employed.

Our games were of our own arranging. We played cricket on the fields adjacent to the semi-slums in which I lived. They were not really fields; we called them 'brickcrofts'; already the jerry-builder was at work upon 'greater Manchester'.

I must have taken very early to the game. I can clearly recall looking at the stop-press scores in the *Manchester Evening News*, and reading 'Tyldesley, b Anthony, 222", tidings of great joy from Trent Bridge, where Lancashire were that day playing 'Notts'. The date was round about 1900. It was certainly in this same summer that I entered the county cricket ground of Old Trafford for the first time, the first time of many.

More than forty years ago! Old Trafford was almost in the country then, Stretford was a village and there was no British Westinghouse. At the top of Warwick Road stood the Botanical Gardens; for some reason or other, gardens devoted to botany were supposed to serve as a means towards culture amongst the masses. I saw William Gunn in these gardens one evening; but I don't think he was studying botany. More than forty years ago, when a small boy nine years and three months old first saw the dread sign outside Old Trafford: 'The public takes its own risk of the weather. No money returned.' A year or two later, on a Saturday in July, 1902, I hesitated outside these forbidding gates; heavy rain-clouds darkened the sky. Then I heard a roar of agony from the crowd within and I risked my sixpence. This was the afternoon on which Australia won the rubber by three runs; I saw the collapse after Maclaren had fallen to a catch in the deep in an attempt to get the runs before the rain came. I think it is the truth that as Ranjitsinhji sat on the amateur's balcony waiting for his turn to bat on this afternoon of agony, he carved his initials on the window-ledge without knowing what he was doing. When in his turn he had to face Trumble and Saunders, he was marvellously and incredibly reduced to impotence, and failed miserably. This story is old and historical. The father of Maurice Tate came in when eight runs were needed, and by reflex action achieved four of

9

them, then died the death. A year or so ago I saw and spoke to one of the few surviving members of this nobly tragic Test match, none other than Clem Hill, who caught out Lilley running yards and yards after what seemed a certain four from a low skimming drive. Hill claimed that he turned two somersaults after gripping the ball. Also he declared that Maclaren's language was spontaneous and empurpled.

They say it always rains at Old Trafford. But weather or industrial gloom or what not, the frieze of Old Trafford's cricket, the great sequence, comes back to mind as though lighted by eternal sunshine. Hornby and Barlow, the roaring ruddy Cheshire squire and his dour henchman. Briggs and his sad Grimaldi grimace; the stately Albert Ward, a whole Sunday School of batsmanship in himself. Maclaren, Spooner and J. T. Tyldesley, the three most brilliant batsmen that ever opened any county's innings one after the other. Walter Brearley, who bowled fast from morning till night until his eyes were coming out of his head and his face was as red as a boiled lobster. The rich Lancashire stuff of Harry Dean, Lol Cook, who always bowled into the wind, and knew that his demand for leg-before would fall on stone-deaf ears. Richard Tyldesley, emerging from three sweaters on a cold day; Duckworth crowing like a cock. I think I was the first man he ever stumped at Old Trafford; it was a so-called friendly match, and when I missed the ball and Duckworth shrieked his appeal and swept up all the bails and the stumps, I felt as though I had been sandbagged. And there was Parkin, lovable stormy petrel, spin and high spirits; when he was in form and getting wickets every over he used to sing comic songs.

Victor Trumper scored a century before lunch at Old Trafford in the same famous three runs Test Match of 1902. At Old Trafford, Ranjitsinhji not only ended his Test Match career but in 1896 performed there one of his most oriental conjurations against the Australian fast bowler, Ernest Jones; he glanced greased lightning from his left ear down to fine-leg for a four of a velocity rendered almost visible and luminous.

Another great Australian fast bowler—the most beautiful of them all—found his happiest hunting-ground at Old Trafford, his name McDonald, and his graceful ghost will be seen in the sunshine that falls on the next Lancashire and Yorkshire match played there. There were Makepeace and Watson, too, determined to stay in all day against Rhodes and Emmott Robinson; no boundaries before lunch, lads, on principle tha knows. Lancashire and Yorkshire, the greatest match of all, certainly the funniest. Think of it—Rhodes bowling protectively, with determination not to drop a ball anywhere within the hitting zone, bowling with all his cunning on a 'safety-first' spot to a Makepeace who would have died rather than have hit the easiest half-volley—at any rate before lunch.

Many years ago, during the calmer moments of a Lancashire v. Yorkshire match, I wrote a passage as follows: 'At three o'clock there was no place on earth where I would rather have been than at Old Trafford. Sunshine fell on the field, and the venerable pavilion stood in the summer light; white clouds sailed in the sky and the Lancashire colours, with the Red Rose, fluttered in the gentle breeze. And the crowd indulged the old humours, never growing weary of them. Grand cheers greeted a piece of dashing fielding; roars fit to split the heavens went out when Lancashire passed the Yorkshire first innings total. A golden day, a noble crowd, and the greenest grass in England! Many a Lancashire man, exiled from his blessed country, now imprisoned across the seas, was thinking yesterday of Old Trafford and saying to his heart, "Oh to be there—whoever's batting!" '

Those lines were written in August, 1926; and it is myself, as I write these lines, that am now the exiled one, far away in Australia, saying to his heart, 'Oh to be there'; and saying also, 'Greetings, Old Trafford, even if it's Lancashire that is still batting!'

It is a mystery to me that I was able in time to learn to play cricket more than competently. I was not physically strong, and my eyesight from the beginning was so myopic that a ball vanished into a mist in front of me after travelling a matter of thirty yards. No poor boy of the period would willingly wear spectacles; spectacles were considered a handicap to one's prospects at getting a job at a real 'trade'; and no boy of the working classes was encouraged by his parents to become a clerk. There was no interest in cricket amongst my family. By temperament as well as by physique I was almost the last in the world ever to stand forth as an exponent of one of England's manly field sports. I cannot attempt to explain why by the time I was twenty years old I was proficient enough at cricket to make my living during summers as a professional. The point to be emphasized here is that it was through cricket that I escaped from the seemingly blind-alley of my lot in an existence as clerk, handyman or any pitiful job; for I had no visible means of support, no technical training whatever, and no capacity to 'rough it'. Cricket opened my door of escape; cricket brought to me enough economic independence whereby to educate myself. That I was gifted to play the game, and to overcome weaknesses of temperament and physique, cannot plausibly be accounted for by any known theories of the influences of heredity or environment. A great county cricket ground was within reach of my home, true; but to watch a first match and to go from it and straightway knock a middle stump aslant almost without seeing it—this is another and different story.

I could not even join a club when I discovered my skill. The only available grounds in and round Manchester forty years ago were the privileges and possessions of the middle-classes. Half a mile from my backyard, where I bowled for hours at a bucket shielded by a broad piece of board, even as Albert Trott learned *his* arts of spin, was the beautiful cricket field of the Rusholme club. After I had gathered a little confidence in myself I would go there on summer evenings to field at net practice; the gentry were not above availing themselves of boys who were content to run about on a summer evening chasing balls and throwing them back to the bowler for not even a 'thank you'. Nobody dreamed of asking you to come forward for a trial. I hated them very much; and years afterwards when at last I played against Rusholme on this same delectable and green sward, I bowled them all out with a relish that counts amongst my most satisfying memories.

Imagine this youth, now beyond shy boyhood, thin and be-spectacled but in possession of power over people at last. On a worn piece of turf I would spin an off-break without effort, so that it would whip upwards viciously straight at the most important and tender part of a man's anatomy. And not every player in those days used a 'box'. I am not ashamed to confess that I seldom hesitated, as soon as a batsman came to the crease, to let him have a quick one bang in the penis; after which a quick, simple straight one would invariably remove him from the scene.

I was not very good as a batsman because in the pre-spectacles stage of my career I could only play a back-stroke. I was obliged to wait for the bowling to pitch before I could see it, though I would crouch low, like Jessop, when the bowler began his attack, so that I might catch a glimpse of what was coming against the skyline. When I arrived at professional status, playing for clubs here and there and at Shrewsbury School, where I was assistant first to Attewell, then to Wainwright, I was content to bat number eleven, in which position I usually hit at least one boundary before succumbing. I do not remember ever scoring twenty runs without making three or four hits to the boundary.

My very first cricket match is as vivid in my mind more than forty years after as on the May afternoon of its occurrence. I was chosen as one of an eleven representing a theological training college in a Manchester district called Whalley Range. Why a theological training college took an interest in me I cannot tell. This team belonged to a league which fought out its battles on Saturday afternoons on pitches crude and unrolled, hard brown earth most amenable to spin. I firmly believe that on such a wicket in those halcyon years I could easily have bowled out an England eleven within a couple of hours.

The first ball I delivered for the theological training college was smitten for six, all run, by an uncouth denizen of Hulme, a slum adjacent to my native Rusholme. I was a passionate young man where my bowling was concerned, though I kept my feelings to myself. I never, as long as I took active part in cricket, summoned enough courage to appeal for leg-before wicket in an audible voice; but the sight of this huge hit off my first ball, a hit by a barbarian, and against the spin, too, the bat most horribly and blasphemously crooked, made me see red as seldom before and seldom afterwards. I 'went through' the side forthwith; I took nine wickets for eight runs additional to the egregious six aforementioned.

But the theological training college lost the match. They lost, as a fact, nearly every match in which I played for them, in spite or rather because of my unplayable spin. As I have written, the pitches were 'nasty, brutish and short'—in a state of nature. No wicket-keeper extant could have prevented byes from bowling that transgressed all known laws of ballistics. As a consequence, though I would capture on an average seven or eight wickets every match for next to nothing, the 'extras' would pile up so high a total that our batsmen were set a task beyond all reasonable hope of achievement. On these incalculable grounds 50 all out was a winning total. An inspection of the score-sheets of the theological training college would eloquently tell the same story every week; something like this:

Ancoats Settlement

Boggs, b Cardus	4
Moggs, b Cardus	0
Dodds, b Cardus	2
Podds, b Cardus	0
Stoakes, b Cardus	1
Noakes, retired hurt	0
Stiles, b Cardus	1
Thompson, b Cardus	0
Wiffle, l.b.w., b Tupman	1
Waffle, not out	0
Woffle, retired hurt	0
Extras	42
Total	51

Theological College

27 all out

At the end of the season, my first and last in this league, I took some 60 wickets for 80 runs; and I was, I fancy, on the winning side once.

Such single-handed mastery I have not experienced since. My next season opened my eyes to my limitations. I played on rolled pitches, and to my astonishment discovered that the persuasiveness of my right forefinger was not all-powerful. To feel the leather spinning from the hand, to see the ideal flight and length—then the ball would go straight through, with time left for the batsman to make a drive past cover—past cover, mind you, off a potential breakback! . . . It is little wonder that this was the year of my absorption in philosophy.

Ah, but now came the most exquisite of the game's delights—the arduous cultivation of stratagem, the patient preparation of a bowler's snare against a good batsman on a flawless pitch, the preliminary investigation of his tricks and the sizing-up of his temperament; then the choosing of the likely bait and the subsequent angling, based on a 'feeding' of his pet stroke; it might all be spread over many overs and all the time you are terrified lest your captain should lose patience and take you off. At last the moment is here; you drop the ball on the spot of your heart's desire; sight, judgment and supple right arm and fingers are your sure ally; the ideal length and spin are vouchsafed unto you—and the batsman 'bites' and up she goes, a mishit to cover. If the catch is held, God's in his heaven; fieldsmen stand round you in a circle, while you explain the trick; the umpire (an old soldier) confidentially tells you he could see it all coming. The westering sun falls on your face, and while you are now resting awhile, you are aware that a breeze is running deliciously over your body. Many such times might a cricketer chant Nunc Dimittis; he may subsequently go through many varied days and experiences and nevermore will satisfaction, so deep and full, suffuse the whole of his being, and give him better reason to say 'This is a good life!'

On the other hand, after the cunning unhurried laying of the decoy, cover-point might easily miss the catch, in which case all is ashes and unspeakable injustice and mortification. The poor fool of a fieldsman approaches you with a 'Frightfully sorry, old chap—but she was spinning like——' and you are supposed to laugh it off with a 'Well tried', or some such lie.

In 1921 I became definitely known as a *Manchester Guardian* writer, not, maybe, dealing with the subjects I had set myself to expound, such as music, metaphysics, all literature, drama, economics, politics and God knows what all. To retain health I was asked by W. P. Crozier to write for the 'M.G.' on cricket throughout the summer, to go up and down the land day after day. The Australians were in England; this was the season of Armstrong's conquering hosts. So at the last the dearest dream of my boyhood came true. I went to Lord's one spring afternoon to watch the Australians at the nets. The time of day was towards half-past five; rain had fallen slightly, but now the sun shone and the grass glittered and the fresh breeze was sweet and the birds sang in the trees at the Nursery end. Years and years before, when I roamed the streets of my native city or played cricket on the brickcrofts and waste lands, I had murmured to myself the wonderful phrase which so many times appeared in the cricket reports of the period: 'Richardson relieved Lockwood at the Nursery end'; 'Ranjitsinhji glanced Jones to the ropes at the Nursery end.' And here I was, at long last, actually present at the Nursery, walking from net to net, watching Australians at practice. And all around me London, London waiting on a summer night.

I have loved every minute of the many days I have lived at Lord's, and not only when I have actually been there but when I have journeyed to it on summer mornings. The ritual began from the moment I came out of my club and called a taxi and said 'Lord's!' The taxi-man felt some pleasure in it too: 'Lord's, yessir!'

With the leisure that only a London taxi-man retains amongst drivers of vehicles in this age of pace, propulsion and explosion, we would proceed along the Haymarket, across Piccadilly, and soon we would be in Baker Street, which was still freshly aired; with the shops pleasantly occupied and old ladies out with their dogs, and one or two tight-trousered old gentlemen doddering along. Baker Street, where Sherlock Holmes had lived! I had read about it in the *Strand Magazine* in the free libraries of my remote youth; and here I was on the way to Lord's in a taxi. Also I had read, when I was a boy, about the West End clubman, and I had imagined him as of rich purple visage, sitting in the windows of Pall Mall, with nothing to do all day but function as West End clubman. And here, mirabile dictu! was I myself a West End clubman. I never seriously believed that I looked the part.

Along Regent's Park the taxi ambled and the boats were sailing on the lake and the children played with the ducks and offered them pieces of bread by tentative holdings out of their tiny hands, and the spring day and the spirit of London blessed the scene.

The taxi drew up at last outside the W. G. Grace gates; inside we could catch a glimpse of the crocuses, brought up to sport the M.C.C. colours. Now the vision of the pavilion and the field and the high white stand near the Nursery where the trees beyond barely rippled. Then the first sojourn, sitting on the Green Bank; you could see the cricket in snatches from under the awning over the seats in front. I have sat on the Green Bank at Lord's through a lifetime of June afternoons, when the play has not protested too much, but has moved to the evening's slanting light, as gentle as muted strings accompanying the summer's passing show at Lord's; all the life of the town in promenade; not a menacing cloud in the heavens.

But Lord's was not all patrician and school tie. It was (and is, God willing) a microcosm of London itself. For Lord's had its East End as well as its West End. The pavilion and the terrace near the Green Bank were not more a part of the pageant of Lord's than the humour and elbow-to-elbow traffic outside the Tavern. Here was the 'crowd', a motley of Camberwell and Putney and St. John's Wood and Balham; artisans, actors—some of them visibly 'resting'; butchers, bakers, candlestick-makers; Chelsea veterans vibrant with medals; Cockneys and comedians and keepers of stage-doors; scribes from Fleet Street and trombone-players from Queen's Hall. Now and again one of the nobility, direct from the pavilion, might come to the

Tavern and drink a tankard, talking with the next man at the counter and watching the game out of the corner of his failing eye. Hearts just as proud and fair may beat in Belgrave Square.

There are all sorts of nooks and crannies and 'backstage' activities at Lord's. I have seen gilded ducal chairs being carried out of the pavilion's doors at the rear ('tradesman's entrance'). The printing shop under the grandstand is busy all day with the 'fall of the last wicket'. Hens used to pick their way about the practice ground and once I saw a hen go into a gentlemen's lavatory at Lord's. A notice in severe type, rather in the nature of a Proclamation, warns small boys that if they ask the players for autographs they will be 'removed' from the premises; but no small boy at Lord's has ever been known to s.. r removal.

Lord's is representative of London in a way beyond the understanding of the foreign visitor, representative of that nice social balance held by the English, whereby privilege and prerogative may hob-nob with the servants downstairs and not feel too sure of themselves either.

As the afternoon comes to an end, the pavilion is draped in a great velvet shadow; the sun shines now on the high stand opposite the far Nursery end. The pigeons walk under the feet of deep long-off; the Tavern empties and goes reluctantly home. The bell of the clock in the tower covered with ivy chimes half-past six, and the cricketers come from the field in groups of twos and threes, and last of all, the umpires follow with the stumps gathered in their arms.

Other games, they tell me, have their like felicities and their crowns of thorns. No cricketer believes it; no cricketer, if he is honest, will admit that of all the pleasures he may dwell upon in the evening of his days, any one will return with the poignancy of those vanished hours on the summer field; for we can, to the very end, partake of other delights, of reading and music and wine and conversation and candlelight and even of love. But sure as sure, the day will come too soon when (happily he never knows it) the cricketer hits a ball for the last time, bowls a ball for the last time, and for the last time walks home with his companions to the pavilion in the evening glow, his sweater flung across his shoulders.

ONCE LONG AGO

ONCE LONG AGO

SOMETIMES when I am looking through an old 'Wisden' I find to my astonishment that I could not possibly have been present at a match which for a lifetime my mind has seen in all its detail, with the field of play sunny, and all the great heroes fixed in eternal attitudes. The explanation is that boys used to read the cricket reports imaginatively—perhaps they read them that way yet. 'Richardson relieved Lockwood at the Vauxhall end'—the old phrase was enough. Vision was stimulated; I could see it all; for many times had I looked at photographs of Kennington Oval, looked at them until I entered the picture and became part of the crowd represented, a Victorian crowd wearing straw 'cadies' or 'billy-cocks' and coats that buttoned high up the chest. I used to buy every edition that came out, and on summer evenings I would wait for the close-of-play papers, suffering hope and fear. Often I would be afraid to look at the score; I would carry the paper still folded up, and walk some distance, knowing that I held in my hand tidings either or joy of misery. When at last I looked at the news I dared not go at once to the stop-press column; I began on the inside page and approached the scores gradually. I knew that J. T. Tyldesley went in first wicket down, and that the figures which came third in the Lancashire list told of his performance that day; my heart sank whenever I saw a single figure, and I prayed a quick prayer that it would be preceded with 'not out'. And the prayer being granted I would then turn to the stop-press—always, of course, fearing the worst; for the paradox of a schoolboy's hero-worship is that at one and the same time he thinks his gods are marvellous and terribly prone to error. Ah! the bliss of reading 'Close of play: Lancashire 198 for three, Tyldesley not out 87'! But occasionally the stop-press score would state only that Lancashire had lost another wicket in addition to those set down in the main pages of the paper—which meant that I could not know whether Tyldesley was still unbeaten or not. And I would make calculations from the Lancashire total printed inside the paper and that given at the close of play, trying to assure myself that even if my hero was out he had made at least fifty. It is a mystery to me that my hair did not turn grey during my boyhood, so acute was my anxiety about the doings of Lancashire in general, and of

Spooner and Tyldesley in particular. But I shall not need to consult 'Wisden' for proof that I was at Old Trafford on Coronation Day, 1902, when Tyldesley scored 165 against Surrey, and A. Eccles and I'Anson flogged the tired bowling unmercifully and sent Lancashire's total soaring beyond 500, a rare aggregate in those times. Of course I was present; I remember the hot sunshine and the sight of Tom Richardson bowling his heart out, hour after hour. The Coronation had been postponed owing to King Edward's illness (he made appendicitis a familiar word and a complaint within the reach of all people of means). The day was June at its most glorious; there was a blue sky over Old Trafford, a place in the country then.

In those days I lived at Timperley, also a place in the country. I set out for Old Trafford; the day before Tyldesley had been not out at close of play. I had to walk the distance to Old Trafford— schoolboys were not taken to cricket matches in state then. I remember that I got on to the wrong bank of the canal which travels from Timperley in the direction of Old Trafford; I did not know how to get off it, and so I had to run on and on, hot and terrified at the thought that Tyldesley was making brilliant runs or getting out —and I not there, I not there! Some men in a barge cheered me as I ran, a pitiful object, but not, I hope, untouched with grace in the eyes of the Lord. I received full consolation for my torments and sweaty toil along the canal bank; when I reached Old Trafford the crowd was vast, and I ran round the sixpenny side in a panic as I heard the multitudinous cheering. At last I crawled through the congested ranks and got a place on the grass. I saw Tyldesley cut Richardson for four after four—bang, crash against the pavilion rails, until a white line of powder, dried paint, could be seen on the grass, knocked off by the power of Tyldesley's strokes. I saw D. L. A. Jephson bowling lobs, and—joy beyond compare!—I saw Johnny jumping out of his ground and driving high into the crowd, who made holes in their mass for the safe reception of the ball. Tyldesley's innings was as brilliant as the day, and it came to an end in a glory which even a partisan schoolboy could appreciate—the middle stump was hurled out of the ground by Tom Richardson's grandest breakback. What a picture Richardson made in that furnace of sunshine and Tyldesley's cuts—a swarthy, handsome giant, with a leonine moustache and curly hair, who ran over the earth with mighty but beautiful strides and leaped as he swung his arm over— the wave going to its crest and breaking in splendour.

That same day Sidney Barnes bowled for Lancashire and caused a rout of the Surrey Guard—Abel, Hayward, and Brockwell! And as each Surrey wicket fell the crowd stood to stretch themselves, shouting to one another, 'Up! up! up!' Then, when the next batsman reached the wicket, the crowd resumed their seats, shouting, 'Down! down! down!' The Surrey situation was retrieved by a dashing innings by V. F. S. Crawford and by some stubborn defence by Captain H. S. Bush. I saw Vivian Crawford hit a ball first bounce into the practice ground, high over the sightscreen. And as Lancashire were winning easily I could appreciate art for art's sake. The crowd became satiated with the day's boundaries, and to amuse themselves they sang something about 'Tottie will you go Down by the Ohio' in four-part harmony, ending with a languorous cadence, at the end of which the crowd would applaud themselves. Ah, spacious, happy days!

I went home that evening tired, hungry, and hot, but with a happy heart. I ran along the Bridgewater Canal again, but I was conscious of no canal this time, right bank or wrong bank; the barges were of burnished gold now, and I saw in the sunset the islands of the blessed. Ah, the cricket I have seen with mine own eyes—and, ah, the cricket I have not seen!

THOUGHTS IN THE RAIN

Summer, 1923

THE wet has made our cricket fields into places of quiet melancholy. Down on the grass falls the rain, turning green a fresher green, while birds move quickly about the pitch where in yesterday's sun a conquering batsman went his way. Think of the hot pages bad weather has torn from cricket's history, think of the great batsmanship Smith most certainly would have displayed to the world had it only kept fine—for have we not always had Smith's own word for it on dreadfully wet days that these were just the days on which his very bones told him he was going to be especially brilliant? A wet day in the cricket season, we can be sure, washes out many a magnificent episode. It might easily have rained at Chesterfield from morning till night on a certain two days in 1898. If it *had* rained then, would we today be believing anybody telling us that Brown and Tunnicliffe once were possessed of the power to score 554 for the first wicket? On these two days in Chesterfield in 1898 Brown and Tunnicliffe performed a prodigy of skill and endurance never before and never since conceivable. Fate put apart one little period amongst cricket's hoary years for all this mightiness to be accomplished. Brown and Tunnicliffe had fine weather for it—but it might have rained. Oh, the valour and the cleverness washed out by an English summer!

But without remorse for these lost magnificences, the rain it raineth every day. A faint mist covers the field, and here dwells the most pensive silence in the world. Maybe a noise comes of somebody walking through the great hall of the pavilion—a cricketer who, even in moist, unpleasant weather, will not stay away from the beloved place is looking at the prints and portraits on the wall. They are faded, some of them, and tell of the days when cricketers were frequently men with black beards. Here they sit, grouped by an ancient artist of the camera, whose notions of the picturesque were ambitious; some of them sit facing you, arms folded aggressively; some recline at ease; some look eastwards far out of the picture; and one at least of them smokes a pipe, hinting at Victorian manliness. They are lovable relics of a time that seems today to have been rather exquisitely young in its ways. One smiles affectionately and not at all for superiority's sake at the old portrait of the wicket-keeper taken 'in character' behind authentic stumps with a vast expanse of lakeland as a background. These aged prints provoke, for the cricketer of fancy, all the fragile sentiment which comes with the thought of time that has gone, of greatness now dim, of happy spirits whose days in the sun are over. It is in the solitude of rainy days that a cricket field and a cricket pavilion seem to have a personality, a presence; it is in this period of quiet that whisperings from olden times may be heard.

In some such mood as this I walked from a deserted cricket field and came upon a waste of common land outside. The rain had stopped, and here I discovered cricketers who had obstinately declined to abandon play for the day. These cricketers were small boys, enthusiastic despite wet, ragged clothes. Of bricks piled unscientifically one on top of the other was the wicket made, and round it the combatants raged furiously. There was the complicated ceremony of 'tossing for innings' going on. A decrepit bat was flung high into the air, wherewith one boy called out 'Flat!' another 'Round!' The bat fell to the earth with a decisive thud, the face of

the blade pointing upwards. And so the boy that had called 'Flat!'
picked it up and got himself ready to play an historic game. One
mode this of tossing for innings when it is only Wednesday and an
urchin's Saturday penny is a long way off. The boy who went in
first took up a position in front of the wickets, thrust out his left
leg dramatically, flung back his head and shoulders, and stated in a
loud voice: ' 'Obbs!'—the attitude confidently assumed as likely to
be indicative of England's greatest batsman in a punishing mood.
His companions did not receive at all aesthetically this act of
characterization; one of them snatched at the ball a second in
advance of the rest, who, finding themselves frustrated both as
batsmen and bowlers, hung round the crease plainly with one hope
and one hope alone burning in their breasts—the hope that Hobbs
would fail utterly. A boy stood behind the wicket with an old coat
in his hands, and used it to stop the bowling Hobbs failed to smite.
He did not announce that his name was Strudwick. He merely cast
irony, along with his companions, at Hobbs. Laughable it all was,
of course, but not ridiculous. For one looked on recollecting that in
the county pavilion, a few moments ago, one had seen among the
old photographs on the wall a picture of Blythe, the beautiful slow
bowler of Kent. And was not Blythe himself found by his county
on a waste of common land, uncouth and no doubt romantically
aping the heroes of his boyhood? The boy who claimed he was
Hobbs possibly got nearer to the true cricketers' heaven than many
a county man that goes about his play content to get out of it just
the amount of safe utility that efficiency guarantees. Not long ago
Hearne and Hendren, in a match against Cambridge University of
all teams, used pedestrian bats on an easy wicket; they played the
familiar professional game. Could they but have seen and felt themselves Hearne and Hendren, as our urchin sees and feels them
every day, what thrilling cricket Cambridge might have experienced!
The small boy's hero-worship of cricketers is a happy matter for the
game. Surely the warmth of it is communicated in time even to the
canniest of those canny fellows whose every innings is so much
hard labour worth a decent wage. Surely the cricketer is a better
man for the knowledge that little boys are in his thrall, that wherever
he may be, whether in his own county or miles away from home,
little boys are talking about him, wishing him well, sad when he is
out of fortune, happy when he is playing a great game. A boy known
to the writer used to pray at nights in the summer for a century by
Tyldesley. And so anxious was he about his hero that he would

offer up his prayer in terms explicit: 'Please let J. T. Tyldesley make a century (100) for the Lancashire County Cricket Club against Yorkshire County Cricket Club tomorrow, 6th August (Bank Holiday), 1902.' You see, he wished Providence to be under no misapprehension about the time and the occasion on which the century from Tyldesley was desired; every assistance was given in order that beneficence might not be misplaced, that a mix-up might not get the heavenly guidance somehow bestowed on George Hirst instead. Does the professional cricketer sometimes forget he is a god in the eyes of countless small boys? Else why does he frequently go about his play with so little spirit that the admiration crowed out to him by the young faithful moves one sadly at times, like devotion offered up unsuspectedly in a deserted shrine? But this is a sophisticated thought of which none but those with mature years could be guilty. To small boys the professional cricketer can do not wrong; he is a hero to them even when he plays back to a half volley with his heart in his mouth. And whether he has made a hundred or nothing, his autograph is priceless. Abolish autograph-hunting on our cricket fields? Banish little boys from the proximity of county cricketers? Then banish the young heart and romance; banish the world.

AN OLD ENGLAND PLAYER

I MET him in a village far from the noise of cities, a village in which it was easy to think that time had stood still and the land was the quiet place it was in the years of his fame. Now, in his old age, he performed for livelihood some mechanical duty in a hosiery factory, and as I looked on him working at his bench one dark December afternoon and saw his white hair and the spectacles down his nose, I thought sadly of his days in the sun. He would not at first talk of cricket when I sat with him in his cottage after his work was over. He pretended to me that never in his life had he been so comfortable as he was now. He even affected to believe that with his life to live again he would not be a professional cricketer. 'It's no more'n a game,' he said, 'and in a lifetime at it you prodooce nowt!' These were the sophistries it was necessary for him to cultivate, that he might not too sharply feel the pathos which age and faltering flesh bring to the cricketer whose love of the game to the end burns a bright light.

And love the game he did in his heart. His eyes began to flash as slowly I led him on to a talk over the old times. And at last, the spell of memory began to work; he was back again in the 'eighties and 'nineties, England's great bowler, in the company of Tom Richardson, Lockwood, Peel, and Lohmann, with summer passing before him like a pageant. He spoke of Lord's, and recollected June mornings in London when he walked to the ground down the St. John's Wood Road, with polished magnificence of hansom cabs all about him. A day in the sun was before him, green grass for his young confident movements. In his period, Lord's was a different Lord's from the one we know. 'I went there a summer or two ago,' he said, 'and I didn't know it. It was crowded and full o' noise. In my day folk didn't flock to cricket matches, and many's the time as I've played at Lord's (he pronounced it Loard's) and it's been nigh empty and that calm that you could hear the echo of a bat coming over the field. Hey! and the pavilion was a grand place; you were feared to breathe as you walked past all the fine gentry when you went out to bat.' It is easy to imagine the scene he had in mind. Look into the Badminton cricket book and ponder the picture of the immaculates of the pavilion at Lord's in 1880. Shining tall hats imposing on you everywhere. True, one nobleman has his tall hat on his knees while he takes the air, but his tall hat being on his knees you can see and admire the better the classic cast of his forehead. Bone of the finest bone, flesh of the most exclusive flesh, is every scion of them. 'There was some rare gentlemen and no mistake at Lord's in them times,' said my old cricketer. 'It did your eyes good to look at 'em, all shining like and mighty.' I understood he did not consider the stock in the pavilion at Lord's nowadays to be so pure, and I am certain he thought the less of Lord's—just a little the less—on that account.

The wonder and glory of life are in the way my old cricketer first went to Lord's—a raw-boned lad now for the first time in his life out of his native village: one week an old widow's only son labouring obscurely on the soil, the next week bowling 'from the Nursery End', while the fashionable intelligence in the pavilion pronounced his name. 'T' old woman,' he told me, meaning his mother, 'was funny when I told her as I were going to play for t' county. "I reckon nowt to that," she said: "t' village team's good enough for thee." But I knowed she were glad in her heart, only she were feared as I'd get hurt playing for t' county. She allus were worryin' about that, and when I didn't get into t' England team in '93 when I was at t' top of my form she were reight sorry proper, but she made to believe she were glad. Somebody had been reading t' paper to her about Ernest Jones.' In his great days he went on living in his quiet village with his mother, till she died. Can you see him, coming home some summer evening to their little cottage, after a day in a Test match amongst great men and in a great place, coming home and sitting quietly with her at summer in the lamp-light, while at that very moment his name was notable in conversation all over the land? The county discovered his ability when he was playing on the waste land outside his village. One evening 'a gentleman in a top-hat' spoke to him and asked for his name and address. A day or two later he was at the nets at the county ground, and in a week he was moving south with the county team, bound for Lord's to play against an M.C.C. eleven captained by Grace.

On the opening morning of the match he went to Lord's while his clubmates were sitting in the smoke-room of the hotel after breakfast. He hadn't the patience to wait for them: he *must* be 'out and doing'. 'I walked up to t' big gates,' he told me, 'with my flannins [meaning flannels] in brown paper under my arm, but t' gatekeeper wouldn't let me in and I couldn't make out to him who I was. Then a big gentleman come up, and he had a great black beard. I knew it was t' Old Man, and he got me into t' ground. He'd heard about me, he said, when I spoke to him. "Aye," says he, "Mr. Johnson told me about you. So you're goin' to bowl us all out, eh? Well, I'm no good against a colt first time he bowls at me." ' And two hours later this rosy-faced lad was bowling at Grace. 'Mr. Johnson put me on after t' first hour, an' t' Old Man and Mr. Ferris had put up a score for t' first wicket. I can see him now—his big body making t' wickets look so little that you felt t' ball weren't big enough to hit 'em. And when he kept putting his left leg down t' pitch and smothering t' ball—hey, I felt as helpless as a babby!' 'W. G.'s' defence looked so impenetrable on the days he was in form that my old cricketer said Attewell used to say to the umpires, 'Eh, but you ought to get t' gauge out and measure 'is bat. He meks 'em 'isself.'

But not all the grand incidents of his career did my old cricketer recollect clearly. Sadly, I found his memory had failed to hold many a great moment's splendour. It was as though days and days had passed through him like water through a sieve. 'Often I looks at

Wisden's,' he said, 'and sees t' scores in matches as I played in, but I can hardly believe I was the same man when I finds my name there.' But there were things he would never, never forget. 'Ranji!' he said, 'I s'll remember him till my dyin' day!' He witnessed again, as he sat there looking into the fire, the dark grace of the man, the lithe body, the silk shirt fluttering in the breeze, his bat seemingly more supple than other cricketers' bats, making movements in curves so swift that you might easily have imagined it was flexible, like a cane. On a fast wicket his first stroke told you that he was there for the afternoon. He flicked you anywhere he chose in the casual way a man flicks off a daisy's head with his stick. 'When he come in to bat we all used to try and get 'is wicket first, for the pride o' the thing, and bowl us selves for all as we were worth. Then we sort of knew it would be no good. It come over you all of a sudden like, and I used to feel summat give inside me.'

It was not Ranji, though, who was the bitter torment of the souls of bowlers in the old cricketer's time, but one name of Shrewsbury. He was past his best when this old man played the game, 'and,' said he, 'when they told us that we used to thank the Lord for it.' There was always a chance for the bowler who was tackling Ranji: even as he conjured your best length ball from the middle stump to the fine-leg boundary you could hope on, grasping at the idea of human fallibility, telling yourself he would do it once too often. Besides, Ranji in one of his long innings would in time persuade even the bowlers into the magic circle of his art, and once there, they were spell-bound by his charm even as the crowd. It was different bowling at Shrewsbury; nothing here but naked antagonism, nothing for the poor bowler to think on but the toil of getting him out. On the hardest and most perfect turf he never strayed from the eternal verities of his art, and whether his score was none or 200 his play went on with the same cool scrupulousness, the same self-control. 'His bat were all middle,' said the old cricketer, 'and even on a sticky wicket you couldn't make him look awkward.'

Gunn and Shrewsbury at the wicket on a hot day, and how pitilessly bowlers were scourged! Lockwood and Richardson in action against their defences, hurling down the fastest that was in them as though by some great convulsion of nature, and in vain! When Notts won the toss in those days on a firm ground bowlers gave themselves over unashamedly to affliction; and if it was a match at Brighton the rest of the Notts men went down to the sea to bathe. To watch Gunn and Shrewsbury in partnership was to have a classical education in batsmanship. This period, my old cricketer's period, saw the classic style touch perfection. The rough grounds of the 'seventies and 'eighties had flawed the work of many a master perhaps not less gifted than Shrewsbury; but now the smooth wickets admitted the precision which is three parts of the classic manner. And not only was the batsmanship of the day pure in style; bowling, too, had the same clarity of outline. Length, length, length! Poise and balance! The ball pitching on the mythical sixpenny-piece, the bowler making a beautiful movement. Even the fast bowlers had the classic rhythm, and none so beautiful as Richardson to look upon. It was the day of first principles, and in the cricket field Shrewsbury and Gunn and Attewell and my old cricketer announced the validity of them even as the Spencerian philosophers were announcing them to the workaday world outside. The age of rationalism, of men who disliked the oblique! Soon there were to come to cricket the first touches of decadence, the 'rococo allurements', of Ranjitsinhji, his music drawing to ruin all the innocents of the field. But my old cricketer and the men he played with, though they heard the first call of the magic pipe, little dreamed of its significance. To the end of their cricketing days the straight bat and the honest length ball were enough for them. This old man showed me a worn cricket ball. 'I clean bowled the Old Man, W. W. Read, and A. E. Stoddart in a couple of overs with that ball, on a plumb Oval wicket, and every ball of 'em as straight as a whistle!' I took the ball in my hand and wondered if the fragrance of many a golden day was not in it somewhere.

And now I had to leave the old fellow. 'Sorry to have to say good night to ye,' he said, 'but I mun see about putting on t' alarm clock for t' morning.' As I left his cottage he was tinkering with the clock and setting it for 6.30. On my way home it so happened that the train passed the county cricket ground that had been the old man's heaven on earth. I peered through the carriage window-panes, but the field was hidden in the December night, and it seemed that summer and cricket could never come there again.

THINGS THAT MATTER

A WONDERFULLY English game is cricket. One morning last summer at Kennington Oval the umpires walked magnificently on to the field a few minutes behind the clock. Arrived at the wicket, one of them bowled a ball to the other—just to remind us, it seemed, that he, too, in his time had been a mighty hunter before the Lord. Then the Somersetshire men moved easefully into view, and, after another dignified lapse of time, out came two Surrey batsmen. Whereupon one of these engaged himself with the umpire over the urgent matter of taking his guard. It was easy to imagine the conversation: 'Middle and leg as usual, Tom.' 'That's the off stump.' 'How's this?' 'Covers the leg.' 'That better?' 'Covers the two, 'Arry.' 'Thanks, Tom.' Meanwhile the captain of Somersetshire, in earnest consultation with the bowler, had been waving his fieldsmen here and there; a gesture from him and some man in white passed far away into the bleak distances of the Oval field. And all the time the crowd waited. And at length the game went on. And the first ball, bless us, upset a wicket which was the last Surrey wicket of the innings. Whereupon the cricketers all moved out of our ken once more, the umpires last and looking impressive—Dogberrys of the cricket field! And the vast spaces of the Oval were empty again. Such is cricket—one sane thing, anyhow, in our mad world. Cricket, obstinately declining to take part in the general movement to brighten old England out of existence! Did the crowd at the Oval complain bitterly at this dilly-dallying of cricket, this lack of 'dynamic sweep', as the man in *Kipps* would say? It did not. It watched the comings and the goings of the cricketers devotedly, and it filled the blanks in the play with its own humanity. As the crowd waited for the game to stir into life in time it expanded into reminiscence. One man informed us—rather, he threw the news upon the morning air negligently—that he had witnessed Bobby Abel score 357 not out for Surrey against this very county of Somersetshire in May, 1899; he thought it was May but wouldn't swear to it. And another man informed us, but not negligently at all, that he had witnessed every run that Bobby Abel had ever scored in his life at Kennington Oval, so help him if he hadn't. This announcement was not, I think, widely accepted, but none the less the crowd was amenable; in its cosily huddled ranks fellow-feeling ran warm. This in spite of cricket which apparently seemed to stand in need of the 'brightening' process the newspapers a year or two ago told us was the only means of saving the game's life.

The fact is, cricket is more than a game. For one thing, it is part of summer. How many of us have gone home after watching cricket and taken with us no impression more likeable than that we have seen during the day the sun climb up the sky, pause over us for a while in beneficent noon heat, and then descend towards evening while the field turned a softer and softer green? The leisureliness of cricket, the room in it for graces and amenities deliciously irrelevant!—all these make for the poetry of cricket; yes, and make for the urbane Charles Lamb prose of cricket. And it is these graces of cricket that the literature of the game has not attended to amply enough in recent days; we have made, perhaps, overmuch of the technique of cricket. In the first year of the game after the war the cry was: 'Speed up cricket!' *The Times* came out with an ingenious suggestion involving the banishment of the left-handed batsman because he interferes with bustle. But we are finding out, at last, that the summer game is not as other games; that the rhythm of it may be as lazy as June's and yet enchant us. Why, only the other day *The Times* itself printed a graceful prose poem in praise of those very parts of cricket which are not to be got into a matter-of-fact inventory of a match.

Think only of the crowd at cricket! The crowd matters a deal to the game and to one's love of the game. And it really is part and parcel of cricket; you will find nothing like it at other games. It sits for so long a time in one place that personal reserves cannot exist in it: in a cricket crowd an intimacy is bred which breaks down all class distinctions. And because cricket frequently takes a placid course the crowd has liberty for self-expression. Think of it—twenty thousand men (and some women), most of them certain to possess a share of the more or less shabby worries that afflict the race nowadays—they will sit in the air, throughout the long day, attending on a game that can charm but can hardly inebriate! The foreigner may well gasp at the spectacle of Lord's on a Saturday afternoon in June. Go about the 'popular' side on any county cricket ground and you are with the salt of the earth. A man is talking of Parkin; he knows him, meets Parkin every morning. He has the ear of the multitude, but, such is life, the voice of the sceptic is sure to be heard in the land. 'You know Parkin—I'll *bet* yer do!' No more words than these, but enough to spoil the day of the man who

claims he knows Parkin. That he has the confidence of the majority
about him is now nothing—ashes are in his mouth. Romance
demands complete and intimate faith! And again, there is the fellow
who turns up late in the day, say, at a Lancashire and Yorkshire
match in the present year of grace, and turns up slightly drunk. He
contemplates the cricket for a while with a hard gaze and suddenly
unlooses the question: 'Wish—wish ish John'y Briggsh?' Somebody
endeavours to adjust his historical sense. He is informed that Johnny
Briggs no longer is in the land of the living, that we are now in 1924.
This information, though put in more emphatic terms than those
used here, has no considerable effect on the seeker for knowledge.
He goes into meditation; again he looks hard at the cricket. And at
last, with a curiosity as fresh and genial as ever, asks: 'Wish—wish
ish John'y Briggsh?' Would not a cricket crowd have moved the
warm heart of Henry Fielding to more and more warmth? Would
he not have loved to come on that common enough scene on the
'shilling side' of a county ground, wherein individuals hot with
futile argument grow stern in language because argument is futile?
'I tell yer 'e played for Essex in 'ninety-five.' 'Played for Essex—
played for Essex! 'Ow could 'e 'ave played for Essex in 'ninety-five
when 'e played for Kent?' 'Don't I tell yer 'e played for *Essex* in
'ninety-five?' And so they go on, round and round in a circle. And
language gets sterner and sterner. And in the very heart of the
argument, and the language, sits a parson, who most accommoda-
tingly tries to look either stone-deaf or a jolly enough fellow of the
world, in his own way, as any of 'em . . . It is not to the point to say
that this crowd is not strictly a part of cricket because also it goes to
football matches. It has to go somewhere in the winter! It is of the
game—the part which adds the salt touch to a dish that without it
might seem a little precious; cricket, a poem of a game, is kept by
the crowd on the good round earth. Things that matter are all
these—the runs and the stumps upset and the fielding; the 'wigs
on the green', the championship; the summer setting; the urbani-
ties, the crowd and its humours, and the airs and graces—all these
are parts of cricket, and no part greater than the whole. Brighten
cricket? Then seek to brighten the comfortable sun. Tired of
cricket? Then you are tired not only of a graceful game but of
summer and communion with fellows of excellent heart.

WHITSUNTIDE AT OLD TRAFFORD
(Or, for that matter, on Every County Ground)

LET any Whitsuntide only be reasonably fine and warm and a great multitude will march every morning on Old Trafford. The advance guard of it will be small boys possessed of sustenance in paper parcels, and these small boys will occupy the first row of circling benches round the 'popular' side long before the cricketers themselves are likely to come into view—occupy them, in fact, even as Hallows, say, is shaving himself at home. Happy pilgrimage of youth to Old Trafford at holiday-time in the summer —surely it goes on yet as fervently as it went on a score of years ago.

Unforgettable the vigil we who were lads then passed through on many a Whitsun morning—a vigil which began at half-past nine and lasted till the first glimpse of the umpires' white coats—a long time to get through when you were dying to see Lancashire bat first. Not for us eager boys the diversions old men employ wherewith to cheat tedium during this waiting period; not for us a cup of tea in the refreshment-room while one's seat was held in reserve by one's coat. Perish the thought in every healthy youngster's mind that, once settled in a good place on the ground, he could risk taking his eyes from the stretch of green for a minute. What might not happen of great significance behind his back? There was nothing but to hold on in patience. True, the first hour was overcome easily enough. To begin with, one was kept alive by the feeling of being here at all, so splendidly in possession of a front seat, the hallowed grass right in front—to be touched by a mere stretching of the legs. There was also the animation of the gathering crowd; the warmer and warmer heat of the sun as it climbed the sky; the first of the day's delicious slakings of thirst with ginger-beer (remember the sudden 'Pop!' down in the shady depths of the packed seats, the squishing noise, the 'Hey up!' of the laughing crowd around). Also to ward tedium away for a while there was the advent of the man selling picture post cards of the Lancashire XI, and the game of guessing the portrait of one player after another without looking at the printed names; the sudden glimpse of somebody in flannels moving across the pavilion front (Who is it? Maclaren? Jackson? Tyldesley? Too far away to see.); the rumour that Lancashire had won the toss and the counter-rumour that Yorkshire had won it.

34

Yet despite all this high and excited life tedium *would* gain bit by
bit on us. Some extraordinary lads there were who could actually
get absorbed in the latest boys' paper, but how we others despised
this sovereign detachment! Unashamedly we would give ourselves
over in the last hour of the vigil, between eleven and twelve o'clock,
to the fidgets and an aching sense that the fingers on the pavilion
clock were simply crawling round . . . It was in this period—
straining as it was boyish patience to the breaking-point—that one
suddenly succumbed to the temptation to open the parcel of sandwiches hours in advance of the recognized adjournment for lunch.
At first one untied the string intending to take only a tiny bite—the
bulk had to be saved for the proper time. Seldom was it saved,
though; the lunch interval invariably found us without a crumb
between us and utterly empty inside. The taste of those sandwiches,
dry and flavoured with last night's evening paper, comes back
blissfully to the palate even now.

We men of years may rest easy that these boyish sensibilities were
not peculiar to ourselves; today and for ever and ever youngsters
at Old Trafford in Whit Week will get as much as we did out of the
moments as they pass. Makepeace and Hallows look just as fine and
large in their eyes as Albert Ward and Maclaren did in ours. And
as unchanged and unchangeable as the boys themselves is everybody
else in today's holiday crowd at Old Trafford or on any other
County ground. This crowd, indeed, is something more than the
sum total of the individuals in it; it has a being of its own; it was
born in the dim past and will outlive us all. Man and boy, this crowd
has been going to Old Trafford in Whit Week these fifty years; man
and boy, it will be going there in thrice fifty years to come. A crowd
it is of immense humanity, and on a warm day the mellowness of
sunshine enters into the ranks. Talk of the hard, grinding North,
ignorant Southerner—poor man, have you never seen Old Trafford
settling down after lunch, all of us huddled intimately, basking in
the afternoon's light, the old pavilion seeming to drowse? The
rigour of the game is appreciated keenly enough by Old Trafford's
crowd, but it is in its most lovable moment towards a golden day's
fall just as the play gets a little stale and attention on the cricketers
begins to dwindle. Then the multitude seeks for amusement of its
own making, and now's the time for men of humour. A policeman
is walking in dignity along the boundary's edge. The crowd suddenly
sees him with one eye. And with a single voice chant the packed
thousands: 'Left, right! Left, right!' keeping time to the solemn

35

movements of the policeman, who endeavours hard to seem utterly oblivious that a cynosure is being made of him. In this hour of Old Trafford's 'sweet doing nothing' have you ever heard the crowd entertain itself by singing in two-part harmony a ditty about *Down by the Ohio*? A good time to have the ears ravished by this musical performance is in the middle of an interminable partnership against Lancashire's bowling, when some impregnable bats have seemingly put the game to a standstill. Then is it that music is made to soothe Old Trafford's breast: *Down by the Ohio*, with a cadence of linked sweetness long drawn out, goes into the mild air. And after the protracted dying away of that cadence the crowd, as a man, applauds its own waggish self. 'Hooray!' it says, laughing the broadest laugh that ever was. Does a wicket fall at last? Very well, Old Trafford now loosens its legs. 'Up! Up! Up!' the multitude chants, and every man jack of them stands up. Does a new batsman come in? Very well, again; the multitude chants, 'Down! Down! Down!' and down once more it sits. Behold Old Trafford's crowd in this hour of its content and call the critic a fool who talks of the unbending North and its economic man.

The cricket on view in Whit Week at Old Trafford is as good as the crowd every year, and that is saying a lot. Lancashire against Yorkshire, and afterwards Lancashire against Kent—there's spice and variety for you—the one match of Cerberus and blackest midnight born; the other making for us a sunshine holiday. It is an excellent idea to let the Kent match follow the Yorkshire match—Kentish Sir Byng after the Ironsides; cricket as pastoral after cricket as intolerable drama. Think of Kent at Old Trafford in Whit Week, and a Lancashire cricket lover will find his mind astir with memories of many a gracious day in the refreshing air. Who forgets the '97 match when Mold shot down his seven wickets, Kent having led Lancashire by 78 runs? Lancashire then wanted 207 for victory, and Johnny Briggs won the game by three wickets with a fierce outburst of batsmanship worth 60. Who forgets C. J. Burnup and his day's innings on Whit Monday, 1900? He was on view from midday to the time of shadows, working away as quietly as a mouse. The surprise of us all when the scoreboard announced his 200 was tremendous. Who forgets that Whit Thursday, a day of scarifying heat, which saw J. T. Tyldesley smite the Kent attack right and left till his total was 295? Who forgets the heroic labours of Fielder that day—his sweaty shirt, his noble determination? This was Woolley's first game at Old Trafford; he had a time of tribulation at first. He was out for nothing, missed catch after catch, and got a solitary wicket for some 60 runs. But on Whit Saturday he let us see his quality in a dazzling innings. Who forgets E. W. Dillon, the graceful lefthanded batsman, and the catch with which A. H. Hornby got him out on a Whit Friday years ago? Who forgets Bradley and his long run?—the man went almost to the boundary before beginning to bowl. Who forgets Blythe, loveliest of all slow bowlers, and Kenneth Hutchings, image of South Country grace, dark, sinuous, his black hair ashine in the sun, his soft flannels? Kent has ever sent happy cricketers to make Old Trafford's Whitsun holiday; sparkling wine of the game Kent has to give wherever she goes, wine all the more refreshing if it washes down—as often it has done—a bitter pill just administered to Lancashire by Yorkshire. This year, as ever, Kent will have a glowing welcome from Old Trafford; from the small boys; from their fathers, who, though they may be looking with admiring eyes at the art of Woolley, yet bear in mind Frank Marchant and J. R. Mason; from their mothers, even, sitting in the ladies' pavilion, some of them in love still with a memory of Kenneth Hutchings. Yes, Old Trafford will greet Kent gladly enough any year; and should Collins get down on his bat and stay there, as he is usually inclined to do at Old Trafford, it is possible Old Trafford will once again say unto itself: 'Let there be music; let *Down by the Ohio* steal upon our ears with a dying fall.'

ARTISTS AND CRICKETERS

TELL the average English sportsman that cricket is in its way an affair of art and the chances are he will regard you, eyebrows raised, with some suspicion. He has come to abhor the word, especially when it is written (or pronounced) with a capital A. None the less, his reactions to the game, the manner in which he frequently talks about it and appreciates it, make convincing proof that he is never so much the artist as when he is at a cricket match, looking on from the popular side or from the pavilion. Go among the shilling crowd any fine day at the Oval and what do you hear? Little technical jargon, little talk of off-breaks and the position of the left funny-bone in the late cut. Instead, you will hear many delighted cries of 'Beautiful stroke—*beautiful!*' Now that same word 'beautiful' is one which average Englishmen are not in the habit of using; it is, indeed, a word they commonly distrust quite as much as they distrust the word 'art'. The truth is we are as a people prone to be ashamed of living the life aesthetic; we see and feel beauty even in our games, but we rarely confess to it. Yet that 'Beautiful!' which a glorious cover drive by Hobbs will bring warmly from our tongues tells the truth; Hobbs is for us an artist. It is not merely the fact that the crowd is shouting for Surrey, keen on a big score by Surrey. If the crowd were keen on naught but Surrey's chances in the match, a cowshot by Hitch would cause as much satisfaction as Hobb's master-stroke; for all hits look alike on the score-sheet—the score-sheet does not mark the difference between the utility value of a Hitch and the utility value plus aesthetic value of a Hobbs. The fine art of cricket is such, in fact, that even if you are a Kent man anxious for your county to thrash Surrey, you are likely to witness with mixed feelings the dismissal of Hobbs for next to nothing. 'Good for Kent', you will find yourself saying as the champion walks home along the lonely track to the pavilion, 'but my afternoon is the worse for it.' Hobbs out for 3—good for Kent, but bad for the art of the most artistic of all games!

Art, when all is said and done, is simply the expression of personality, through a stylish technique, making for our pleasure. Is not, then, Woolley an artist? Is not Woolley a 'personality', is not his technique stylish, and is not our delight in Woolley enormous?

At cricket style is certainly the man. The old notion of style of batsmanship will not do—I mean the notion which insists that the left leg forward and the elegant straight bat are the be-all and end-all of style. In cricket, as in any other pursuit, good style is never a standardized matter; it does not cause all men to look alike. Style must never be confused with Fashion. The ancient view held by the public school coach of other years that style in batting is a certain conventional way of playing the ball—it was called the forward method—this view did not help, but hindered the development of personality in the game. There is no such visible thing in cricket as good style as we commonly and narrowly define it—there are only styles. Good style, in truth, is that very character in a man's play which marks him off from other men. The style is the man. Palairet was a stylist and so was Hirst. Spooner was not a truer stylist than Gilbert Jessop. Each of these masters played the game as their temperaments compelled them to, and the style of each was true to character. What is bred in the bone will come out at the wicket. And because cricket is a game that takes time for its unfolding; because of that very leisureliness which those who are not cricketers do not like, because of cricket's occasional static quality, it gives scope for the expression of personality and the individual style.

The pace of football is too fast for an artist's indulgence in his own particular way of getting a thing done; your cleverest footballer is at the mercy of the rest of his team, dependent on them and sent here and there pell-mell according to the sheer chance of the ball's movements.

But at cricket a Sutcliffe, a Hearne, is able to dominate the field for hours; he stands there in isolation, so to say, poised on the peak of his own egotistical ability; for the paradox of cricket has always been that the great masters serve their sides best when they serve themselves best. The great batsman, in his three hours' traffic at the crease, seems master of all he surveys; the bowling is his material, and out of it he can, if he be a Woolley, carve beauty before our eyes, beauty that is characteristic.

Amazing game of cricket, so flexible in technique that all sorts and conditions of character may be revealed through it. Watch a cricket match from this point of view and it will never be dull, no matter how little grinding of the competitive axe is going on. Before you is a microcosm of the world itself: human nature 'giving itself away'. For let me see a batsman at play and I will tell you what sort of man he is. Take Quaife, of Warwickshire, for example. A dapper little batsman, scrupulous, tidy—even 'finicky'. See how fastidiously he grounds his feet before taking the bowling. Observe throughout his longest innings—and how long some of them could be in his best years—how he crosses his t's and dots his i's. The neatest batsman surely that ever was. Well, you would be amazed to learn that in his everyday life off the cricket field Quaife was a roaring, dishevelled man, slack in dress, tie all wrong, and bootlaces loose. And you would be right to be amazed. Quaife the man is as neat, as polite, as much lacking in boisterousness and abandon as Quaife the cricketer. At the extreme of Quaife as a man was Brearley; here we had a very gale of humanity, a man who lived his life always in rare gusty humours and energies. Such a man was bound by character to be the tempest of a fast bowler that Brearley was.

In the 'nineties a miracle of self-revelation happened on our cricket fields. Up to that time our summer game had been English through and through—the straight bat, the unsubtle, honest technique of 'W. G.' had set the type. Then suddenly black magic came into cricket, for a strange un-English artist began to play. Cricket, the game that served so well 'W. G.' and hearty English souls like Bobby Peel, A. N. Hornby, and Briggs, served also the dusky Eastern grace of Ranjitsinhji. His cricket was not of our soil and green grass; it had the sinuous beauty and the sense of wizardry which we associate with his own land. Through our English game, born at Hambledon, shone a light from the East, and it passed away for ever with the passing of Ranjitsinhji.

Fry, of academic mind, was ever a batsman who, as I say elsewhere, played by the book of arithmetic. The dry light of ratiocination was in his every innings. Maclaren's superb independence of spirit, his imperious air, came out whenever he spread the grandeur of his batsmanship over the field. Remember that sovereign hookstroke of his; nay, he did not hit the ball—he dismissed it from his presence. So with Emmott Robinson, a loose, shambling man made out of the stuff of Yorkshire county and none other. Imagine that the Lord one day scooped up a great lump of Yorkshire earth, breathed into it and said, 'Emmott Robinson—go, open the bowling at the pavilion end.' . . . And so one could go on, through all the master cricketers, finding character in the style. The game must be very great to contain so much of nature. Go to it, gentle reader, with your imagination's eye, as well as your physical eye, open. To the dullard, who looks merely at the score-board,

> A Woolley at the crease's rim
> A simple Woolley is to him
> And he is nothing more.

But to the cricket-lover of sensibility, this Woolley is an artist, and the game of cricket a little game of life itself.

THE SUMMER GAME

CRICKET has the movement of summer in its growth and budding-time. The game comes to us modestly on spring's rainy days, and like a plant it turns to the sun and is not happy when an east wind blows. But as the season passes, cricket begins to flower; by the time hot June is come it is roses, roses all the way from Old Trafford to Canterbury. Sit on the Mound Stand at Lord's on midsummer morning at noon, and if the sun be ample and you close your eyes for a while you will see a vision of all the cricket fields in England at that very minute; it is a vision of the game's rich seasonal yield; a vision of green spaces over our land, of flashing bats, of thudding, convulsive bowlers, and men in white alone in the deep or bent low in the slips.

June and July bring in cricket's gold of the year; August finds the game, like the sun itself, on the wane. Now the sands are running out every evening as the match moves towards its close in yellow light; autumnal colours darken play at this time of the year; cricketers are getting weary in limb, and even the spirit has lost the first rapture. The end happens at far-away Eastbourne—or if it doesn't it ought, for poetry's sake, to do so—and after the last drawing of stumps a leaf falls from a tree and a faint mist touches the field. Summer is over, and cricket, too. Goodbye a hundred happy days in the open air; good-bye Lord's, Tonbridge, Gloucester. The North of England cricketer who packs his bag for the season's last time away down at Eastbourne lets his cab take him to the railway station and it is twilight, with the street lamps shining bitterly on the sea front. The homeward journey to Manchester is a period of sentimental reverie; what can life possibly contain for a fellow tomorrow? No Old Trafford—only the ache of festival cricket. Pass, now, summer game, late September is on you, dark winter not far behind; you are only for the light. . . .

It is the brevity of a cricket season that makes the game precious. And the shyness of its coming on early May days makes it lovable. Other games burst on us in all their plenty; the first afternoon of football is as challenging, as multitudinous, as any of the season's maturity. The arrogance of football's advent, the sudden activity and conquest, it is all surely a little brazen, even vulgar—reminding us of the person who puts on all her jewellery at once. Cricket comes into her own slowly, as though by a patient, affectionate wooing of the year's playtime. The game may almost be said to show itself with a blush in the early May days.

A match at Oxford gives one time for day-dreams; play is not masterly enough to intrude on private meditation. And at the spring of the year cricket fields make much the same effect on me as old ruins by moonlight made on Sir Walter Scott—they cause me to think of something else. The other week at Oxford I found myself now and again dwelling upon Bramall Lane—a digression in thought due possibly to the mind's innate tendency to jump at contrasts and seek for identity in opposites, as the Hegelians say. Can it be the same game that is played at Sheffield and in the Parks? The one breathes the hot smoke of battle, the other is soft and restful, like peacefulness itself. Janus-faced cricket!—in Yorkshire warlike and intolerant, and in Worcestershire as genial and magnanimous as an English landscape . . . And we must think not only of county cricket; there is the club game, too, letting us see yet another facet of this jewel our cricket. I do not mean the highly efficient club cricket of Lancashire and Yorkshire; I have in mind the village green, where skill is not everything so long as you contrive to be a man of spirit. On Saturday afternoons during a summer, as two first-class batsmen grow prematurely old through responsibility on a county ground, I let my thoughts go to any old-world country place of my recollection. And at once I am lifted to another and more humorous world. Little Slocombe's bowling is in a rare tangle against Eleven of the Constabulary. The parson, who is captain, consults his forces in the middle of the wicket while P. C. Vokes (not out 57) mops his brow. As a last resort the parson asks Huggins, his gardener, to 'send up a few'. Huggins takes the ball, rolls up his sleeves, and as he does so good intentions light a fire in his bosom. Huggins has never before been seen to bowl, and, indeed, does not quite yet know himself whether he can bowl. But the parson, wishful to set a cunning field, asks: 'Fast, slow, or medium, Huggins?' And Huggins ponders for just a second, then replies, 'Well, sir, I caan't 'zactly say yet a while; I s'all leave it to natur'.' Good old village green, do you still find room for cricket? Perhaps the club game is the summer game at its happiest, after all; perhaps village cricket never comes to the autumn, but sustains the freshness of May the season through.

OVER THE FENCE

SIR JAMES BARRIE has spoken of the pleasure which comes of leaning over a fence and looking at a village cricket match. This pleasure, of course, is keenest when it falls on us suddenly and takes us by surprise. All of us born in this land know how it happens, how the happy occasion will spring from round the corner of a lane on a June afternoon. We are out walking; no thought of cricket is in the mind; under the leaves of old trees we wander in hot, sleepy air, with noises of summer about us. The lane is quiet and miles from the city; thick hedgerows are on each side, and from them we hear now and again a quick chirruping, as our footsteps in the dust disturb the lane's silence. A bird moves and darts out of the growth with a flutter of wings. Farther along our track we come to the first gap in the hedgerow; a horse is rubbing his nose on the gate and we stop for a while and stroke his long, hard face. Onward we walk, feeling the ripe contentment of England in summer-time every-where. And now we are visited by extreme bliss: the lane makes a curve—a gesture of invitation. We turn round the bend, knowing that some delectable sight is waiting for us. Here is another fence, a wide casement in the shade of the lane, and sunlight comes through and shines on the road like water. We see through it our cricket match; it is going on in a little field tucked away in the countryside. And, being English, we stop, lean over the fence, and watch the play.

We watch it lazily, disinterestedly. This, indeed, is the very point of our pleasure; it must be an indolent watch that we keep on the game, an interest untroubled by partisan excitation. We are not disturbed as the wickets fall (they are always falling on the village green); we are not driven to a gnashing of teeth as we see a catch dropped (and catches are many times dropped on the village green). We stay there, over the gateway, looking at the summer game, and our enjoyment of it is in tune with the spacious mild spirit and humours of English life on a warm day deep in the heart of our everlasting country.

A wooden pavilion stands some distance from our comfortable point of vantage. In front of it men and women give themselves up to the yielding curve of deck chairs. Through the window of the pavilion we catch a glimpse of somebody struggling in the folds of a shirt; at the doorway a man is putting on his pads, and as he does so gentle applause in the field announces the fall of another wicket. Then the fingers of the man who is putting on his pads are seen to get slightly agitated and lose something of control over the buckles. Genial handclaps welcome back the batsman who has just been bowled; there is the noise of tins rattling, as the small boy by the score-board proudly builds up his proclamation: 34—5—7. The next man in leaves the pavilion hurriedly (strange how one is never quite ready to go out to bat; no matter how long the time for getting ready—there is always a penultimate second of mingled panic and confusion, a sharp sense in the mind that one's pads after all are wrong way round and the straps absurdly loose). The village green again makes genial handclaps while the next man in walks to the middle; everybody knows well enough that he will be back almost immediately, yet everybody pretends that he won't. And the batsman himself, such is the faith within his immortal soul, really believes that this time, by taking great care, he will get at least a dozen runs— a belief not shaken by countless Saturday afternoons' proofs that his ability is justly measured by a snick through the slips.

It is humour that keeps the village green lovable, the fun that is born whenever ambition in fallible mortals vaults well beyond achievement's reach. Rarely comes humour like this to county cricket. For in county cricket, laughter which binds weak faltering man to weak faltering man is often enough expelled by sheer efficiency. A Hobbs commands admiration; never does he set us laughing. Art is austere. With Hobbs it is certain as certain can be that we shall see beautiful and scientific cricket; its very perfection, though, can easily hold it at a distance from common humanity; its very ease and mastery will place it outside the world where Disrule is merry king, bursting our pretty bladders of vanity with a cudgel of hard fact—the hard fact of our essential limitations.

The captain of the village team is the village parson; every week he opens the innings with Simpson, his gardener. And every week, without exception, the Rev. P. P. Jenkins goes to the wicket believing that somehow he is about to play, at last, the innings of his life. He hits his first ball for four, a stroke which is impressive because of its great power and rashness. He attempts a like stroke from the next ball and he is comprehensively bowled. As he departs from the wicket Simpson, his gardener, says, 'Aye, but Maister Jenkins 'e does have a terrible shortness of patience for a minister of the Church.' And laughter that makes for fellow-feeling is born forthwith.

Hobbs and Sutcliffe stealing runs against a swift field—an admirable sight this, but where's the humour of it? as Corporal Nym would ask. We do not laugh at the thing that is well done. Watch the Rev. P. P. Jenkins and his curate as they steal *their* runs. The curate plays a ball nervously towards cover and cries out 'Yes—No', an ambiguous remark which leaves the Rev. P. P. Jenkins suspended, so to speak, in thin air, mid-wicket. Frantically

44

he doubles on his tracks, flings himself along the earth and gets home by the skin of his teeth. He picks himself up; his heart returns from his mouth to its proper place. He looks down the pitch at his apologetic curate and says, choosing words with much self-control, 'My dear Tompkinson, do try to be definite. I hate a "Yes—No"; it is very confusing.'

I am not, of course, unmindful of the skill the village game is able to boast; from country cricket have come Rhodes, Tyldesley, Hirst, Blythe. My point is that cleverness is but a by-product (to borrow Mr. Shaw's term) in village cricket; they do not insist tyrannically on skill down at Old Slocombe. All that is expected there of a cricketer is a good heart and some decent flannels—though, for that matter, I have seen the blacksmith score his runs while his trousers' braces dangled about his body and his grimy shirt hung loose at the neck; he used his bat like a hammer, and for yards around the wicket it might have been a red-hot forge. . . . The very language of censure invented by cricketers for the incompetents is full of the milk of human kindness. 'Butterfingers' and 'Rabbits' are cheerful, tolerant epithets, and both of them come from the village green. Even the man who leans over the fence, if he gets there in good time, may easily find himself taking part in the game; there is usually 'one or two short' at Little Puddleton. And if the parson asks him to field long-on at both ends he is not likely to complain; to his dying day he will cherish the pleasure got from walking through the long grass, his face burning in the falling sunshine. After the match, let him call at the Spotted Cow. There he will hear Simpson, the parson's gardener, making a magnanimous review of the afternoon's play: 'An' parson, when 'e were bowled, well 'e said—ay, 'e did too —"Dang me," says 'e, "if ever I play again!" But this were only 'is proud spirit. 'E's spoke rash like that for more 'n twenty year.'

OLD ENGLISH

THE records of 'W. G.' that have lately been equalled were merely his minor achievements. What, indeed, was a mere matter of 50,000 runs in a lifetime to him, and 2,000 wickets (some of which *must* have been out)? He took his cricket in his stride, the while he went about the main purpose of his existence, which was to be, as Emerson would say, a Representative Englishman. Grace was an Institution (to use a term which, surprisingly enough, Mrs. Micawber never used to describe her Wilkins); he was as Institutional in this land and in his age as Mr. Gladstone. Is Hobbs, in this sense, a national possession? Do folk talk of Hobbs who know not what a break-back is? Grace was, in his prime, a Topic of Conversation; after dinner, lean and spectacled professors of moral philosophy would ask 'How many has Dr. Grace made today?' The Royal Family was in the habit of inquiring publicly, at proper intervals, about the health of 'W. G.'. And when it was known in the clubs of the West End that 'W. G.' was not out at lunch they emptied immediately, and along the St. John's Wood Road, on the way to Lord's, the tinkle-tinkle of hansom cabs would be heard on the sunny air.

Grace is a legend now, but to hundreds of folk who never looked upon him in the flesh he is more real than living men. I saw him only once—praise the Lord, he spoke to me, and when I was a little boy! Yet it seems today that I saw him often, and knew him well. Never can I hope to know, say, Hearne half so well, though I have seen Hearne not once but many, many times. Grace's fame, the tradition of him, not only as cricketer but as man, has become part of the land's inherited memory. Innumerable fathers have communicated to innumerable sons a sense of 'W. G.', an idea, a feeling, an emotion of him. This is immortality.

We were discussing his records; the essential ones are still unapproached, let alone broken. Where is the next cricketer capable of weighing 18 or 20 stone and growing an immense black beard at the same time? Where is the next cricketer capable of 'W. G's.' never-ending energy, gusto, and enjoyment of the game? Where is the next cricketer capable of carrying out his bat for 300, then fielding the whole length of the other side's two innings, and then, on the last evening, immediately the match is over, capable also of running uphill to the station for the last train, hugging a cricket bag, whiskers blowing in the wind, while a mob of happy, cheering urchins follow after? For years he 'diddled them out' and hardly a batsman grew the wiser. Perhaps some great stand was going on against Gloucestershire. At length the Old Man's high voice would be heard: 'Here, you, give me that ball. You kaint get 'em out; you kaint get 'em out. Let me have a try, I'll see what I can do.' He would lumber along to the wicket and his arm would come half-

46

over, heavily, laboriously. He would give, apparently, the most
tremendous twist to his fingers, making a grunt as though the act
of putting on so much break were hurting him. And the ball would
pitch and go quite straight on—straight enough, anyhow! 'Heh's
thaat?' the high voice would demand, and probably would itself
give prompt answer:

'Out! You kaint put your legs to a straight ball. Out! Well
pla-ayed, well plaayed! Who's next? Give me that ball; he's a
young 'un, this lad; I ken get him out! I ken get him out!'

What a man! He was bound to be loved, for he was constantly
happy in his play. Did he ever use his wits unfairly? Let me quote
an old Gloucestershire professional—he was a cricketer who served
under 'W. G.' and would have gone through fire and water for him:
'I never knew the old 'un to get up to sharp doings,' said this
henchman of the Master; 'no; he kept the ring of the Law all right.
But, goodness me, the Rum Things he did do inside it!' Grace
played cricket with the whole man of him in full action, body, soul,
heart, and wits. He would have had caustic things to say about any
notion that winning in cricket doesn't matter. 'What, what?' we can
easily imagine him saying; 'winning don't matter, eh? What the
hangment are we all pretending to be doing here, then? What's the
scorers for? Best side ought to win, eh? Best side, eh? Well, ain't *we*
the best side? Eh? Get on with the ga-ame; get on with it. Give me
that ball; you kaint get him out nohow. Pla-ay—Heh's thaat!' Old
artful dodger he may have been at times, yet nobody has ever heard
an unaffectionate word spoken of 'W. G.' by any cricketer who knew
and played with him.

Cricket was for Grace more than an affair in which the aim is to
set high skill precisely against high skill. He, perhaps the most
scientific of batsmen, never allowed himself to fall into that mechanical kind of play and that blankness of mind which are the bane of
the game. His nature was always alert, his spirits agile. If sometimes
he was so keen that he would appeal for leg-before-wicket from a
position at right angles to the ball's line of flight—why, he got so
much glee out of stealing a march on his enemies that human nature
had no choice but to smile at his artfulness—and wish him luck.
Once, when Grace was fielding at deep square-leg, Fred Roberts,
the old Gloucestershire bowler, hit a batsman on the pads with a
fast ball and did not appeal. At the end of the over 'W. G.' came
thundering over the earth and in a voice of terrible rage he demanded: 'Why in hangment's name didn't you appeal, Fred?' Poor

Fred, wishing he was dead, and trembling all over his body, stammered, 'W-w-w-well, s-sir; I-I-I was w-w-waitin' for you, s-s-sir!'

I see his long, happy life always with the West Country for a background, a far-off England now, peaceful and simple of heart. Morning after morning the summer's sun rose for him, and he went forth and trod fresh grass. Every springtime came and found him ready for cricket; when he was a boy he learned the game in a Gloucestershire orchard white with bloom. He grew in the sunshine and wind and rain; the elements became flesh within him. Why did this natural man ever die? On June days when the trees beyond the Nursery End at Lord's are moving gently in the light, and cricketers are on the field with hours of the game before them—on these gracious mornings it is hard to understand why 'W. G.' should not have been permitted to go on living on the ripe earth, playing the game he loved until he was tired of it.

A SENTIMENTAL JOURNEY

A TAXI was taking Jolyon to Lord's, running quickly along and passing Regents Park on the right. The old man felt a flutter of strange excitement; not for years had he been to Lord's—he couldn't remember the last time. He was always intending to watch a cricket match again, but somehow other things turned up, and he loved his garden in the summer. He remembered, as if it were only yesterday, the match in which Grace reached his 1000 runs in May. Grace had wanted about 50, and for a quarter of an hour his score stayed at 49. A long time ago; the 'nineties seemed to Jolyon often to be farther away than the days when he was at Oxford. He played in the Parks in a Freshman's match and remembered it well. But he often mixed up the names and events of the 'nineties.

There was something strange about this journey to Lord's; what was it? Ah, of course, he was being taken in a taxi. Never before had he gone to Lord's in a taxi; it had always been a hansom. But there was much to be said for taxis; they went quicker, saved time, and, besides, that hole in the top of a hansom was a fool of a thing, and you felt ridiculous when the cabby looked at you through it.

The taxi turned into St. John's Wood Road. Jolyon recognised every part of the pavement of it; time after time he had come here on forgotten June mornings. It was quieter then, not so much traffic. He once saw Richardson and Lockwood walking along the pavement. They were very big men, and they wore blue serge, with watch-chains over their waistcoats. Both were dead now, Jolyon supposed, but you could not easily believe it; they had seemed the sort of simple, rough men that go on for ever. 'Institutions,' said Jolyon as he thought about them.

He saw at once, as soon as he got into the ground, that the place had changed a bit. He was not sure about the Nursery end. Where were the arches? That stand was in the way; that was new for certain. Well it was a change for the better; it looked handsome, and there was no doubt that many more people watched cricket nowadays. He bought a match-card off a boy on his favourite Mound stand; he never did sit in the pavilion, not enough sunshine there after midday. He looked at the card: 'Gloucestershire *v.* Middlesex; a three-day match.' He liked the formality of Lord's. A splendid place; he really must come oftener. The pavilion possessed dignity; the whole place stood for something. Jolyon remembered a phrase he had read the other day about Lord's—'Eternal England'; rhetorical, of course, but true in a way.

He was glad it was Gloucestershire who were playing: he wanted to see Hammond. He read the names on the card. Where did C. L. Townsend bat nowadays? But what was he talking about; C. L. Townsend didn't play any longer. No, it was not a piece of bad memory; he prided himself on his memory. C. L. Townsend had given up county cricket early on in life; he could not be much more than—well, fifty or so. Jolyon saw Townsend at Lord's bowling left-handed slows, fresh from school, a tall, thin boy. Then there was Jessop. Jolyon chuckled. How the field used to spread; four or five men in the deep and the stumper all alone! But Thornton had been a bigger hitter even than Jessop; and then there was that Australian fellow, Blackham; no, Bonnor—that was his name; he had a black beard.

The players came into the field, and Jolyon joined in the hand-clapping. He found it hard to sort out the cricketers, though he admitted the score-board was efficiently worked. 'Bowler 10,' Goddard; a new man, evidently. And Middlesex, not Gloucestershire, were batting. He turned to a parson sitting next to him. 'Which is Hammond?' he asked. The parson pointed out Hammond

49

fielding in the slips. 'Ah yes, of course,' said Jolyon. 'He's thickened out since last summer.' He was pleased with that reply; he was not going to give himself away.

'They are making the new ball swerve a lot this morning,' he said to the parson after a while. That was another score for him. He had read in the newspaper all about the new ball—no fresh idea, of course, because he recollected old Wright of Kent and Rawlin of Middlesex. The parson became a little restive. 'Very slow batting,' he said. 'They don't play forward enough; I'd like to see Stoddart tackling this stuff.' 'They've got to play themselves in,' said Jolyon, and he applauded a stroke through the slips which went for a single. 'Stoddart would have cut that ball for four,' said the parson, 'but you never see any cutting nowadays.' Jolyon fixed his attention on the game. He admired the quick movements of Hammond in the slips. When Hendren and Hearne came in he told the parson who they were.

At lunch he went in the room where a long time ago he used to take his young nephew. He ordered cold salmon and tasted it again after many years. It brought back a Gentlemen v. Players match; he could feel the day and the occasion. Curious how a man sometimes feels he is doing something he has done before, feels he is living through a scene and an act which, as though in another existence, he has already lived through. That day he had given young Stephen a birthday, and after Lord's had taken him to the club and then to a theatre to see W. S. Penley. They left Lord's an hour before close of play, and in Pall Mall they bought an evening newspaper and saw that Arthur Shrewsbury had reached his century. He could have sworn, as he ate the salmon, that it had all happened only last year; the sense of everything remained fresh and near.

He returned to his seat. Hearne was not out, and Robins was in with him. He liked the young man, so eager and full of life. He applauded vigorously and several times cried out 'Well hit, sir!' He told the parson what he thought of Robins. The parson answered, 'I wish this man Hearne would bestir himself.' Jolyon told him that the bowling was very good. He was sad when Robins fell to a catch at cover.

Another professional joined Hearne. The sun shone down on his old head, and the chimes of the clock in the ivy-covered tower made a sweet sound. He nodded, and saw the haze of heat on the meadows beyond his garden near the Thames; he saw dappled shadows on the grass at his feet made by the sun falling through the orchard trees. He told himself he would have to see Wilson about some wasp-bands. . . . He woke up with a start. Confound it, he had fallen asleep at Lord's. He was annoyed with himself. Perhaps, after all, this man Hearne was rather dreary; but he had enjoyed Robins. He liked the noise of the hand-claps as it rippled round the field from time to time. Yes, he would come to Lord's oftener. Another wicket fell, and he looked for his match-card. It had dropped to the ground. He picked it up, and after examining the scoreboard he wrote with his pencil '*c*. Sinfield, *b*. Parker'. 'Parker must be getting on in years,' he said to the parson next him. Hearne was in the nineties, and Jolyon became nervous. 'Leave them alone, he murmured as one or two offside balls went by Hearne's bat. The parson told him there was no danger. At last Hearne hit a four and reached his century. 'Well played, sir,' said Jolyon, 'a fine innings, I think.' 'Too slow,' said the parson. 'He's played the right game for his side,' retorted Jolyon, and then felt ashamed of his heat. Still, he was right, surely, to stand up for Hearne. He looked at his watch. Ten minutes to six—he must be going. The parson was calculating the time Hearne had been batting; four hours for 102. 'They don't hit the ball,' he maintained. Jolyon chuckled to himself; a lovely thrust had occurred to him. He got up ready to depart. 'Too many people nowadays living in the past,' he said.

Outside the ground he was still chuckling; that was a Parthian thrust, he told himself. He got into a taxi, and soon he was passing Regents Park again. An idea struck him; he would round off the day at Lord's in the way he used to; dinner at the club and then a theatre. Once he saw Irving in *The Bells* a few hours after he had seen W. G. Grace make a big score. Well, there was Gerald du Maurier at the Prince's, as good an actor as any of them.

DUCKWORTH

MEN often tell us by their physical appearance what they do for a living. Lawyers look legal; colonels look belligerent; ostlers look like horses about the mouth; and wicket-keepers look like nothing on earth but stumpers. George Duckworth was made by nature to sit close to the ground; he bends nicely, and his voice would have been wasted in any occupation but the one he adorns so perfectly. Duckworth's appeal is famous at this end and at the other end of the earth; sometimes it is so penetrating that both ends of the earth might well be able to hear it at the same moment.

He is a most hostile stumper, no mere accomplice to the bowlers. Duckworth is not content to wait for the attack to deliver batsmen into his clutches; he is warlike in his own right, out for destruction of his own. I have seen him in his best days plunder catches from unsuspecting and honest glances to leg, held up and ruined on the direct and open highway to the boundary. Old Trafford will never forget the sight of Duckworth crouching low to the fast bowling of Macdonald. Along the earth came Macdonald with his own supple and sinister silence; the wrist was poised for a second before the ball flashed through the air: the beautiful poise of the cobra's head before the spitting of venom. Then would Old Trafford see the poor batsman's pathetic reflex action, and hear a snick, and a triumphant shriek as Duckworth hurled himself yards to leg and caught the ball with a voracity which made the faltering batsman not his victim so much as his prey.

There are stumpers who do their work by stealth. Oldfield is the gentlemanly Starkey of wicket-keepers; he whips off the bails quietly and turns his head to the square-leg umpire and formally asks, 'How is that?' He seems to apologize to the batsman as though saying, 'Terribly sorry to have to stump you like this, sir—and behind your back!—but I have no alternative. Anyhow, I'm doing it as nicely as I can, only the leg bail. Good afternoon; there's the pavilion on the right. Mind the step.' Duckworth stumps his men out in a frenzy of mingled exultation, rage, and indignation. His appeal says at one and the same time, 'Out! How dare you lift your right toe? I'm here. Out! Hop it! Out, umpire! I'm telling you.' Duckworth's appeal is frequently the judgment itself, not the petition asking for judgment. Up goes his right finger when he appeals for leg-before-wicket, and his legs are aggressively a-straddle. A terrific little fighter, the Game Chicken, palpably a Lancashire lad—nay, better still, a Warrington lad.

Duckworth is a creative stumper; he makes many of his catches himself and has a disdain for the passive watchfulness of those stumpers who hope to serve by just standing and waiting. I have seen Duckworth get his gloves to snicks and mis-hits which would not seem to go in the territory at all of other wicket-keepers. And because he has not been able to hold the absolutely elusive chance he has been reported as having missed a chance. People of dull mind will tell you that Duckworth is brilliant but erratic, as though anybody can be brilliant and consistent.

The power exercised over a great batsman by a great hostile wicket-keeper is not estimated by half on the score-sheet; it is not merely the catches and the stumping that tell the tale; the aggressive presence of a Duckworth prevents a batsman from attempting strokes which would be safe enough if the wicket-keeper were only a more or less passive accessory after the bowler's act. Duckworth is attacking from behind as directly and violently as the bowler is attacking from the front. I have myself felt the force of Duckworth's ravenous presence behind the wicket, and in the batsman's eyeless rear; I believe that I was the first cricketer ever to be stumped by Duckworth on Old Trafford's historic grass. (It happened more than a dozen years ago; further details would not be relevant here; I will add no more than that I lifted my toe for not more than two-thirds of a second and that when Duckworth stumped me I felt I had been sandbagged.)

Oldfield and H. Martyn of Somersetshire are the two most stylish wicket-keepers I have seen. I was much too late for Pilling. Martyn was an intrepid genius; he 'stood up' in a Gentleman v. Players match to N. A. Knox and Brearley. He 'stood up' once to Kortright, the fastest bowler of all time, so they say. His captain said, 'Do you know who's about to bowl?' 'Yes,' answered Martyn. 'Well, then, get back a few yards unless you want to be knocked out.' 'I prefer where I am, if you don't mind,' replied Martyn. And then he proceeded to stump somebody, just outside the leg stump, off Kortright. Duckworth is nimble, galvanic, rather than stylish; he is the Spring-heeled Jack of stumpers.

Since his first season in county cricket Duckworth has held 539 catches and achieved 283 successful acts of stumping. These figures do not, of course, give the faintest notion of the number of times Duckworth has appealed. He has won honours on all the fields of cricket; they know him and love him in Sydney, Melbourne, Brisbane, Adelaide, Capetown, Johannesburg, Sheffield, Lord's and Maidstone. He has held up an Australian attack for an hour and a half; he can be very obstinate with the bat, and I love to see him get down on his bat and stick out his chin, and scamper across the wicket shouting 'one run'. He is a character as well as a cricketer, a dweller upon the fine points of strategy, a man of views outside cricket; a shrewd man and a Lancastrian to the bone's marrow. The boys and girls worship him, and that is a fine thing to say of any cricketer.

ONLY A GAME

FAR away at Trent Bridge there has been a Test match, seen by a congested crowd, while all the press and megaphones of the world made the air a showman's rostrum. Far away from where? Why, from the cricket field of Puddleton-in-the-Hills. I can see it still, as I saw it years ago, at two o'clock on a Wednesday afternoon. In the pavilion there was a sound of somebody setting out teacups; it was Mrs. Simpson, the old lady who attended to the refreshments. She assured me that it was going to be fine because of the drawing pains in her legs in the night. 'They always draw,' she said, 'when there's one of them anti-cyclones which the B.B.C. talk about.' She was anxious for a fine day because her boy Johnny, aged thirteen, had been chosen to make up the eleven for Puddleton against Watch-over. She had washed and ironed his cricket-shirt that morning.

Out in the sunshine the groundsman was pottering about. I walked through the long grass of the outfield to the brown oblong which was the pitch. He said he expected to see a few 'shooters' during the afternoon; he was umpire as well as groundsman. 'I'd like to see that feller Bradman batting here.' He was proud of his wicket that assisted 'shooters'. 'He'd have to jump about,' said the old man, with a chuckle. 'There's nothin' like these here worm-casts for bowlin' on,' he added, with another and deeper chuckle. I gathered that he took a lenient view of leg-before-wicket until the batsman 'did it twice', by which he meant a second case of a 'shooter' colliding with a pad or a big toe. 'I like to see 'em dancing,' he said, not in an unkindly way, but as one who liked to enjoy himself.

The match began as soon as the cows behind the bowler's arm opposite to the pavilion had been chased into the next field. Later in the afternoon, during a misunderstanding between the two batsmen in the middle of the wicket, a certain run-out was averted because long-off got his hand entangled in the grass where the cows had been. It was a young clerk who worked in the solicitor's office in the Watchover High Street; if it had been Bowker, the Watchover blacksmith, the Reverend H. H. Pinching would not have scored anything like 26. The Reverend Pinching always batted first; he played cricket seriously, remembered that Tom Emmett had coached him at Rugby, and found only one flaw in his love of the game at Puddleton: the outfield robbed him of four after four. 'He won't hit 'em in the air,' explained Giles the umpire to me; 'he's a stickler for style.' I confess it seemed to me a shame to hear and to see the Reverend Pinching's off-drive crash from the bat and go with a swishing sound into the long grass and stop dead there, so that extra-cover had to come forward to retrieve the ball.

Bowker naturally employed less fastidious methods when Watchover went in; he clumped into the air, and sometimes the fieldsmen had to grab wildly about them and tear up handfuls of grass as they hurled in their returns. Bowker was clean bowled by the Reverend Pinching with a high full toss; he called it his 'head' ball. Whenever he went to Lord's the Reverend Pinching sat on the seats near the Tavern and drank a glass of ale with his sandwiches, and in the lunch interval got into conversation with somebody, and said, at last, 'I can't think why the modern bowlers don't send a high full toss now and then, straight on to the bails.' He also thought that modern batsmen were too apt to use their pads. And he disliked maiden overs; from time to time he would send a letter to the newspapers arguing that a maiden over should count as one to the fielding side.

Watchover's captain was the village grocer, and when he tossed for innings with the Reverend Pinching he did so with a certain deference. 'Heads,' he said, as the coin went into the air from the parson's fingers. He was too polite to look down eagerly to the earth when the coin fell and the Reverend Pinching said, 'We'll bat.' Watchover dismissed Puddleton for 68; the boy Johnny went in last and scored two runs, a single through the slips and a single stolen by a sharp run from a ball blocked just outside the crease. The bowler was Smith, the Watchover constable, and he bowled fast and did not slacken his pace for Johnny. 'Stand up to 'im,' whispered the umpire to Johnny, 'he'll not hit you, and I'll not give you out if I can help it.' Johnny's mother saw him batting through the little window of the pavilion, while she cut the cake for afternoon tea. Then, when Watchover batted, Johnny was long-stop at both ends, and he walked up and down the wicket, as the field changed over, looking very tiny amongst so many big men, but very industrious and loyal. It was not his fault that Watchover won the match.

The game finished with cheers and handshakings. Somehow there was a general overlooking of Johnny; he was too shy to go into the pavilion when the Reverend Pinching called for three times three in honour of the victors. Johnny went home and waited for his mother, who, of course, stayed behind to lock up. But when she did come home she told him she had watched him batting. 'You were a good lad,' she said. And that night there came a knock at the old woman's door, and the Reverend Pinching looked in just to say that he wanted to thank Johnny for making up the side. 'He played very well, Mrs. Simpson; I'll give him some coaching—some instruction, you know.'

After the Reverend Pinching had departed, waving his hand to Mrs. Simpson as he rode down the lane on his bicycle, she ran upstairs to Johnny's bedroom. She woke him up and told him what the 'minister' had said; and Johnny went to sleep, the happiest boy in England, at ten o'clock exactly, just as down at the Rose and Crown they were turning out the saloon bar, and old Giles, the umpire, was explaining that the parson had really been out leg-before-wicket before he had scored. 'But,' he said, 'I gev him out last week 'gainst Hortford, 'fore he 'ad scored, and it were not fer me to gev him out agean so soon like; now were it, George?'

A DAY AT TRENT BRIDGE
(MAY 11, 1929)

THE main challenge to Lancashire is likely this season to come from Nottinghamshire; that was one reason why I went to Trent Bridge today to see the cricket between Nottinghamshire and Kent. But it was not the chief reason. I made the journey because this match is always gallant; the antagonists are led by courageous captains who, when they toss for innings, say, 'One of us is going to win, and one of us is going to lose.'

The play gave me more pleasure than anything I have seen on a county ground for a long time past; it was none of your canny trench warfare, with men burrowing underground, afraid to show themselves to the enemy. This was an action that went forward openly on the green earth. From noon till evening, batsmen, bowlers, and fieldsmen played cricket; the good ball was respected, the bad one was attacked; bowlers never ceased trying to get wickets, and batsmen were constantly looking for runs. Not once all day did I observe an instance where a batsman declined the opportunity of a hit from a ball of loose length. In less than six hours 430 runs were scored and 12 wickets were taken.

When I reached Trent Bridge the match had been in progress for nearly half an hour. As soon as I passed through the gates I looked at the score-board; it told me that it was not a Lancashire and Yorkshire match, for I saw that 40 runs had already been hit for one wicket. Then my eyes saw Woolley leaning on his bat at the end opposite to the one which Hardinge was about to defend. Woolley leaning on his bat is amongst the loveliest sights a cricket field has to show—the tall and slender shape, the inscrutable face, the air of negligent mastery. I had scarcely settled in a seat before Woolley was cutting and driving the Nottinghamshire bowling at his sweet will; twice in one over he sent the ball to the boundary with a bat which curved effortlessly; he leaned on an off-side delivery, and at once it was running silently over the grass with the quickness of light in summer. Kent lost Ashdown's wicket, caught by Lilley, when their score was only 18; then Hardinge and Woolley reached 50 in just over half an hour. Hardinge drove through the covers in a style which named the period of his first culture; you need to go to old-fashioned batsmanship for simple beauty, even as you need to go to old-fashioned music for mellowness and simple song. But when Hardinge had made 24 I thought he was leg-before-wicket to the Shrewsbury schoolboy, Bland, who is on trial just now for his county. The ball made pace from the turf and quite defeated Hardinge's broad bat. From where I sat, it appeared that the pads alone saved the stumps. Kent were 67 for one, and the match merely fifty minutes old when Woolley's innings came to a cruel end. He was playing at his most felicitous; his long easy strokes made the bowling seem a yard shorter than actually it was. He countered, by means of his own composed but strong back-stroke, a ball from Barratt which pitched just short of a length and came sharply upwards. Woolley played the ball into his wickets. A hundred runs, with bloom on every one, were thus cut sinfully down. But Woolley's innings of 24 was worth any century built parsimoniously up by (as Ko-Ko in *The Mikado* would put it) What d'ye call him—

Thing'em-bob, and likewise—Never-mind. Woolley is about to celebrate his forty-second birthday; he has seen cricket pass through many phases; he has seen the various fashions of swerve and spin and off-theory and leg-theory, seen them all wax and wane, but has gone his own ways, to the honour and bright renown of cricket. What does he think in his heart of all the current chatter about the need to 'liven up' cricket? Given the right sort of cricketer, the right attitude of mind, the rules are good enough. Today Woolley is as great a batsman as ever he was. The gods preserve him, for there is no winter in his bounty; his autumn grows the more by reaping.

Ames came in after Woolley and put a ball from Barratt through the slips off the edge of his bat. He played confidently nevertheless, and according to the custom of the day he hit two boundaries in an over. Kent reached 100 in eighty minutes, and Carr looked worried. Just after one o'clock Larwood returned to the attack, and now the turf was slightly faster. He bowled Ames with a ball of glorious length and speed. And almost on the point of lunch he got Hardinge caught at the wicket. Hardinge was disgusted that he had touched the ball, but Larwood does not often leave the batsman free not to play some sort of stroke. In five minutes under two hours Hardinge made 73 by vintage batsmanship. At lunch Kent were 138 for four.

The interval gave me a pleasure which was in keeping with a day that I will try always to cherish. There is efficiency at Trent Bridge, yet not so much that homeliness is dispelled. You can walk on soft grass on one side of the ground. And behind the old pavilion is a hen-run, with chickens just out of the shell; and a little orchard where the trees are in blossom. The pavilion itself is touched with age, but I would not have a single coat of new paint on it. Inside the pavilion there are many fine old prints and portraits which tell of the great traditions of Trent Bridge. You can see the picture of Richard Daft, most lordly of men. There is a score-card of a match between the Ladies of Nottingham and Veterans of the Crimea and Indian Mutiny. The Ladies won easily, and five of the Veterans were run out—perhaps some of them had the rheumatics or were hard of hearing. And there is a score-card of a game in which R. H. Spooner made 249 at Trent Bridge; I watched the innings and I can see it in my mind's eye yet, an innings of gold and silver.

After lunch we were granted the spectacle of Larwood at his best. He bowled Deed by a stupendous breakback. Legge, the Kent captain, tackled Larwood with a big heart. Twice in quick sequence he drove to the off boundary the man who has blighted Ponsford's life. Larwood's pace hereabout was as fast as Macdonald's, to say the least. Legge was out at 166 in a way that set the crowd buzzing. He gave a lightning chance to the slips; the next ball he drove to the off for four; the next ball whipped in and wrecked the stumps.

The Kent innings seemed ready to fall into ruin on a splendid Trent Bridge turf. Two amateur batsmen, proper cricketers of Kent, saved the day partially. Mitchell, son of the famous Frank Mitchell, now joined Bryan, who since one o'clock had been defending with capital skill and judgment. Mitchell showed fight—a laughing antagonism it was, for at every blow of his bat, even when he missed the ball, Mitchell showed a gay smile to the grim men of Nottinghamshire—especially when Larwood shaved his wicket. Larwood was rested and Voce, who today bowls fast left-handed swingers to a leg-trap, 'went for' Mitchell's wicket for all he was worth in young, abounding vitality. Once Mitchell clouted high to the straight deep field a fast short ball from Voce. Fizzing white wine of the best of games!

Bryan and Mitchell held the Kent seventh wicket for fifty-five minutes and scored 61. A few moments later Bryan's high-minded innings was ended by a catch by Payton which was all in tune with an afternoon of ideal cricket. With the Kent 'tail' in Bryan began to hit, and after two or three drives and pulls in the grand manner, he drove a ball from Voce loftily past mid-on. The bat was too much 'under' the ball for safety, but the hit seemed to be going clear of Payton, who turned instinctively as though to run to the boundary. He put out his hand as the ball was leaving him and—it stuck. Payton did not throw up the ball for a second or two; obviously the truth of his wonderful catch did not dawn on his mind all at once; when it did he threw up the ball like a schoolboy. Bryan's innings lasted one hour and fifty minutes; every stroke told of uncommon cricket sense and a principled technique. At four o'clock Kent were all out for 255, made in twenty minutes under four hours. Nottinghamshire bowled steadily all the time, and, as I have tried to suggest, Larwood had mighty moments.

The boy Bland interested me—perhaps most of all because he has played cricket at Shrewsbury School. That means he is one of the blest of the earth. He knows what it is to walk down the avenue of limes to the river, to call out 'Boat!' to the ferryman, to climb the hill, to walk through the gate near the little chapel, to come suddenly upon the playing-fields stretching to the west. He has seen the 'cotton' tree shedding its blossom in July, and has known the peace-fulness of summer in a place where at high noon the earth seems to stand still for a brief moment in the heat. And he has heard (or ought to have heard) the crow flapping back to its nest in the high dark branches over the chapel at the day's silent end.

At twenty minutes past four, in none too good a light, George Gunn and Whysall began the Nottinghamshire innings masterfully. The batting was in excellent contrast. At one end Whysall drove ponderously; his massive blows reminded me of heavy artillery. His bat moved matter from one part of the field to another. But there was nothing of matter to be moved in Gunn's play; his strokes were as flickers of wit and personality coming from him through the bat's end. Every stroke by Gunn has 'touch'; it is not made merely by a bat striking a ball. The bat itself seems to possess sensibility; one can easily imagine that a bat in Gunn's hands is alive and able to relish the sensation of willow cutting and driving cricket ball. All his strokes are his very own; even the classical cover-drive, which he let us admire several times today, is somehow put into the light of his own whimsical mind. For, of course, he might easily decide not to make the drive at all, but instead block the ball for us tantalisingly down to the earth. The man is made all out of whimsicality. Gunn and Whysall scored 50 in thirty-five minutes, and 100 in just over an hour. At 119 Whysall was bowled, and a dozen runs afterwards Freeman defeated Gunn. Between them Gunn and Whysall hit no fewer than twenty boundaries. The day went to a rattling end with Carr at the wicket. In two hours and ten minutes Nottinghamshire scored 175.

The delectable experience at Trent Bridge was rounded off happily—a journey home to Manchester on the London train caught at Derby; dinner in the restaurant car, with the Peak outside my window quiet and gleaming in the evening sunshine.

ARTHUR MAILEY

THE most fascinating cricketer I have known was the Australian Arthur Mailey, an artist in every part of his nature. On the field of play, he bowled leg-spin, with the 'googly'. A man of his gift for fantasy could never have contented himself with 'seaming' a new ball. Mailey would tell me how much he revelled in the 'feel' of a ball spinning from his fingers. 'I'd rather spin and see the ball hit for four than bowl a batsman out by a straight one.' Such a view or attitude was not exactly attuned to the main idea (the only idea nowadays) obsessing a cricketer: the lust for victory, the fear of defeat. Yet Mailey could win a match devastatingly, spinning the greatest batsmen to immobile helplessness. Once he bowled Gloucestershire out single-fingered, or rather, with three fingers and a thumb. He took all ten wickets in a Gloucestershire innings for 66. Then, later, when he wrote his autobiography, he called the book *10 for 66, and All That*.

His life as a boy was not unlike my own, born in a semi-slum, the so-called Surry 'hills', a Sydney excretion, eighty years ago. He was 'dragged up', and worked as a labourer, a plumber's mate, at any casual job. All the time he educated himself, learned not only the most difficult sort of bowling; also he cultivated a talent to paint pictures and draw cartoons. He became, at the height of his career as cricketer, a well-liked cartoonist in Sydney newspapers. He sketched in the manner of the 1890s, broad and unsubtle, yet humorous. He painted landscape canvases, with trees and skies recognisably green, brown or blue. In London, he had a private exhibition of his paintings. Queen Mary did him the honour of inspecting these landscapes. She was graciously approving, on the whole; but she paused in front of one canvas, saying: 'I don't think, Mr. Mailey, you have painted the sun quite convincingly in this picture.' 'Perhaps not, Your Majesty,' replied Arthur, 'you see, Your Majesty, in this country I have to paint the sun from memory.'

'If ever I bowl a maiden over,' he assured me, 'it's not my fault, but the batsman's.' He enjoyed himself; he explored himself; he was whimsical. One Saturday in Sydney I saw him on the ferry boat going to Neutral Bay, a mile or two's journey—it couldn't be called a voyage. We chatted and parted at our suburban destination. A few days later, I read in a newspaper that he had arrived in London —in wartime. Not a word had he spoken, as we journeyed that Saturday afternoon to Neutral Bay, of his flight to London. I would run into him at Lord's, not during a tour of an Australian team here, run into him and cry out in surprise, 'Good Lord, Arthur, what are you doing in London? When did you come?' 'Oh,' he would say, 'I've just dropped in from Hong Kong—via Neutral Bay.' He was slender of physical build, well-shouldered; his face good-looking, with a touch of aboriginal, was wrinkled with incipient fun. He never laughed loudly; he smiles, as the play of his whimsical mind tickled his nerve of risibility. He was one of the New South Wales bowlers pitted against Victoria at Melbourne, in the Australian summer of 1926–1927, in the match in which Victoria amassed 1107 runs in a single innings. Mailey contrived to take 4 wickets for round about 350 runs; but, he maintained to his life's end, the scorer's analysis on the occasion did him less than justice, because three catches were missed off his bowling—'two by a man in the pavilion, wearing a bowler hat.'

He tossed up his spin to the batsman slow and alluringly; never have I seen on a cricket field such undisguised temptation as was presented to the batsman by Mailey's bowling. It was almost immoral. He once clean bowled the incomparable Hobbs with a slow full toss, also at Melbourne, after the Master and Herbert Sutcliffe had scored 283 together, undefeated, on the third day of the second Test match of the 1924–1925 rubber. First ball next day Hobbs missed Mailey's full 'floater'. Mailey needed to double-up his body to express the humour of it. If a catch was dropped from his bowling, he seldom complained; he would go to the unhappy fieldsman and say: 'I'm expecting to take a wicket any day now.' No bowler has spun a ball with more than Mailey's twist, fingers and right forearm and leverage. He lacked the accuracy of, say, Grimmett, another Australian leg-spinner; but Mailey bowled his spin with the lavishness of a millionaire. Grimmett bowled it like a miser—as Ray Robinson, Australia's wittiest cricket writer, once put it, or suggested the simile, to me.

He took to cricket in the manner of nearly every Australian boy in his period of penniless nonage, playing with a kerosene tin for the wicket. At once he discovered that he could, with the sensitive education of his fingers, persuade a cricket ball to go through a kaleidoscope of changing curving flight and capricious gyrations from the earth; he could by spin and flight express his own mazeful mind. He was a romantic in the sense which is regarded as completely outmoded these days, a time of history described by Sir Thomas Beecham as 'the most barbaric since Attila'—and that is going back somewhat. Mailey when young was staggered one Saturday, in his head and his heart, to learn that he had been chosen to play in the first XI of his district 'Grade' contingent. (In Australia every suburban community has two or three cricket teams.) Moreover, young Arthur would, this very Saturday, be playing against

Victor Trumper's side. And Victor then was in his prime, the idol worshipped by all Australian boys—and by English boys, myself included—the most chivalrous batsman of all time, the most gallant, versatile and youthful. His grave, in a churchyard outside Sydney, is to this day covered by fresh flowers. Young Mailey spent this Saturday morning, preceding the afternoon of his personal contact with Apollo, in an utter misery of anxiety. No; he wasn't worrying about his own likelihood or unlikelihood of performing ably in his baptism into top-class Sydney cricket, first rung on the ladder to Test matches. His concern was all for Victor—was he well, not afflicted by a chill? Would he get run over in the streets by a cab? People, sixty or so years ago, did somehow get run over by four-wheeled cabs, so Arthur's fears could be justified, considering the way God had made him, responsive to any romantic suggestion. Victor survived the morning's dangers; he did not cut himself dangerously while shaving, did not scald his hand with hot water, did not get run over in the streets. He played for his XI *v.* the XI containing the tyro Mailey. And Mailey couldn't believe it when his captain asked him *to bowl at Victor*! Arthur did bowl at the Incomparable. Victor enchanted Arthur by some strokes from his bowling which, Arthur remembered years after, were like strokes made by a bat of conjuration. Then, incredibly, Arthur clean bowled Victor. And, wrote Mailey, in his autobiography: 'I was ashamed. It was as though I had killed a dove.' Language to bring a blush to the cheeks of the latest of cricket's sophistical fellow-workers.

Mailey really was an incorrigible romantic. Throughout his life (and he passed his eightieth year), he remained, for all his show of worldliness, the poor boy of the Sydney slums, never stale at whatever life brought to him, always *experiencing* events with the boy's wonder—'how has all this happened to me?' On board ship, on his many voyages to England and back to Sydney, his crowning moments occurred whenever he gave a champagne cocktail party. Champagne was, for him, the symbol of the miracle which had changed him from a ragged urchin to one of the best-beloved and most magical of cricketers. He would often, in his cabin on the ship, listen to a gramophone record: Tauber singing about Vienna. He rented a flat in Park Lane during one of his summer visits to London. He gravitated naturally, on holiday, to Montmartre. He died happy. In his last moments of delirium, he imagined he was on board the Orient liner *Orion*, entertaining the ship's captain and officers to a champagne party. He squandered his imagination to the end, even as he tossed up his spin, with the millionaire's generosity. In heaven he has probably already clean bowled the Holy Ghost—with a 'googly'.

TWO SHASTBURY CHARACTERS

RICHMOND was master of mathematics at Shastbury, and he played cricket passionately and statistically. He kept a record of every one of his innings, written down in ledgers of leather binding, carrying the inscription: 'H. Richmond. Cricket. 1893.' And so on. The first volume began much farther back. He was grizzled grey in 1912, a little man squarely built with a ragged moustache and keen, kind eyes. When he was not in form, that is to say when he was not making runs, he would walk through the Shastbury streets absent-mindedly and sometimes he was obviously worried. He was, of course, a bachelor.

His stance at the wicket dated him as decisively as an early Victorian shilling. He stood legs astride, with the upper part of his body bent at an acute angle and even then he appeared to be placed at quite a distance from the line of the bat, wicket to wicket. His left arm suggested an inverted letter V; his bat was scrupulously straight and held upright defending the middle stump so exactly that the bowler might well believe that he could see the off- and leg-stumps. He played off a stationary right foot, the left one going up in a sort of prance. If the ball came in from the off, he played back this way. One day in the nets I advised him to put his right foot and pad over the wicket and try to get behind the ball to play over it with the break. No; he wouldn't 'stick' his legs in front. 'That Nottinghamshire fellow—Shrewsbury—began it all. This leg-before pest. What's a bat for?' He made this statement in May 1913.

When he was in the field and the other side batting, he could tell you the score in detail at any minute, each batsman's contribution and the analysis of each bowler. He remembered everything. Seldom did he need to refer to his ledger if any performance of his own was in question; he made an error on one occasion only, as far as I can remember. In a conversation after net practice he confessed that he had made a pair of spectacles once only in his life and that his second o was given to him by a 'shooter' from Woof while playing in a game against Gloucestershire Club and Ground. Next day he corrected himself, having consulted the ledger for the appropriate year: 'No, it wasn't Woof; it was Paish.' But he'd given us the right date.

On a good pitch he was, for all the 'openness' of his stance, hard to get out. He watched the ball all the way, played extremely late, seldom lifted the bat from the ground and was content to get runs by taps through the slips. After he had scored ten, he would remove the pad on his right foot and give it to the umpire; after he had scored twenty he would remove the pad on his left foot and give it to the umpire; after he had scored thirty he would take off the glove of his left hand and give it to the umpire; and arriving at last at the total of forty he would take off the glove of his right hand and give it also to the umpire. He wore cricket shirts with sleeves the lower half of which could be detached; after the completion of his fifty he would detach both and give the removed parts to the umpire. One afternoon 'Ted' Wainwright, the senior cricket professional, was umpiring and he had not seen Richmond before; it was Ted's first season at Shastbury. As he called for a boy to come from the pavilion to take away his share of Richmond's discarded accoutrements he was overheard to ask: 'What does this little feller look like when he's med an 'undred?'

On a Saturday night in 1912, strangely hot in a season of rain, I was sitting up late in my lodgings at Cross Hill. All afternoon we had umpired, Ted and myself, in a game between the First XI and the Masters. Ted had gone to bed, tolerably drunk. Towards eleven o'clock our landlady came into the sitting-room to say a gentleman had called to see Mr. Wainwright. I went to the door and there was Richmond. I told him that Wainwright was alseep. 'I'm terribly sorry to disturb you at this time of the night,' he said; 'in fact, I've been to bed myself but I couldn't sleep. You see, Cardus, I'm bothered about Wainwright's decision today—he gave me out l.b.w. to a left-arm bowler from round the wicket. Now, I'm not of course doubting Wainwright's judgment but as you know I never stick my legs in front of the wicket; and the main point I'd like Wainwright to explain is how can a left-arm bowler get a man out l.b.w. from round the wicket on a plumb pitch?' He asked me if I could possibly go and see Wainwright, wake him up and get his point of view. There was nothing else for it; obviously Richmond was in danger of a sleepless night. So I took courage and, after some trouble, brought Wainwright temporarily back to consciousness. I jogged his memory

c   65

about the afternoon's doings in general and his Richmond judgment in particular. 'Silly old b——;' he said, turning his pillow over: 'tell 'im ball coom back inches and would a' knocked off stump to 'ell.' Then he went to sleep again. But Richmond was satisfied. 'I didn't see the ball turn, but no doubt that was my fault.'

It was the custom at Shastbury for the First XI to go into the nets every Monday, Wednesday and Friday from a quarter to one until a quarter to two—that is, until mid-June set in and the House matches began. The practice was strenuous, especially for the professionals, who were supposed to keep the attack challenging all the time. After a particularly gruelling session on a sweltering Monday, Ted and I were resting at the open windows of the professionals' dressing-room at Shastbury, still in our flannels and enjoying our pipes (Edgeworth was one shilling an ounce then, and a Dunhill pipe seven shillings and sixpence), while we looked over the shimmering cricket field, stretching away to the distant Wrekin. Suddenly Richmond knocked at our door and came forward. He had been dreadfully out of form for a month and on the previous Saturday had been clean bowled first ball while opening the innings for the Shropshire Gentlemen. 'Would you please give me a net for half an hour or so?' he asked. Wainwright consented, and Richmond went away to change into flannels. I was furious. 'He knows he has no right to ask for a net after School practice,' I protested. 'Doan't argue,' said Ted. 'Coom on and get it over. There'll be half a crown for thi, anyhow.' I told him I didn't want a half a crown. 'It's the principle,' I argued. 'Well,' said Ted. 'If tha doesn't want to bowl at 'im, tha knows what thi can do?' 'No—what?' ' 'It 'im in cobbles.' 'Oh, don't be a fool, Ted—come on then, let's go and have it done with.' Besides, I was too young to know what he meant by 'cobbles'. As luck would happen, the nets had by this time of a dry summer become worn and dusty. Richmond duly appeared in the brown canvas shoes he invariably wore for the purpose of practice. His bat was very yellow and bound in two places with twine. Wainwright's first ball pitched outside the off and just missed the leg stump. 'Coom forward—it were well up enoo', sir.' Then Richmond studiously went through the correct movements to an invisible ball of the same kind; once or twice he went through them, lost in contemplation. He was beginning to play with some certainty of touch when one of my off-breaks pitched on a very bare spot, came back like a knife, and sped upwards at an acute angle smack on to Richmond's bladder. And he never wore a protector or 'box'. He bent double with a stifled groan; but before we could get down the wicket to render first aid he drew himself erect and waved us away. But he decided he had better not continue practice today. He tipped us and apologized for putting us to inconvenience. 'But,' he said, in reasonable extenuation, 'it *was* a beast of a ball, wasn't it?' Then he added, 'And it would have missed the bails by inches.'

After he had departed and we were alone again in the professionals' dressing-room, Wainwright chuckled richly. 'By gum,' he said. 'Tha's a seight better bowler than Ah thowt. Anybody as can 'it batter in cobbles when he likes is a bit of all reight. . . .' In vain I protested that I had hit Richmond's bladder by accident. 'Tha's tellin' me,' replied Wainwright; and this was probably the first really relevant use of the term.

A. F. Chance was master of cricket during my terms as a junior professional at Shastbury. He was tallish and rather saturnine of aspect; I think of him always as I saw him in cap and gown walking near the Speech Hall at change of lessons, or when he came behind the nets at practice (not in cap and gown) and severely considered not only the play of the boys but the bowling and coaching methods of the two professionals. He wore a drooping moustache; his jaw was long and firm; his eyes intent and without obliquity; and he was a scholar. He was known by his House as 'The Man', and seldom have public schoolboys, with their genius for nicknames, so aptly penetrated in two words to the essence, the quiddity, of any individual or character. It was Chance who signed the professionals' weekly cheque—£5 for Wainwright, £2 10s. for myself, small fortunes in those days to my way of thinking, though Wainwright thought I was a 'foo-il' for not asking for another ten shillings. The cheque was brought to us every Friday afternoon by the Hon. Treasurer of the School XI. One year the position was held by Ellis, and one Friday he neglected for an hour or two to disburse, and while Ted and I waited—Ted eager to get down to the town and to the George Hotel—I uttered my first and last pun in a lifetime: 'Where the Ellis Ellis?' I asked, which amused Ted so vastly that he said I was a rum young begger and wondered what would become of me.

Chance not only kept his eye on the actual cricket at Shastbury; he would come regularly and inspect the nets, the netting itself, and ask Wainwright if the quality of it, and the price, were the most durable and economical possible. He was a thrifty man, yet in his

House he could be hospitality itself. His cellar was exceptionally good, and his face was that of one who lived well. He was a confirmed bachelor. His House usually won the School competition, and most seasons six or seven boys from 'Chance's' were in the XI. In my time 'Chance's' produced Donald Boumphrey, possibly the best public school batsman who never got his Blue at Cambridge; M. C. Dempsey, now Sir Miles Dempsey; Ellis, a brilliant Welsh boy who might have played for Glamorganshire given the opportunity; little Onslow, one of the first boy 'googly' bowlers in cricket's history; his period was round about 1913. (Miles Dempsey in the same period actually bowled a left-handed 'googly'.) There was also R. B. Stone in 'Chance's', of strong defence, with a clean and powerful drive to the off; and there was in my first summer, which was 1912, 'Gertie' Millar, a bowler of pace and unbridled energy. None of these young players went into county cricket but, none the less, I have seldom seen or known better since. None of them apparently came under the influence of Chance's classic erudition.

One summer during the celebrations of Speech Day, M. C. Kemp, who was captain of the historic Oxford University XI which beat the Australians in 1884, stayed with Chance, and he asked Wainwright for a net, though he was well beyond fifty and hadn't touched a bat for years. We bowled at him half an hour and he flayed both of us, ball after ball, cuts and drives of much ferocity. Each stroke racked him with pain and after each violent hit he emitted anguished, involuntary and quite unselfconscious cries and shouts, such as 'Ooocher!' 'Ouch!' and 'Godalmighty'. At the end of his practice he was streaming with sweat and twisted with muscular torment, but happy. 'I can still see the ball,' he said, and he tipped us generously. Chance, who had watched him from behind the net smiled his sardonic smile. 'Too much Cockburn coming out,' he remarked. 'Not a glass,' answered Kemp. I have seldom known or seen a batsman who could hit as hard as Kemp that day.

Chance had a liking for ruminative allusive comment as he watched a match or practice in the nets. During a Shastbury v. Rossall game he paused in his steps as he was changing class (the school in general was not liberated from work until after lunch). He stayed only a few minutes, but long enough to see a boy in Alington's House caught from a stroke incompetent and hideous. 'That boy's a fool,' he murmured, without emotion, 'so was his father.' He spoke entirely to himself. He took no interest at all in the doings on the river, and when the Bumping Races were in full swing and all the School watching them, Chance would wander alone over the vacant cricket field, the season at an end now. A boy from his House came up the hill from the river flushed with jubilation. He saw Chance and rushed up to him. 'Oh, sir!' he exclaimed, proud to be the first to deliver to Chance himself the good news. 'We've bumped Moser's and gone to the head of the river!' 'Are we in the Bumps this year?' queried Chance, then went on with his scrutiny of the turf. For all his interest—I cannot associate him with passion—he was never heard to refer to any other form or category of cricket except Shastbury cricket, not to University, county, Test, or to any other public-school cricket; and I suspect that he thought old Richmond was vain and foolish.

One evening, at the term's end, a melancholy time for me because it meant a return to Manchester, compelling a readjustment of spirit and body not easy to achieve by a youth of twenty, he invited me to dinner in his house in Kingsland. He opened a vintage claret. I can see him to this day fondling the bottle. I had never before tasted wine and not for many years after did I taste wine again. But I owe to Chance the awakening of the palate to its most truly aesthetic function. Shastbury, Chance, his junior 'pro', and claret, the mahogany of his dining-room, with the twilight falling in late July, more than forty years ago. . . . It was a queer epoch, and there were some queer folk in it.

THE IDEAL CRICKET MATCH

FIRST DAY

IF some good fairy were to ask me to pick out one match of all I have seen, to relive it as I lived it at the time when it happened, my choice would be easy: England v. Australia at Lord's in June 1930. I was at the prime of forty years then, fulfilled in work and happy in home, love and health, the mind still unstaled, yet critical enough. This game could be laid up in heaven, a Platonic idea of cricket in perfection. It was limited to four days and finished at five o'clock on the closing afternoon; 1601 runs were scored and 29 wickets fell. Bradman batted in a Test match at Lord's for the first time, scoring 254 in his first innings. England batted first and made

425, but lost by seven wickets. Glorious sunshine blessed every moment's play. London was at its most handsome; 1914 forgotten and 1939 not yet casting a shadow for all to see. I can still catch the warmth and the animation of the scene, feel the mind's and the senses' satisfaction. I can see Grimmett bowling, his arm as low as my grandfather's, his artfulness as acute; and I can still see Chapman as he played one of the most gallant and dazzling and precarious innings which has ever cocked a snoop at an Australian team ready and impatient to put to rout and ruin an England team apparently in the last ditch, the ghost about to be given up.

In the two teams were some of the greatest players of history, names already classic or legendary: Hobbs, Woolley, Hammond, Duleepsinhji, Hendren, Tate, Woodfull, Ponsford, Bradman, Kippax, McCabe, Victor Richardson, Oldfield and Grimmett. From one of the boxes near the grandstand, K. S. Ranjitsinhji looked on; and the fact that he was present in the flesh relates the match more even than the heroism and splendour of the actual cricket to the realm of the fabulous past. Only twenty-six years ago? It is hard to believe. Every department of cricket was seen at its best during this match; fast bowling, slow bowling, spin; all varieties of batsmen from Woodfull and Bradman to Duleepsinhji; with wonderful fielding everywhere.

Sutcliffe was unable to play, and when Chapman had won the toss and England's first innings was about to begin, the vast crowd saw Woolley walking to the wicket with Hobbs. Not since 1921 had Woolley gone in first for England, though he had taken part in thirty Test matches against Australia. And how he opened the England innings now!—the cricket at once seemed as though ignited by the radiant sun. Woolley's strokes were as brilliant, as much a matter of nature as the rays dazzling the field from the blue sky. Wall attacked at a superb pace, supported by the virile dangerous fast-medium swing (both ways) of Fairfax, from whose bowling Hobbs was soon and most courteously caught by Oldfield, a wicket-keeper who, judging by his quiet charm of manner, might well and always have kept wicket in the kid gloves in which he was married. The overthrow of Hobbs cast no gloom over the morning's sheen as Woolley cut and pulled, combining power, poise and felicity. He scored 41 in half an hour; his strokes changed Lord's and a Test match into Canterbury with all the tents and bunting and white wine.

Fairfax changed over to the pavilion end. His first ball rose to cutting height. Woolley lay back, lifted up his tallness and cut hard.

We looked to the boundary, and the fieldsman at third man ran in in anticipation; but Wall at backward point scooped up a catch, though the impact of the ball against his hand sent him reeling back. This, though we did not know it yet, was the match's *leit motif*; we shall see how the same kind of catch marked the great climax of the last afternoon. Duleepsinhji and Hammond batted for England with the scoreboard announcing the loss of Hobbs and Woolley for a mere fifty. Though Hammond was forced to the defensive and Duleepsinhji likewise, none of us suffered anxiety. England were bound to get ample runs on a fast pitch during a dream of a June day.

But on this occasion, at Lord's in June 1930, Grimmett bowled Hammond, luring him out by flight, defeating him by spin. A few weeks before this, at Trent Bridge, Grimmett on a lovely wicket for batsmen, had shown us spin bowling unparalleled; in half an hour he deceived and drew into his web Hammond, Woolley and Hendren, each put under his influence by hypnotic flight—then the poison of spin performed the dispatch. There has never been a cleverer slow leg-break bowler than Grimmett. He is not really properly described as a leg-break bowler, because the term usually suggests a certain inaccuracy of length. So I shall here call Grimmett a length bowler, a meticulous length bowler, who had control over leg-spin and googly: he was a little man, with a shining dome of intellect or cunning, who ran a few nimble steps to deliver the ball, as though on the velvet of a cat's paws. And his arm, not above the shoulder, could toss the ball along an arch of wicked temptation; or send it along with a subterranean deceit.

This day he cudgelled his brain vainly for hours. Duleepsinhji and Hendren used quick feet, making strokes while the ball was coming to them. In half an hour 50 runs flowed over the field, or cracked and thundered when 'Patsy' hooked. This also was a Golden Age. Sunshine and applause, the cricketers' flannels catching the bloom of the day. . . . Ripe and red in the face with contentment, the crowd greeted England's 200 for three wickets, whereat Hendren hit a long hop from Fairfax into young McCabe's hands at long-leg; Hendren greedy for his 50, was out for 48 and came home to the pavilion with his face more or less concealed by the width of his smile. As a fact, England's innings hereabout suffered unexpected indecision. Chapman and Allen failed, so the score 239 for 6 was not good or safe enough. Tate was next man in and as he walked through the Long Room on the way to the wicket he saw me sitting on a table; at once he flourished his blade, envisaging a scythe-like cut, and said to me, out of the corner of his mouth, as though in confidence, 'Batsmanship!' Just that and nothing more. He went forth, splay-footed, to join the elegant Duleepsinhji and lost no time before he was driving and heaving the confident Australian bowlers all over the place. He and 'Duleep' added 98 in seventy minutes, Tate's share 54. As England's total arrived at the full tide of 400, Duleepsinhji allowed his freedom of strokeplay to run to licentiousness; and towards six o'clock he was caught by Bradman from a reckless hit to the offside. He had made 173 in his first Test match. He was in a position to enjoy himself, wasn't he? When we review the match as a whole, seeing the end in the beginning, 'Duleep's' impetuousness, so near to close of play, must be counted as a major contribution to England's defeat. His illustrious uncle the Jam Sahib, 'Ranji' himself, severely reprimanded him for carelessness when he reported himself to the enpurpled box at the end of the innings. At close of play, England were 405 for nine.

SECOND DAY

Next day, Saturday, the sun outshone the glory of yesterday and the crowd at Lord's sat in an eternity of content. Woodfull and Ponsford began Australia's innings with grim protective vigilance. Australia had lost the first match of the rubber at Nottingham; now they went in facing 425 and possibly a wicket inclined to get dusty. Woodfull and Ponsford made only 30 in an hour: 'Playing for a draw already' said more than a few irritated patriots, who naturally wanted Ponsford and Woodfull to get out, or assist in the act of their own downfall. Australia's score reached 100 just after lunch, for none; the time of day was half-past two. At a quarter past three the score was 150 for none, Ponsford 77, Woodfull 70. It was at this point in the proceedings that King George came to Lord's and was presented on the field of play to the cricketers. From the first over after the King's departure from the scene, bowled by White, Ponsford was caught by Hammond in the slips. He 'followed' a wide ball. There is no doubt that Ponsford's wicket should really have gone to His Majesty's credit. At half-past three, when Australia were 162 for 1, Bradman walked to the wicket, taking his time. He drove his first ball smack to long off and when he had finished the stroke, he was near enough to the bowler to see the surprised look on White's face; for until this instant minute no batsman had dreamed of running out to drive White; in fact several very famous English cricketers had assured me that to drive White on the half volley was an act scarcely

comprehensible in terms of skill or common sanity. The advent of
Bradman on this Saturday of burning English summer was like the
throwing of combustible stuff on fires that had been slumbering
with dreadful potentiality. Nearly every ball was scored from.
Bradman ran yards out of his ground to White and belaboured him;
White was obliged to pitch short and then Bradman cut him to
ribbons. After tea a massacre, nothing less. Never before this hour,
or two hours until close of play, and never since, has a batsman
equalled Bradman's cool deliberate murder or spifflication of all
bowling. Boundaries everywhere—right and left and in front. The
bowler helpless and at Bradman's mercy even as he ran to bowl.
He reached 100 in one hour and three quarters, with 13 fours. At
5.20 Australia's score was 300 for 1; at 5.30 it passed 350. Tate was
wildly cheered when he sent a maiden to Bradman. But the England
attack was entirely at a loss; not to get Bradman out—that wild hope
had gone long since—but just to stem the flood of his boundaries.
There were not enough fieldsmen available; Bradman found gaps
and vacancies in nature. Ten minutes before half-past six, Woodfull
was stumped pushing out to Robins's spin; and it is a mistake to
think that he was a dull, unlovely batsman. His stiff arms and short
lift-up of the bat distracted the attention of casual onlookers from
the prettiness of his footwork. It is a compliment to Woodfull that
he did not sink into anonymity, or invisibility even, while Bradman
at the other end of the wicket played the most brilliant and dramatically incisive and murderous innings of his career, and played it
without turning a hair. At half-past six Australia's total was 404 for
two; and Bradman, in little more than two hours and a half had
made 155, not once exerting himself, every shot dead in the target's
middle, precise and shattering; an innings which was beautiful and
yet somehow cruel in its excessive mastery.

THIRD DAY

In constant sunshine the third day began and ended, but it had in
it little of brightness or pleasure for English cricket. The Australians
devoted themselves to the twin-souled cause of consolidation and
attrition. Bradman abstained from gaudy hits; he and Kippax began
the morning as though Australia's position in the match still needed
cement in the foundations. Neither batsman seemed likely to get
out, except through some error gross and inexplicable. Bradman, like
Kippax, waited for the loose ball, punished it mercilessly without
going beyond the safe scope of known and practised technique. No

wickets fell before lunch; Australia were then 544 for 2; and after lunch Bradman and Kippax resumed activity or operations exactly where they had left off at half-past one. Somebody in the Press box asked if King George was expected at Lord's again, and I added the hope that he would bring the entire Court with him. The scalded bowlers worked in shifts waiting for the mistake Bradman or Kippax would surely make in God's good time; and at ten minutes to three Bradman lifted a ball from White into the air—the only ball he raised an inch from the ground in all the length and magnitude of his innings. Chapman ran yards on the offside, and held the catch. Bradman scored 254 in five hours and a half; on the third day he made 99 in three hours, playing with a comfort which told us that he was for reasons of policy not moving along at a quicker or more murderous speed. Kippax soon followed Bradman to the pavilion's refreshing shade. He tried to cut White and played on. His 83 pleased the eye of the connoisseur all the time.

Here happened the ferocious Australian onslaught which for hours had been in sinister preparation. McCabe, Richardson, Oldfield, treated the England attack sardonically; every ball was hit somehow, in the air, on the ground, into the crowd, 56 in 25 minutes. The declaration by Woodfull at the total of 729 for 6 was regarded by everybody present not only as an act of policy but also of Christian charity. One of the scoreboards patriotically declined to register the number 7. Australia's innings had lasted ten hours and ten minutes; England were destined eight years later to take revenge for this monstrous spawning and spoliation; but we could not know this on the glorious summer's day of our discontent at Lord's in 1930. A sad day it was to the end. Hobbs and Woolley, when England went in again 304 behind, scored 45 in half an hour by means of strokes good and strokes not so good. Grimmett immediately discovered spots on the wicket, the same wicket which only a few moments earlier had suggested a batsman's field of a cloth of gold. Hobbs walked down the pitch and prodded it. When Bradman left his crease it was always to prod the bowling. Grimmett coaxed Hobbs forward and bowled him with a leg-break. He placed a silly mid-on under Woolley's nose. As a retaliation Woolley hit Grimmett square and trod on his wicket while doing so. Apparently fearing the presence of the 'silly' mid-on, Woolley pulled his stroke farther round than he would have done if no 'silly' mid-on had been in his way; he was obliged in consequence to move back on his stumps in order to shorten the ball's length. Craft as well as misfortune contributed to his undoing. At half-past six, England's 98 for 2 definitely announced that Australia were on the verge of an astonishing and illustrious victory.

FOURTH AND LAST DAY

At the end of this great and enchanting match, I sat on the Green Bank at Lord's, hurriedly writing my description of the day's play just after five o'clock. I could begin my article for the *Manchester Guardian* in no better way than this—'There is a passage in *Tom Jones* where Fielding, having got his plot terribly complicated, calls on all the high Muses, in person and severally, for aid; because he tells us, "without their guidance I do not know how to bring my story to a successful conclusion." As I write this report, I feel also the need of inspired and kindly forces. The day's play, in the old term, beggars description. . . .'

England had virtually lost the match by noon; in the last hour of the afternoon—my God, they nearly won it back; And they lowered the flag only after being forced to submit by sheer odds. When twelve o'clock chimed from the clock covered with ivy at the Nursery end England were 147 for 5; Hobbs, Woolley, Hammond, Duleep-sinhji and Hendren out; and the Australians were 157 ahead and another innings in hand. Grimmett was at his exercises again, wheedling his victims out, by slow flight which hovered before the crease, the ball an Ancient Mariner's eye, fixing the batsman on the spot, until it span with the noise of wasps. Now, as we could hear the England innings splitting on its beam ends, Percy Chapman came in. Before making a run he spooned Grimmett to mid-wicket, totally confounded by flight. The chance was the easiest ever offered to fieldsmen in a Test match. The ball hung obligingly, waiting to be caught. Two Australian fieldsmen dithered—and the ball fell harmlessly to earth between them. I can see at this distant hour and in the distant place where I am writing these lines, the wild incredulous stare of Grimmett's eyes; and I think I can hear also, a slightly demented laugh. Chapman proceeded to play an innings fantastic and audacious, with skill half-blinded by hazard and gallantry. G. O. Allen helped him staunchly in a stand which, coming as it did after the impotence of Hammond and Hendren, seemed absolutely secure, once Chapman had discovered that he could kick Grimmett's breaking away ball (the 'googly' to Chapman's left-handed bat) with his legs and pads; he then proceeded to kick and frustrate it by pedal movements which were scarcely related to

75

any known formulated footwork. At lunch Chapman and Allen were still not out, England 262 for 5. And all Lord's wondered and hoped . . . could the match after all be saved? Alas, after the interval, Grimmett's straight ball ensnared Allen, but not before the sixth wicket had added 125 in 95 minutes. Allen's courage and trustfulness in a straight bat played forward entitles this innings to an immortal place or chapter in the Fox's Book of Martyrs of Cricket. Chapman's cricket was played as though in a strange dimension of unreason with a method in all the apparently inverted science. Some of his strokes, technically to be counted and described as mishits, seemed somehow to have the power and certainty of strokes made and directed from the bat's true middle. With a combination of pushwork with his pads and a delayed forward lunge, he upset Grimmett's tactics in the very first stage of his innings, when England's position was at its worst. Grimmett was obliged to pack the on-side and pitch his leg-break—off-break, of course, to Chapman—wide to the off-stump. But as soon as Chapman had obtained a 'sight' of the ball, he repeatedly pulled Grimmett round, square or to long-on, or in spaces between these two points. No cricketer entirely speculative could hope to hit Grimmett hard and often simply by flinging his bat through the air. Chapman pulled Grimmett for six, pulled or drove him for six three times. In an hour he scored 69. A mighty straight drive from Grimmett lifted the astonished, happy crowd to the height. This was Chapman's hour; he was in a beatitude. His bat performed wonders and it was as if he did not know it was performing wonders. He sent a ball into the deeps of the packed multitude on the Mound stand. Seldom has an innings in a Test match stirred a crowd to such jubilation as Chapman inspired now; it was a jubilation in which people saw visions and experienced unwonted impulses towards perfection. We should probably have to refer to Jessop's rout and rape of the Australians at the Oval in 1902 to find an equal to Chapman's century at Lord's in 1930. His 121 was made out of 207 in two hours and a half; and England in a second innings, broken of back half-way, survived to achieve a total of 375. A run out, which threw away White's wicket when he was defending safely enough with Robins at the other end, no doubt had a subtle and far-reaching influence on the result of the match, a result that was not reached in the matter-of-course way expected by the Australians and everybody else at all interested.

At ten minutes to four, Woodful and Ponsford walked confidently into the sunshine to compile the nominal 72 needed for victory.

Against Tate and Hammond, Ponsford batted as though intent on getting all the runs himself. Two fours from Tate set him in excellent motion. Woodfull then sent a severe chance of a catch to Duleepsinhji at mid-on; and an over or two afterwards Robins, who had found a spot at the Pavilion end, bowled Ponsford beautifully. Bradman, in next, was as usual slow in his progress to the wicket; the crowd remained, of course, to see him bat. People who had seen his first innings told those who hadn't, exactly what they thought he would do to finish off the game. He scored a non-committal single before he lay back and cut Tate ferociously, a great stroke cracking in the air like gunshot. It disturbed the pigeons. Thousands of eyes flashed to the boundary. Chapman was in the 'gully', standing in his favourite position as the ball was bowled, legs apart, arms semi-folded, left elbow resting on the top of the right hand. As Bradman made the stroke, Chapman bent down, picked up the ball an inch from the grass, threw up a catch beyond belief, and assumed his usual upright stance, legs slightly apart, left elbow . . . and so on. The roar of the crowd expressed ecstasy and incredulity simultaneously. I was watching the match at this point in the company of Sir James Barrie, in front of the Tavern. As Bradman departed from the crease, on his way back to the Pavilion, Barrie spoke to me, saying: 'Why is he going away?' 'But surely,' I said, 'surely, Sir James, you saw that marvellous catch by Chapman?' 'Oh yes,' replied Barrie. 'I saw it all right. But what evidence is there that the ball which Chapman threw up into the air is the same ball that left Bradman's bat?'

Spin by Robins ensnared Kippax, caught at the wicket by Duck-worth with a terrible noise and yelping. Australia 22 for 3. Could England . . . but nobody dared tempt Providence by asking. Young McCabe the next batsman was met by Woodfull, who spoke to him. Robins lost his length; McCabe plundered 13 in an over, settling the account and issue. As the cricketers came from the field, the light of a glorious June afternoon shone on them; it shines on them yet. A victory in four days won in the face of a total of 425; England, though needing 304 to save defeat by an innings and though down and out at noon on the last day, in the fourth innings of a dusty Lord's wicket, forced Australia to sweat and strain at the finish. It was the match of everybody who played in it. Victor and vanquished emerged with equal honour; and the chief laurel crowned the fair perspiring brow of A. P. F. Chapman. The match of every cricketer's heart's desire.

ENGLAND

First Innings		Second Innings	
J. B. Hobbs, c Oldfield, b Fairfax	1	b Grimmett	19
F. E. Woolley, c Wall, b Fairfax	41	hit wkt, b Grimmett	28
W. R. Hammond, b Grimmett	38	c Fairfax, b Grimmett	32
K. S. Duleepsinhji, c Bradman, b Grimmett	173	c Oldfield, b Hornibrook	48
E. Hendren, c McCabe, b Fairfax	48	c Richardson, b Grimmett	9
A. P. F. Chapman, c Oldfield, b Wall	11	c Oldfield, b Fairfax	121
G. O. Allen, b Fairfax	3	lbw, b Grimmett	57
M. W. Tate, c McCabe, b Wall	54	c Ponsford, b Grimmett	10
R. W. V. Robins, c Oldfield, b Hornibrook	5	not out	11
J. C. White, not out	23	run out	10
G. Duckworth, c Oldfield, b Wall	18	lbw, b Fairfax	0
Extras (b 2, lb 7, nb 1)	10	Extras (b 16, lb 13, w 1)	30
Total	425	Total	375

AUSTRALIA

First Innings		Second Innings	
W. M. Woodfull, st Duckworth, b Robins	155	not out	26
W. H. Ponsford, c Hammond, b White	81	b Robins	14
D. G. Bradman, c Chapman, b White	254	c Chapman, b Tate	1
A. F. Kippax, b White	83	c Duckworth, b Robins	3
S. McCabe, c Woolley, b Hammond	44	not out	25
V. Y. Richardson, c Hobbs, b Tate	30		
W. A. Oldfield, not out	43		
A. Fairfax, not out	20		
Extras (b 6, lb 8, w 5)	19	Extras (b 1, lb 2)	3
Total	*729	Total	72

*Innings declared closed

C. V. Grimmett, P. M. Hornibrook and T. W. Wall did not bat

AUSTRALIA BOWLING

	Overs	Mdns	Runs	Wkts	Overs	Mdns	Runs	Wkts
Wall	29·4	2	118	3	25	2	80	0
Fairfax	31	6	101	4	12·4	2	37	2
Grimmett	33	4	105	2	53	13	167	6
Hornibrook	26	6	62	1	22	6	49	1
McCabe	9	1	29	0	3	1	11	0
Bradman					1	0	1	0

ENGLAND BOWLING

Allen	34	7	115	0				
Tate	64	16	148	1	13	6	21	1
White	51	7	158	3	2	0	8	0
Robins	42	1	172	1	9	1	34	2
Hammond	35	8	82	1	4·2	1	6	0
Woolley	6	0	35	0				

Umpires: F. Chester and T. Oates

C. B. FRY*

C B. FRY went beyond eighty on 25th April, 1952, according to 'Wisden', a witness to which he paid a certain respect. But he is not likelier to count a matter of eighty years in a man's life as of higher numerical importance than he counted, in his prime, eighty runs made on the cricket field. He was usually sustaining a batting average of round about three-score-and-ten while taking in his stride achievements in other fields and spheres—first-class honours in Classical Moderations at Wadham, association football in the Oxford University and the England XIs, journalism, the captaincy of the England cricket team, acting as a substitute delegate on the Indian representation at the first, third and fourth assemblies of the League of Nations. Nobody will share his diverse distinctions, a century in a Test match and an offer of the Kingdom of Albania. Bradman has equalled Fry's performance which in 1901 seemed to verge on the marvellous: six centuries in six consecutive innings. But Bradman has never sent translations to *The Times* of the English Hymnal and written a speech which turned Mussolini out of Corfu. In his stride Fry did these things.

We should just the same have written something in celebration of Fry's eightieth year if he had never handled a cricket-bat in his life. He himself thinks he might be remembered for his work as a moulder of character and educator of youth on the training-ship *Mercury*. For a while Fry held the world's record long-jump. In these days athletes are schooled from cradle to beat records; the preparation is hieratical. Fry jumped by nature or, let us say, by grace. From zest of living he excelled in many and different callings,

*This portrait originally appeared in the *Spectator*.

mastered by other people mostly by severe application or professional labour. Fry was one of the last of an English tradition or
breed, an amateur in the things of mind and of the body, not bound
to or tyrannised by skill but sometimes free of it, because it has come,
in part at least, by a sort of inspired dilettantism. But here is the
paradox; when Fry gave himself to batsmanship, Apollo turned
ascetic.

The comprehensive cricket skill which won him lasting fame in
two hemispheres was the consequence of hard study and practice.
Not by grace but by reasoning and self-discipline did he in his career
amass 30,000 runs, averaging 50 over his many summers. It was, in
fact, as a fast bowler that nature first stirred the cricketer in him,
until Jim Phillips, the umpire, no-balled him for throwing. His
coaches in the school-nets said he would never make a batsman.
When Fry was seen in his heyday at one end of the wicket and Kumar
Shri Ranjitsinhji at the other, on a June day at Brighton long long
ago, imagination beheld visions of Oriental conjurations in contrast
to a Spartan austerity of exercise. Fry batted by the book of arithmetic and, while 'Ranji' seemed to toss runs over the field like
largesse in silk purses, Fry acquired them—no, not as a miser his
hoard but as the connoisseur his collection.

Fry was so much the student of batsmanship that often he
appeared less interested in the runs he was making than in the
bowling as it presented itself to his intellect almost in the abstract.
Only by staying a long time at the crease could he arrive at the
detachment necessary for scrutiny as objective as this; his centuries
accrued as a by-product. I am certain that in his years of supremacy
as a batsman no thought of personal records or aggrandisement
occurred to him. He was absorbed in the problems of technique; he
was interested in the rationale of strokes, seeking the answer to the
great trick of S. F. Barnes, the ball which 'ran away' very late. (Yet
Fry considers Barnes was not a more dangerous bowler than George
Lohmann.) So lost was Fry to the common and external furniture
and accountancy of cricket, so deeply did he thrust his mind into the
heart and centre of it, that once I saw him, after he had been struck
on the hand by a fast ball while batting, walk beyond the square-leg
umpire, shaking the bruised fingers, then looking closely at them,
as though contemplating pain not as a personal experience or
sensation, but as a metaphysical phenomenon.

At Leeds, in 1930, Bradman scored a triple century on one and
the same day against England. I was sitting with Fry in the lounge

of a Harrogate hotel, over the weekend, and he was recalling a season of the 1900s and a match between Middlesex and Sussex at Lord's. I want the reader to try to imagine the scene; Fry stretched in an easy chair, playing with his monocle, myself and a friend fascinated by his talk, Bradman forgotten. 'At close of play on the second day,' he said, 'I was not out 80 or so, and next morning it was our policy to get runs quickly as some rain had fallen in the night. I reached my century and then—and then . . . Albert Trott clean bowled me, yes, clean bowled me with an off-break.' Here Fry rose from his chair, and his eyes were looking across the distance of thirty years. He walked up and down the lounge, and went through the motions of a batsman playing an off-break. 'I can't think what I was doing,' he said; 'I simply can't.' Thirty years after the event he was still seeing Trott's off-break as a problem to be solved.

By concentration he conquered most bowlers. Against Yorkshire with Hirst, Rhodes, Haigh, Wainwright and sometimes F. S. Jackson, an attack superlative, Fry scored nearly 2,500 runs in all, average 70. In 1903 he made 234 against Yorkshire at Bradford; next summer against Yorkshire he made 177 at Sheffield and 229 at Brighton in successive innings. It isn't possible to convey the amazement felt by followers of cricket in the 1900s as Fry went his processional course. None but players truly great could get anywhere near a score of 200 in a period which saw bowling at its best. The game was still unstaled; the soil had not been entirely turned and morning was in the air, with much to be done that had not been done before. Batsmanship was on the gold standard; the currency hadn't been debased. When Fry scored six hundreds in six consecutive innings in little beyond a fortnight, two on bowlers' wickets, he caused not 'a sensation' but wonder and nothing less.

Equally impressive was a failure by Fry to score. There was that staggering afternoon in 1902 when news came from Lord's that England against Australia had lost two wickets for no runs; and in the newspapers we saw in black staring print:

C. B. Fry, c Hill, b Hopkins	0
K. S. Ranjitsinhji, b Hopkins	0

This same season Fry and 'Ranji' were both dropped, in their pomp, from the England XI, for they had momentarily disclosed a mortal fallibility. It all seems legend now; great figures in the sun, sure of themselves. They remained at a distance from us; there was no means of rendering them familiar to us off the field, or ubiquitous.

I don't fancy schoolboys of the 1900s thought of Fry at all as an ordinary man who wore ordinary clothes, a stiff collar and the rest. On the field he was a sight for Phidias, the living sculpture of upright masculine grace and handsomeness, with just a hint of a Sir Willoughby Patterne hauteur. As he stood at third-man, on the boundary, waiting for the bowler to get to work, he would make movements on his toes suggesting a waltz. When he chased a ball, his long effortless strides kept the indignity of hurry at bay; and his aquiline tawny face flushed in the sun and air. He was past sixty when he went to Australia to write comments on the Test matches there. I saw him one evening stripped and about to dive in the swimming-pool on the liner *Orion*. The balance of him, the upraised arms and the suggestions expressed by nerve, sinew and limb of unstaled satisfaction in living, the rays of the setting sun on him and the deepening blue of the Pacific sky above—somehow I think of him today as I saw him then, even before I think of him as I saw him in his prime, batting with 'Ranji', while the bowlers toiled and sweated and wondered which end of the wicket was the one really to avoid.

'Play back or drive.' 'Watch the ball and deliver the stroke at the ball itself and not at a point in space where you hope the ball will presently be.' This was the Fry-Ranjitsinhji doctrine that brought revolution to the game. The 'classic' lunge forward, which extended the batsman to a point where stretching allowed little freedom of action, and where the ball could only be guessed at to inches, fell into obsolescence amongst the great players. 'Play back or drive'—and no cricketer has driven a ball with more than Fry's easy power and imperiousness of swing. 'The only way of getting on top of Barnes,' C. B. Fry has written, 'and it was not often done, was to drive him over his head.' Think of it!—advice to batsmen: drive S. F. Barnes for purposes of defence. It all sounds strange language in the 1950s, and indeed to read of Fry's prowess at cricket, and of the luxuriance of it all, impels us to imagine that the game once upon a time was part of a sort of Arabian Nights Entertainment; it certainly reads that way in 'Wisden' now.

Every lover of the game will fervently wish, a private indulgence, that he could just for an hour look again at Fry and Ranjitsinhji in conjunction; flicks and magical passes at one end of the wicket, while at the other Fry moves calmly towards close of play, the scholar athlete in excelsis.

GLOUCESTERSHIRE CRICKET

THE strongest giants of the North would tremble whenever Gloucestershire invaded Lancashire, Yorkshire or Nottinghamshire led by the Graces. But the county was scarcely less formidable under the leadership of Beverley Lyon. Three years in succession, from 1929 to 1931, Gloucestershire missed winning the Championship by inches; fifteen matches were won in 1929 and fifteen in 1930. It is a fact that two English cricket captains of brilliant opportunism, swiftness of mind, and courageous conviction have not had the opportunity to inspire an England XI; for Fender was not less bold and original than Lyon. Lyon's stroke of genius was to close an innings after one over had been bowled on the third day of a match apparently dead because of rain and no play on the first two days. By this device the winner of what was virtually a one innings game received the full award of points obtainable from a three-day match. Lyon, of course, saw to it that the captain of the other side fell in with his plan. Law and tradition frowned on Lyon; we prefer a bourgeois conformity even in the direction of our national games and manly field sports, where the artist of temperament is even more suspect than elsewhere.

Lyon was fortunate to have under his command a number of truly gifted cricketers, including two brilliant and audacious stroke-players; one of them a New Zealander, C. C. Dacre, as flashing, fresh and uncertain as an April day, the other Charles Barnett, one of the most daring of contemporary English batsmen. Dipper, pale and lean, straight out of Falstaff's army, was a solid corrective of unbridled enterprise, and Sinfield also kept a wary watch. And there was Hammond in his pomp. Lyon, too, ready to cut and drive to rout any faltering bowler. His own attack included one of the most dangerous left-hand bowlers of his or any other day—on home-grown Gloucestershire wickets especially—Charles Parker his name. And the best slip fielder of modern times, Hammond of course, was there to take the catches sent by blind reflex-action from the edge of the bat that was rooted out by Parker's slow to medium-paced spin. Tom Goddard at the other end turned the ball from the off over after over; but originally he bowled fast, or at any rate, that was his idea. Sinfield exploited inswingers of beautiful length; and of course Hammond could on his day use the new ball with a destructive late-swing as vicious almost as Tate's. But for all the excellent

83

material at Lyon's disposal Gloucestershire cricket would scarcely have achieved as much destruction and as many victories as came their way if Lyon had not schemed every action with a decisive end in view, and at the risk sometimes of finding his plans turned against him. Today, Gloucestershire are in a low state, yet there is ability in the team: Graveney, good enough to be chosen for England, Emmett, one of our most delightful stroke players for years; Milton, whom I regard as a better batsman than Graveney in point of character and power of resistance (and he has strokes too); there are the solid Crapp and Young; and the obstinate Wilson. McHugh is no negligible bowler with the new ball; Lambert has been on the fringe of representative games; Cook (mirabile dictu!) has already bowled left-hand for England and useful he is; and we must not overlook Wells, an 'original', a cricketer of independent character, with humour and determination to enjoy himself. At Lord's the other day he fielded at long-on and applauded Denis Compton as though not himself responsibly in the game but somehow a spectator straying from the crowd momentarily. Not a great nucleus, maybe; but much could be done by leadership of initiative and benevolent dictatorship to make the most of it. To say the truth, no county except Warwickshire has not suffered a decline in achievement and idealism after a professional has succeeded to an amateur captaincy. Dollery is the exception that proves the rule. Even if the professional turns amateur the result is much the same. A sergeant-major is one thing; a commanding officer is another. When I first saw a Gloucestershire XI, W. G. Grace had left for London County. Gilbert Jessop was captain; and F. H. B. Champain went in first with Wrathall. Nobody remembers Champain today, any more than they remember P. R. Johnson of Somersetshire. Yet if I were a drowning man with all my days in a cricket field returning in mind before the final oblivion, I am certain that I should again see just for an infinitesimal vibration of memory a cover drive by Champain, a straight drive by Johnson. Other players for Gloucestershire on a distant day at Old Trafford, which I was visiting for the first time, truant from school, were W. S. A. Brown, C. O. H. Sewell, C. L. Townsend, Jack Board, Paish, Roberts and Jessop himself. Townsend as a boy was, with A. G. Steel and J. N. Crawford, one of the three most gifted cricketers in the game's history; he bowled slow right-arm leg-breaks and batted left hand. In an essay in which I attempted an imitation of Galsworthy and described an afternoon spent at Lord's by Old Jolyon, I made Jolyon get confused in his memory and think of Townsend as a left-handed bowler and a right-handed batsman. It was a deliberate slip intended to suggest failing memory on Jolyon's part. Innumerable correspondents have since written to me putting me right. Fred Roberts bowled fast and W. G. Grace worked him hard for hours. Towards half-past six he would still be toiling away on a perfect pitch in the hot sun and 'W. G.' would call out to him from point: 'Keep your arm up, Fred.'

The sight of Jessop merely going forth to bat would cause a cricket crowd today to wonder what on earth was about to happen to the game. Before he had walked purposefully half-way to the wicket four fieldsmen were to be seen journeying to far-flung positions, going there as though by instinct and not by official direction. The spectators in their seats got ready to make a hole in the mass of themselves into which the ball might drop without damage to skull or small of the back. There is still a notion in circulation that Jessop was a 'slogger'. He was in fact a scientific quick scorer who watched the ball. He could score at a great pace because he could both drive and cut. No batsman can hope to disperse a good attack into headlong retreat and confusion if he does not command these two strokes. The quick-footed leaping drive of a Jessop compels the bowler to pitch shorter than he would wish; and when he pitches only a shade short he is cut to ribbons. Jessop's square-cut was as ferocious and as much over the ball as his drive. No slogger could have reduced great bowlers as frequently as Jessop did to disorganization and havoc. Here is a record of one or two of his performances:

Against the West Indies in 1900, he scored 157 between half-past three and half-past four; in 1903 he scored 286 against Sussex in three hours; against the Players of the South, in 1907, he scored 191 in ninety minutes. Four times he scored a century in both innings of a match, each time at the rate of 100 an hour.

The thickest pads were needed by Jack Board to defend his shins sometimes from Jessop's catapultic throw-in from the off-side. Board for years was Gloucestershire's wicket-keeper, excellent at his job and, moreover, a batsman equal to a double century against Somersetshire. He belonged entirely to the West of England; his speech was slow and rich of twang. I sat one wet day in a Gloucester inn listening to his happy flow of talk. He, of course, had served under 'W. G.'. 'Sometimes,' he related, 'when a big stand was going on against us, the Old Man would come to me pulling his beard and he'd say: "Have you nothing to suggest, Jack? What's use of bein'

behind the wicket and seein' everything? How can we get 'em out?"
So I might say; "What about Mester Champain, sir?" "Mester
Champain?— what you talkin' about, Jack? Mester Champain
can't bowl for toffee." But he might give Mr. Champain an over or
two of his "dollies" and if he broke the partnership the Old Man
would come to me and slap me on the shoulder and say: "Well done,
young Jack, well done. Stumpers sees most of the game!" But if, as
was more likely to happen, two or three fours were hit off Mester
Champain's first over the Old Man 'd come tearin' down the pitch
saying: "You're a young fool, Jack Board, a young fool, Jack Board.
I told you he couldn't bowl for toffee!" '

    Time goes on and names which for years were read in the cricket
scores like lasting rubric or incantation give way to others 'st Board
b Dennett', 'c Board b Paish',—names which in conjunction were
as familiar in Bristol and Gloucester as 'c Tunnicliffe b Rhodes'
or 'st Hunter b Rhodes' in Leeds and Huddersfield. Charles Parker
who succeeded Dennett as Gloucestershire's slow left-hand bowler
began as a fast-medium 'swinger'; there was no room in the
Gloucestershire XI for two slow left-hand spinners; and Dennett,
astute and clever, was kept out of the England XI only because
Blythe and Rhodes blocked his way. Parker himself played only once
for England against Australia, at Old Trafford in 1921, when he
dismissed Macartney and Pellew for 32. But he was invited to be
present at Leeds in 1926 and was omitted from the team, even
though A. W. Carr won the toss and sent Australia in first on a soft
wicket. Macartney scored a century before lunch and Parker appeared in the field with refreshments. He was a man who could smile a
sly ironic smile and he appreciated the situation. He was a limp, tall
bowler, who often appeared to wilt with melancholy. One day at
Bristol, some batsman snicked one of Parker's best balls past Dipper
at first slip. As the field was heavy with rain no third man had been
thought necessary so Dipper went off in steady but persistent chase,
accompanied by wicket-keeper Bloodworth, as pace-maker. Smiling
wanly Parker watched them go, then turned to Reeves, the umpire,
and said: 'Look, Bill, there go mi ruddy whippets.' On the Bristol
wicket, dusty on a third day, or at Cheltenham, Parker's spin was
often unplayable; and on a sticky pitch anywhere the greatest of
batsmen seemed at a loss against it. But at Cheltenham when the
turf was 'glue' and Parker's spin was humming like wasps, George
Gunn played throughout a Nottinghamshire innings, scoring round
about 50 out of 70, walking in and out of his crease at will, and with

time to spare. 'You're a grand bowler, Charlie,' said George. 'You make tide come in regular and it's easy playin' with tide.' It was at Cheltenham that Lancashire went in after lunch on the third and closing afternoon to bat out time. They might just lose but scarcely; it all depended on the state of the pitch, for there had been rain and the sun was beginning to shine, though only dimly. Hallows and Makepeace batted comfortably, so that after an hour's amiable stonewalling, I decided to take the opportunity to slip out of the ground and have an aching tooth out; for we were journeying that evening to Bournemouth or some other distant place and I dreaded a night of toothache in the train. I found a dentist in the road running alongside the ground and after some agonized durance with *Punch* in a waiting-room the tooth was removed. I returned to the cricket field and found it empty. The small crowd had dispersed. And the scoreboard's figures announced that Lancashire had lost ten wickets. In my under an hour's absence, Parker had won the match and in one over had taken four wickets. There was, none the less, a vivid and closely analytical description next day in the *Manchester Guardian*; for I knew well enough how Parker got his wickets on a spinner's pitch.

Gloucestershire once on a time could put into the field eleven amateur cricketers and yet defeat Surrey and Nottinghamshire. Recently it has been an entirely professional team, led by two of the most charming of all professionals, Jack Crapp and George Emmett. But the flavour of traditional amateur batsmanship has never been absent from a Gloucestershire innings. Charles Barnett batted for love and to this day Emmett bats for love. Granted he is in the mood and the turf trustworthy, Emmett has no superior in county cricket of the moment for supple wristy strokeplay. He cuts late with the bat giving a touch of intimacy to the ball even as first slip or the wicket-keeper is bending forward in certain anticipation. He can drive with power almost concealed by his easy, indolent, but all the same swift movements. He is one of the few batsmen playing county cricket at the present time of whom we can say that if he stays at the wicket an hour he will certainly delight us with some personal and fascinating strokes. The scoreboard and the averages tell us next to nothing about a batsman of Emmett's rare gifts. There should be some other than the scoreboard's way of estimating such a batsman. And there is—we remember an Emmett innings, keep it affectionately in mind. He belongs to the free pleasures of cricket, and not at all to its competitive pains and penalties.

If cricket had remained a game and pastime and had not been transformed into real industry, we could pick an ideal XI from the lists of players of Gloucestershire. For example: W. G. Grace, Barnett, Hammond, Emmett, Graveney, C. L. Townsend, G. L. Jessop, Sinfield, Board, Goddard and Parker. A fast bowler?—why, Jessop, of course, in his form of 1900, when he took a hundred wickets and scored 2200 runs, both feats being done with alacrity.

YORKS. *v*. LANCS.

THE great game must have pageantry about it and bring forth variety of a man's nature, especially humour of national character. The crowd must take it to heart and get upset and brood during the week upon its ups and downs. It must at times lay heavily upon the minds of the people and render them gloomy. Years ago Lancashire defeated Yorkshire, in a cricket match at Leeds, a victory by some twenty runs. On the third morning Yorkshire had wanted a mere fifty to win, with all their wickets to fall. During an epic August Bank Holiday Lancashire had collapsed in a second innings, all out just before close of play; and the crowd went home content that the issue could be regarded as settled. Next day hardly anybody visited the ground, except those necessary to go through the formalities attendant upon obtaining the correct statistics of a ten-wickets victory for Yorkshire—the players, the scorers, the umpires, the press, with perhaps a handful of members as witnesses, and a few cloth caps with 'nowt else to do' and anyway t' bars would be open while Sutcliffe and Holmes were knocking off t' runs.

Gentle rain in the night had made the turf capricious, and before we knew what was happening the Yorkshire innings fell into rack and ruin. When the last batsman was overwhelmed and Lancashire had really and truly won the match, I rushed from the ground eager to carry the good news back to Manchester. I leapt on a tram, sat down inside, and the guard came with his tickets. 'What's they won by—lost any wickets gettin' them?' I told him that Lancashire, not Yorkshire, were the victors. He expressed some impatience. 'Ah'm talking' about t' cricket,' he said, presumably under the impression

I had come straight from a polo match or archery tournament. I repeated to him the dreadful truth, and he suspended business at once. He didn't give me a ticket but turned his back on me and walked from the almost empty tram, conveyed the news to a trolley-boy, who relayed it to the driver. The tram proceeded to travel some three miles into Leeds by its own volition.

When I reached the railway station, I was a little in advance of the departure of the train to Manchester, so I entered a refreshment-room and sat down at a little table. Shortly afterwards, a man sat down next to me, cap and muffler, and spoke in the speech of Laisterdyke. 'Eh, dear,' he said, 'who'd a' thowt it? Faa-ncy Yorksheer crackin' oop like that. Ah'd never a' thowt it.' There was no anger in his voice, no tone of abuse directed at the faltering Yorkshire eleven. There was only the accent of sorrow. 'Eh, dear,' he repeated, 'it's a rum 'un.' He eyed me carefully, then said, 'Tha doesn't seem to be takin' this very much to 'eart'; and I was obliged to explain to him that, as I came from Lancashire and Manchester, born and bred there, I couldn't be expected to 'take it to heart' exactly. He looked at me from a different angle.

'So tha'rt from Lankysheer art tha, eh, dear; and tha's from Lankysheer?'

'Yes, from Lancashire.'

A slight pause.

'And tha's coom all way from Manchester to watch match, ast tha?'

'Yes, that's it,' I answered.

'And tha's goin' back to Manchester by two-twenty train, eh?'

Yes, I told him, I was indeed returning to my native city by the two-twenty train. After another short spell of meditation, he said:

'Tha'll be feelin' very pleased with thisell, won't thi'?'

'Naturally,' I replied, taking care not to look too triumphant.

'Eh, by gum. Faa-ncy Yorksheer crackin' like that. Aye. Tha'll be feelin' very pleased with thisell. Ah shouldn't wonder.'

And he repeated the question:

'And tha's goin' back to Manchester by two-twenty train, art tha?'

Feeling now a little access of irritation, I answered:

'Yes, straight back.'

'Well,' he said, without the slightest heat, 'Ah 'opes tha drops down de-ad before tha gets there.'

If a game doesn't exhibit elemental character, and loosen springs of unselfconscious humour, I can find no use for it. I can remember happenings at cricket which seemed to have been devised by a great Comic Muse who very much loved the English, especially the North English people. On a certain morning in another Lancashire and Yorkshire match at Old Trafford, in 1939, the cricketer Mitchell arrived at the wicket early, and stone-walled through the afternoon. In other and less passionate matches, Mitchell was not above a brilliant stroke or two; but he reserved himself especially for Old Trafford, when the crowd, many of them liberated at Whitsun from the pits and factories, had come out to take the air and enjoy themselves. In dead silence everybody ached in resigned boredom. Maiden over followed maiden over, and Mitchell got down lower and lower over his bat. Thirty runs he made in two hours.

Suddenly the stillness was broken by a voice, weary and outraged:

'Every bloody year; every so-and-so year 'e cooms 'ere. This so-and-so Mitchell, and 'e spoils Bank 'Oliday. Every so-and-so year.'

Silence again, disturbed only by the sullen and muffled bat of Mitchell. More maidens. The voice, of a man in a hard bowler hat, was raised again:

'Every bloody year, every so-and-so year.' Thus far he had addressed nobody in particular; it was an apostrophe to abstract reason and justice and toleration. But now, he directed himself to the crowd around him.

'Every so-and-so bloody year 'e cooms 'ere. I said to my missus this mornin', "Ah goin' to Owd Trafford and what's more that so-and-so Mitchell 'll stay in all bloody day, that 'e will. Every so-and-so year 'e does it, and 'e'll do it agen." That's what Ah said to ma missus. And look at 'im; 'ere he so-and-so bloody well is.'

Another descent into a dreadful stillness. And now, the man in the hard hat spoke to Mitchell personally.

'Thee, Mitchell!' he called out. 'Ah'm talkin' to thee. Every so-and-so year tha's been coomin' 'ere spoilin' Bank 'Oliday. Every bloody year. But listen to me, Mitchell—aye Ah'm talkin' to thee and doan't pretend tha can't 'ear. Every so-and-so year tha's been muckin' up Bank 'Oliday 'ere. But Ah'll tell thi summat tha doesn't know.' He took a deep breath. 'There's goin' to be a so-and-so war, me lad, so tha won't bloody well be coomin' 'ere next year. Good afternoon and t' 'ell wi' thi.' He gave Mitchell a last look and went home.

HERBERT SUTCLIFFE

HERBERT SUTCLIFFE was a player in one of cricket's golden periods, from 1919 to 1939, and few players at the outset of their careers so handsomely caught the public eye as Herbert Sutcliffe did. He immediately became a pin-up boy in the bedrooms of countless Yorkshire girls, for this was an epoch in which girls insisted that their glamour heroes should be elegant and eye-catching —Rudolph Valentinos of their respective callings. Into that dour Yorkshire team of Rhodes, Emmett, Robinson and the rest, the young Sutcliffe appeared as some Lothario might have appeared among Cromwell's Ironsides. Immaculately flannelled from his first match onwards; glossy and dark of hair, he was utterly unlike any Yorkshire professional we had ever seen.

Sutcliffe immediately announced not only his ability as a batsman but also, in his baptism to nerve-challenging cricket, his self-confidence; that amazing self-assurance which was always an asset beyond mortal estimation. It is the solemn fact that he never expected to get out; never dreamed of it. One day at Lord's he was bowled by an unplayable ball which swung away, then whipped back and took the leg stump. 'Bad luck,' I said, as he walked down the Long Room. Sutcliffe was clearly surprised at this comment. 'I was unsighted by a man moving in the pavilion.'

At The Oval in 1926, the famous Percy Chapman struggle brought back the Ashes after a long time in Australia. England were 22 behind in the first innings when Hobbs and Sutcliffe opened the second innings towards the end of the second day. In the gloaming, they scored 49 without a wrinkle of care or concern. But during the night a terrific thunderstorm drenched the ground which, in those days, could turn quite nasty. When the England openers resumed they remained calm and in absolute possession until the 'Master' was bowled for a century at 172. Sutcliffe went on to score 161 and was then bowled by Mailey in the last over of the day. He smote his pads in open disgust, outraged that he, of all men, should be bowled a few seconds before the close.

Sutcliffe had his first taste of Test cricket in Australia in the 1924-5 series. His first game was at Sydney when he opened the innings with Hobbs. Sir Jack told me that he, as usual, took the first over, a difficult one from Kellaway, who swung the ball late. 'He was so late swinging, just past the off stump,' said Sir Jack, 'that I had to withdraw my bat at the last split second. I knew what I was doing, but perhaps it looked a little risky to anyone else. At the end of this pretty hot over young Herbert came down the pitch and said: "I think I'd leave them alone, Jack, if I were you." ' 'Then, added Sir Jack, 'I knew we'd found the right opener for England.'

Everything that he did was done with character; never was he anonymous. On the rare days which found him out of touch, he couldn't be ruffled. If a ball should beat him he would appear to be interested rather than worried. When the crowd applauded him, as he reached a century, he acknowledged the applause with a wave of the bat which said, 'Yes, yes, dear people, I know, I know. Thank you, but really, really.' I have seen him suddenly hold up a bowler's run while he went out of his crease to remove some almost invisible foreign body from the pitch.

I have seen him wave a Lord Chief Justice from behind the bowlers' arm on the pavilion at Lord's, wave him away as though not just out of sight but out of existence. No event or circumstance on the cricket field seemed able to put him off the Sutcliffian poise. Once, while fielding in the leg-trap, he received a terrific blow on the ankle. Momentarily he was brought low, bent in pain. Yorkshire colleagues came forward solicitously. He at once stood upright, unflinching, and waved them back, as though saying, 'Pray do not be concerned. But, thank you, we Sutcliffes do not suffer pain.'

He was a strange decoration on the stern main structure of the Yorkshire cricket of this time. Yet for all his airs and graces he had, not far under the surface of hauteur, the tough bone of his county, none, in fact, tougher. After he had taken guard and marked his block hole mathematically, he would pat the crease decisively three or four times, and never worry about it again. The upper part of his body was stiff, as he waited for the bowler, the knees slightly bent and suggestive of caution. The head, inclined forward, was alert, concentrated, with radar and antennae.

He commanded strokes enough, a leaning beautifully propelled cover drive, cuts hard down from the wrists, a swinging drive, and a most majestic hook. But for the cause—Yorkshire's or England's— he could deny himself. Well did he know, better than most batsmen, that there is a time to make strokes and a time to abstain from making them. At Sheffield, one sun-burnt afternoon, just after the 1914–1918 War, he was handsomely immobile through a succession of maiden overs. A friendly voice from the crowd asked him 'What dost think tha art—Herbert? A ruddy War Memorial?'

Sutcliffe was born in Pudsey in November 1894, and because of the 1914–1918 War could not enter first-class cricket until he had gone into his 25th year. In his first season for Yorkshire in 1919, he scored 1601 runs, average 48·51, heading the county's batting averages. But he had to wait until 1924 for his first England cap, such was the distinguished Test match company he had then to face. In his very first Test match, at Birmingham in 1924, he scored 64, and, with Hobbs, began the first of the great opening stands for England.

For a decade he was indispensable to England, a first choice almost as a matter of personal right. Of all his rare assets of temperament and intelligence, maybe the most valuable was his close under-standing of his own technical scope. If, say, Sir Leonard Hutton had been obliged to depend on no more than Sutcliffe's technical equip-ment, I doubt if he would have played as many times for England as he did; for Hutton was always well aware, as he faced an attack, that he was only a man and that all men are mortal. Such a thought probably never occurred to Sutcliffe.

Still, I sometimes got the impression it wasn't for him as easy as all that. Often he had to live rather above his technical income. He had, remember, to keep up with the Hobbses and the Hammonds. He didn't inherit a rich technical dowry; he was self-made. He was not born to greatness; he achieved greatness. His wasn't a triumph of skill only, it was a finer triumph, a triumph of character, application, will-power.

NEW HEROES

LEN HUTTON

THE characteristics of the classical style in cricket, or in anything else, are precision of technique, conservation of energy, and power liberated proportionately so that the outlines of execution are clear and balanced. Hutton is the best example to be seen at the present time of the classical style of batsmanship. He is a model for the emulation of the young.

In our own day, Hutton comes as near as anybody to the classical style, though there are moments when the definition of it, as expounded above, needs to be loosened to accommodate him. Dignity, and a certain lordliness, are the robes and very presence of classicism. Frankly, Hutton many times is obliged to wear the dress or 'overhauls' of utility; moreover, his resort to the passive 'dead bat', though shrewd and tactical, scarcely suggests grandeur or the sovereign attitude. The truth is that the classical style of batsmanship was the consequence of a classical style of bowling—bowling which also observed precision, clarity of outline, length, length, length! It is as difficult to adapt classical calm and dignity of poise to modern in-swingers and 'googlies', as it would be to translate Milton into Gertrude Stein, or Haydn into Tin-pan Alley.

But Hutton, in the present far from classical epoch, follows the line of Hobbs, and if all that we know today of batsmanship as a science were somehow taken from our consciousness, the grammar and alphabet could be deduced from the cricket of Hutton, and codified again; he is all the text-books in an omnibus edition. Compared with him Bradman, who has been accused of bloodless mechanical efficiency, was as a volcanic eruption threatening to destroy Pompeii.

We need to be careful of what we mean if we call Hutton a stylist, which, we have agreed, he is. Style is commonly but mistakenly supposed to be indicated by a flourish added to masterful skill, a spreading of peacock's feathers. (The peacock is efficiently enough created and marvellously beautiful without that.) Style with Hutton is not a vanity, not something deliberately cultivated. It is a bloom and finish, which have come unselfconsciously from organized technique rendered by experience instinctive in its rhythmical and attuned movements. His drives to the off-side have a strength that is generated effortlessly from the physical dynamo, through nerve and muscle, so that we might almost persuade ourselves that the current of his energy, his life-force, is running electrically down the bat's handle into the blade, without a single short-circuit or fusing, thence into the ball, endowing it, as it speeds over the grass, with the momentum of no dead material object compact of leather, but of animate life.

His 'follow through' in his drives is full and unfettered. But the style is the man: there is no squandering in a Hutton innings. Bradman, to refer again to the cricketer known as an 'adding-machine', was a spendthrift compared to Hutton, who is economical always, counting every penny, every single of his opulent income of runs. We shall understand, when we come to consider the way of life that produced him, his *habitat*, why with Hutton, the style is indeed the man himself.

Some of us are obliged to work hard for our places in the sun; others have greatness thrust upon them. A fortunate few walk along divinely appointed ways, the gift of prophecy marking their courses. Hutton was scarcely out of the cradle of the Yorkshire nursery nets when Sutcliffe foretold the master to come, not rolling the eye of fanaticism but simply in the manner of a shrewd surveyor of 'futures'. But Sutcliffe knew all the time that the apprenticeship of Hutton had been served in that world of vicissitude and distrust which are the most important factors forming the North of England character under the pressure of an outlook which thinks it's as well to 'take nowt on trust'—not even a fine morning. In his first trial for the Yorkshire Second XI, May 1933, he was dismissed for nothing against Cheshire. Four years after, when he was first invited to play for England, he also made nothing, bowled Cowie. Next innings he was 'slightly more successful'—'c Vivian, b Cowie 1'. Though he was only eighteen years old when he scored a hundred for Yorkshire in July 1934—the youngest Yorkshire cricketer to achieve such distinction—illness as well as the run of the luck of the game hindered his progress, dogged him with apparent malice. When he reappeared on the first-class scene again it was just in time to take part in that dreadful holocaust at Huddersfield, when Essex bowled Yorkshire out for 31 and 99. Hutton's portion was two noughts. In his very first match for Yorkshire at Fenners in 1934, J. G. W. Davies ran him out brilliantly—for nought. Until yesteryear, in fact, the Fates tried him. The accident to his left forearm, incurred while training in a Commando course, nearly put an end to his career as a cricketer altogether.

He has emerged from a hard school. It has never been with Hutton a case of roses all the way; he had to dig his cricket out of his bones: a bat and the Yorkshire and England colours didn't fall into his mouth like silver cutlery. According to the different threads or warp of our nature and being, a different texture is an inevitable consequence. There is no softness in Hutton's psychological or, therefore, in his technical make-up. And there are broadly two ways of getting things done in our limited world. We walk either by faith or by reason. There are, in other words, the born inexplicable geniuses and those we can account for in terms of the skill they have inherited. They are in a way the by-products of skill and experience accumulated and still pregnant in their formative years; their contribution is to develop the inheritance to a further, though rationally definable stage of excellence. But we know where they come from and how. Hutton is one of the greatest of these. But a Compton, or, better for our illustration, a Trumper, seems to spring into being with all his gifts innate and in full bloom from the beginning. He improves in certainty of touch with experience, but as soon as he emerges from the chrysalis there is magic in his power, something that 'defies augury'; he is a law unto himself, therefore dangerous as a guide or example to others who are encased in mortal fallibility. But I am wandering from a contemplation of classicism and Hutton.

He is a quiet thoughtful Yorkshireman, with widely-spaced blue eyes that miss nothing. And his batting is quiet and thoughtful; even in his occasional punishing moods, when his strokes are animating as well as ennobling the field, he doesn't get noisy or rampagious. His stance at the wicket is a blend of easeful muscular organization and keen watchfulness. The left shoulder points rather more to the direction of mid-on than would satisfy Tom Hayward; but here again is evidence that Hutton is a creature or rather a creation of his environment; that is to say, he is obliged to solve problems of spin and swerve not persistently put to Hayward day by day. With Hayward and his school, the left leg was the reconnoitring force, the cat's whisker, the pioneer that moved in advance to 'sight' the enemy. With Hutton it is the right leg that is the pivot, the springboard. But often he allows it to change into an anchor which holds him back when he should be moving out on the full and changing tide of the game. He is perfect at using the 'dead' bat—rendering it passive, a blanket of a buffer, against which spin or sudden rise from the pitch come into contact as though with an anaesthetic. He plays so close to the ball, so much over it that he has acquired a sort of student's slope of the shoulders; at the sight of a fizzing off-break he is arched like a cat. Even when he drives through the covers, his head and eyes incline downwards, and the swing of the bat doesn't go past the front leg until the ball is struck. He can check the action of any stroke extremely late, and so much does he seem to see a delivery all the way that we are perplexed that so frequently he is clean-bowled by a length well up to him. From the back foot he can hit straight for four; and all his hits leave an impressive suggestion of power not entirely expended.

We shall remember, after we have relegated his 364 against Australia at Kennington Oval in 1938 to the museum of records in sport rather than to the things that belong to cricket, his innings at Sydney in the second Test match during the 1946–1947 rubber; only 37 but so dazzling in clean diamond-cut strokes that old men present babbled of Victor Trumper. He has even while playing for Yorkshire more than once caused some raising of the eyebrows. At Nottingham in 1948 he not only played, but played well, Miller, Johnston and Johnson as though for his own private and personal enjoyment. But usually he subdues his hand to what it works in— Yorkshire cricket. I have heard people say that he is not above 'playing for himself'. Well, seeing that he is Yorkshire to the bone's marrow, we should find ourselves metaphysically involved if we tried to argue that he is ever not playing for Yorkshire.

There is romance even in Yorkshire cricket, though they keep quiet about it. Romance has in fact visited the life and career of Hutton. In July 1930, the vast field of Headingley was a scene of moist, hot congestion with, apparently, only one cool. clean, well-brushed individual present, name of Bradman, who during the five hours' traffic of the crease, made at will 300 runs, and a few more, before half-past six. He returned to the pavilion as though fresh from a band-box; the rest of us, players, umpires, crowd and scorers, especially the scorers, were exhausted; dirty, dusty and afflicted by a sense of the vanity of life. In all the heat and burden of this day at Leeds, more than twenty years ago, a boy of fourteen years was concealed amongst the boiling multitude; and so many of these thousands seethed and jostled that one of them, especially an infant in the eyes of the law, couldn't possibly (you might have sworn) have made the slightest difference to what we were all looking at, or to the irony of subsequent history. The solemn fact is that as Bradman compiled the 334 which was then the record individual score in a Test match, the boy hidden in the multitude was none other than the cricketer chosen already by the gods to break this record, if not Bradman's heart, eight years afterwards.

CYRIL WASHBROOK

WASHBROOK has for years been a representative cricketer for the players at Lord's and for England; he has also attained to power as captain of Lancashire county. He has scored a century for England against Australia; and to this day when a cricketer has scored a century in England *v.* Australia Test matches, he is at liberty to chant a *Nunc dimittis*. Yet somehow Washbrook has not exactly found his way. When he scored 152 in his second match for Lancashire against Surrey in 1933 he was only 18 years old and his cricket was already strong, decisive and, in many ways, masterful. During this same period another young Lancastrian batsman vied in promise with Washbrook; his name was Oldfield and he was more of a stylist than Washbrook. The war that broke out in 1939 stole years from both these players just at the time when talent matures to more than talent. Oldfield missed his footing on the upper slopes of greatness and, likewise, Washbrook, though he actually has reached the summit of reasonable achievement, has not remained there. Yet in point of presence and individuality of stroke-play we must count him amongst the truly distinguished batsmen of his time; moreover he goes without argument amongst the most brilliant and beautiful of all cover-points, a worthy follower for Lancashire on the wing of Vernon Royle and R. H. Spooner.

To measure a batsman who is an artist as well as a consistent run-maker the scoreboard is inadequate. There are cricketers who are able to arrest our attention while they are not at the moment in the scorer's books at all. It is a matter of personality; and this is something which defied definition even in times when personality was omnipresent on English cricket fields. Today, most of our players are so much alike in style and personal aspect that catalogues could scarcely classify them. Personality does not depend on consistently successful performance, though without some distinction of performance it could not very well make itself felt. Many great performers, virtuosi in skill, record breakers of renown, have lacked personality.

It was once maintained that Hobbs himself seldom had a crowd's attention by any personal hypnotism. But if indeed Hobbs was frequently anonymous, it was in the way that Homer is alleged to have been not a man but an epoch. An innings by Woolley was at once 'signed' as soon as he came in, not only because of the easy supple beauty of his strokes, defensive if called for, but by the dominating, yet at the same time unobtrusive poise of him, and the inscrutable face.

Washbrook, from the day of his first match for Lancashire has drawn my eyes to him, whether at the wicket or in the field. I like the way he wears his cap; no cricket cap can seem as confident of peak as Washbrook's Lancashire cap with the lovely red rose on it, or England cap. His shoulders are a cricketer's, also his easy unconcerned movement as he walks on the field, changing from cover to cover, with a jaunty motion, chin up. It is said that he is aloof, unsmiling. A certain prima donna was reprimanded by her concert agent: 'You must smile at the audience.' 'And why?' she asked, 'zey are not fonny.' I like the pouter pigeon thrust forward of Washbrook's chest; and whenever he scratches the batting crease with his right foot, champing it, I know that the bowlers are likely to be put to the sword. And there, by a phrase, is one of his qualities brought vividly to mind. Of how many batsmen in the game at the moment may we say that they can, in a situation of gravity and challenge, put an attack 'to the sword'. I have seen Washbrook cut an advancing attack to ribbons. Better still, and as much to his credit, I have seen him lose his wicket because of daring and contempt. At Nottingham, in the first Test match of the 1948 rubber, he was caught at long leg from a superb hook off Lindwall. At Old Trafford, in the same rubber, he was missed on the boundary from another great hook, MacLarenesque, by Hassett. Not at all daunted, Washbrook immediately repeated the stroke, off Miller or Lindwall, and again Hassett dropped the catch. (Hassett then borrowed a bowler hat from a man in the crowd and held it out in front of him.) The dreary folk who set the standards and canons of contemporary cricket, those who never saw J. T. Tyldesley, severely chastised Washbrook for 'carelessness'. I can see yet, with my mind's eye, the hook by which Washbrook got out that day at Trent Bridge in 1948.

He is essentially a stroke player. In fact, it is not from 'carelessness' with his hooking and pulling that he has not had a long reign in Test cricket; his failures were the consequence of strangely and unnaturally immobile footwork which got him out leg-before-wicket.

Some kind of malaise seems to come over him; a sudden moodiness, inexplicable in a cricketer born confident and sure of himself. At Lord's, in 1950, he reached a century by close of play, then next day made not another run against Valentine and Ramadhin in about half an hour, then succumbed as though changed into a batsman with neither eyesight nor vision. Washbrook is not to be described or defined at all in terms of averages and aggregates or of the steady service of the artisan worthy of his hire. Only the man who is a technician before he is an artist is prepared always to submit to the demands of the machine. He was born perhaps too late; in contemporary Test matches a batsman is not encouraged to make strokes that might cost him his wicket early in the game. I doubt if J. T. Tyldesley could retain his place in the England XI of today's consistent cheese-paring economy. But Washbrook can, of course, exercise self-denial enough. His century at Melbourne, against Australia in 1946, saved England from defeat. I have never understood why he was removed from his position as the player fit to open England's innings with Hutton until a better man was found, or a swifter fieldsman at cover found, or a cricketer who can lend as much of panache as Washbrook at a time when the England team is generally to be recognized at the wicket for industry real and careworn.

So many times has Washbrook done less than justice to himself on great occasions that on the face of it a severe sentence in Mr. Altham's and Mr. Swanton's *History of Cricket* may be justified: 'Hammond, Hutton and Compton were still' (in 1946) 'on any standard great players. Washbrook, if lacking their genius, was much more than competent.' The line that divides talent from genius is thin and precarious. Washbrook at his best can bat with a touch, a mastery, a freedom of style far beyond the scope of competence. A strict technical analysis of his batsmanship might arrive at the view that he is greater as a stroke-player than as a player of organised defence. We must judge any man by his best work; nobody in contemporary cricket can excel an inspired Washbrook innings for combined power, brilliance and the grand manner.

DENIS COMPTON

DENIS COMPTON was a master batsman who allowed no bowler to enslave him. Whenever he ceased scoring quickly we knew that the bowling was unusually good. He enjoyed his own cricket, played the game on his own terms. His technique, though comprehensive and reliable, never tyrannized him. He was a great improvisor, instinctive and free. For example: in August 1947, Kent, on the third afternoon, invited Middlesex to score 397 to win at the speed of more than ninety an hour. And Middlesex lost by only 75. On a dusty Lord's pitch in glorious sunshine, Douglas Wright bowled at his cleverest, which meant that in his every other over, the batsman needed to cope with at least one almost unplayable spinner. Compton scored 168 before getting out to a deep-field catch off Wright.

One of his strokes I can see whenever I close my eyes and wish. He danced out to drive with the spin to the off, anticipating a leg-break. Not until the ball pitched was it revealed as a consummately disguised 'googly', whipping off the pitch viciously. Compton had to readjust his entire physical shape and position at the last split second. As a consequence he fell to the earth flat on his chest; but he found time to sweep to the leg-boundary the fizzing spin from the off. It was a case of delayed science.

The fact is that Compton at bottom batted with respect for and knowledge of rational law, though frequently he appeared to be playing according to a law of his own, and making it up as he went along. He was, like George Gunn, eccentric and original; but George did his stuff with a mature cynicism, Denis pulled science by the beard like a cheeky schoolboy. No cricketer has ever been more of a schoolboy's hero than Compton. Schoolboys crowed like cocks as Denis walked out of the Lord's pavilion on his way to the wicket. They adored him because in him they saw the cricketer they themselves would have wished to be. Compton's cricket was always young of impulse. He ran his runs with a most likeable waddle; when he broke his 'duck' he would scamper along the pitch for dear life, as though, like any schoolboy, he was afraid he might not get another run.

Sir Jack Hobbs used to open his score by placing the ball to an inch, then running a single at his leisure. In Compton's longest innings he was continually eager and adventurous, 'daring' himself to do this or that thoroughly unacademic thing. But no discerning student of cricket was for a moment blind to the fact that Compton, for all his sportiveness, was fundamentally a sound, even a correct batsman. No matter how he seemed to make shots on the spur of the moment, no matter how unconventional his preliminary physical motions, when his supple blade made contact, his feet were rightly placed, his body was over the ball, his nose 'smelling' it. In Australia, he was at first somewhat nonplussed by the bowling of Iverson for Victoria. At the other end of the wicket David Sheppard was batting steadily, but runs were not being scored quickly enough. So David, between overs, approached Denis for instructions. 'You go on just as you are,' was Compton's advice, 'I'll attend to the antics.'

In point of genius he stood above all batsmen of his period. He, the most animated and brilliant stroke-player, also has to his credit one of the greatest defensive innings ever achieved in a Test match. At Nottingham, in June 1948, England began a second innings 344 behind and lost two wickets for 39. Compton proceeded to discipline himself wonderfully. In a dreadful light often, against Miller at his fiercest, he stayed at the wicket six hours fifty minutes, scoring 184. Then a brutal ball from Miller reared shoulder-high, Denis shaped to hook it but slipped on the wet grass, and fell on the stumps. Long and spartan though the innings must have seemed to Compton himself, not for a moment did it try the patience of anybody peering through the recurrent encircling gloom. It was a classic innings in style, reserve power and easy unselfconcious bearing.

While Compton was still adorning English cricket, it was his colleague and contemporary Sir Leonard Hutton who usually was called 'The Master'. But Sir Leonard many times had to suffer to be dictated to by bowlers, Denis seldom, if ever. If he occasionally defended, cutting out his boldest, most individual strokes, the reason was that the situation of the game demanded that he should temporarily play for Middlesex or for England. Whether doing as he liked with an attack, or denying himself 'for the cause', he was always personal, inimitable and fascinating to eye and cricket sense, never merely efficient, never anonymous.

After taking guard at the beginning of an innings, he would twiddle his bat as he surveyed the fieldsmen and their placings. As with all truly great batsmen, his bat looked as though it possessed sensitiveness, as though it were tactile, and as though some current of his own nervous system were running from him, via his fingers, into the blade. He moved to the ball on light fantastic toe. Now and again he would skip out of his crease as the bowler was more than halfway through his run. If he found that the ball, when pitching, was too short for a forward stroke, he would skip back to his crease and perform a neat late-cut through slips which, having expected to see him drive to the off, had stood up and relaxed.

Again, like all great players, he made bowling adapt itself to his own extraordinary notions of what is a hittable length. 'He sometimes makes a bowler look silly', said a master-spinner who was a contemporary of Compton; 'but it is grand fun to bowl at him.'

His 'wonderful year' happened in the summer of 1947. He scored 3816 in this season, a record, with eighteen centuries, also a record. His batting average for 50 innings, eight times not out, amounted to 90·85—breathtaking figures to the credit of a batsman who collaborated so frequently with the bowler in his own dismissal. In 1947 summer sun blessed England, which was still licking war wounds. Never have I been so deeply touched on a cricket ground as I was in this heavenly summer, when I went to Lord's to see a pale-faced crowd, existing on rations, the rocket bomb still in the ears of most folk—see this worn, dowdy crowd watching Compton. The strain of long years of anxiety and affliction passed from all hearts and shoulders at the sight of Compton in full sail, sending the ball here, there and everywhere, each stroke a flick of delight, a propulsion of happy sane healthy life. There were no rations in an innings by Compton. Men, women, boys and girls cheered him to his century, running all his runs with him. The gods had been good to him, endowing him with the ideal cricketer's looks and the ideal cricketer's delight in the game. But, in his prime, the gods treated him churlishly; they crippled him almost beyond repair. Nothing could daunt his spirit, though.

Knee-cap or none, he remained an artist-batsman, beyond the powers of assessment of the scoreboard. I doubt if any cricketer has been so much loved as Denis in his heyday. All eyes at once were fixed on him as he came into the field, padded or with his team-mates. Round about 1947-48 I sometimes took Kathleen Ferrier to dinner in the 'Ivy Restaurant'. Not many of the people at the tables knew who she was. But once, when Denis was my guest, one diner after another came to him asking for his autograph: 'Next time I invite you out to dinner,' I told him, 'I'll book a private room.' His face was known to thousands never present at a cricket match. His portrait was to be seen on hoardings everywhere, advertising a hair-cream—and on the field of play, at any rate, Denis's hair was unruly beyond the pacifying power of any cream, oil or unguent whatsoever.

He was always 'in the game', not a virtuoso batsman exclusively, in the eyes of the public. The crowds followed all his movements wherever he fielded; sometimes he was placed near the wicket and he would bend, hands on knees, like a schoolboy playing leap-frog. As a bowler, he could spin the ball left-handed from the back of the hand; what is more, he was really a dangerous bowler of his kind whenever he found the right length. He sent down his overs at quick motion; no time-waster here. (Imagine Compton wasting his precious moments of fun on the cricket field!) He brought his arm over after a few steps, and frequently was bowling another spinner before the batsman had resumed 'position' again.

He might have won a Test match at Leeds in 1948, the game in which Australia in the fourth innings scored 404 for three wickets, and achieved one of the most remarkable victories in cricket's history. The pitch was dusty—no use to seamers, no use to Laker; but 'made' for leg and 'googly' spin. Norman Yardley, the England captain, put Compton on to bowl straightway; and Compton straightway caught and bowled Hassett. He span really viciously and, as I looked on, I expected him to take a wicket every over. Arthur Morris, who eventually amassed 182, was goaded into running out of his ground to cope with Compton; and Godfrey Evans missed a difficult stumping chance. Then—lo and behold!—Bradman, baffled by a swift leg break, sliced to first slip, where Jack Crapp dropped him. During the lunch interval the Australians decided that Denis had to be knocked out of action, and when play was continued a fierce assault on his slow spin was made by left-handed Morris. Denis, taken off, didn't bowl again until Australia had virtually won the match. If Compton had been given licence to bowl all through that astonishing afternoon, I fancy Australia would have lost. Compton's analysis might have worked out at something like 7 for 200. But England, with 400 runs to play with, could have 'closed' one end of the wicket with the length attack of Alec Bedser and Pollard.

Compton would, as certainly as anything in cricket can be certain, have sent along one pretty unplayable ball every three or four overs. To this day Denis regrets that he was not trusted at Leeds in 1948 to win a Test by his bowling—after getting rid of Hassett, and having both Morris and Bradman missed off him in his opening overs. Not that Denis is given to regrets. His temperament is happy and resilient. It is absurd that he had to grow up into middle age; in his case growing up was against nature. Some cricketers—especially batsmen —are born old; some have old age thrust upon them, while in the act of batting. Compton at one time threatened to keep the advancing years at bay indefinitely, so the fates had to do something about him; and they crippled him. Whom the gods love. . . .

All, or nearly all, the laurels of the game came his way. For M.C.C. v. N.E. Transvaal he scored 300 out of 399 in 181 minutes. In his first-class career (so far) he has scored 38,635 runs, average 51·99, with 122 centuries. Maybe there is more to come, even yet. The other summer, at Lord's, his innings of 71 against Cambridge University was virtually a restoration, not to say a resurrection, of his genius, brilliant, original, happy. 'Happy', that is the operative word in a description of Denis. The greatness of any artist, his abnormality of technique, sometimes seem to weigh heavily on him. The crowd look at Great Men with something of amazement—anyhow, they don't count the Maestro, as a rule, one of themselves. Compton, for all his prowess, his comprehensive skill and his accumulating renown, never lost touch with the crowd.

Last summer, while a match was in progress at Lord's I came across three schoolboys behind a stand busy getting paper cups of coffee out of a machine. 'Why don't you watch the cricket?' I asked. 'When I was a boy I wouldn't have missed a ball for anything.' And the eldest boy answered, 'There's not much to watch, sir, is there?' 'Not much to watch?' I retorted, 'how old are you to be blasé already?' 'Thirteen,' he replied. 'And,' I said, 'so you think there's nothing worth watching in cricket nowadays?' 'Well,' answered the boy politely, but very firmly, 'there's no more Denis Comptons, are there?' The good old days! Has any cricketer, alive or dead, received a tribute as splendid as this boy's? 'No more Denis Comptons. . . .'

W. J. EDRICH

BILL EDRICH has always been the right cricketer for the crowd, who love a fighter always and a man who, small of inches, gets to the top by determination as well as by skill. He was not born with genius like Denis Compton. There is something about the chosen few, the abnormally gifted elect, that the English distrust.

As a people we are not comfortable in the presence of the stylists and the poets. The fact that our poetry is the greatest and most varied in the world is proof that action and reaction are equal and opposite; we have, as a nation and an environment been obliged to escape into poetry. Edrich is neither stylist nor poet. There is not a man sitting in the 'Free Seats' at Lord's any day watching Edrich who doesn't feel 'There, but for the grace of God, go I; that's the way I'd play cricket myself if I were good enough.' Again Edrich appealed to the English sentiment of sport by struggling through a terribly sticky patch at the beginning of his career as a Test player. In 1938 against Australia he failed at Trent Bridge— 'b O'Reilly, 5'. He was given another chance at Lord's and again he failed— b McCormick 0, c McCabe, b McCormick 10'. In the fifth game in this rubber, in which England scored 903 for 7 wickets at Kennington Oval, O'Reilly got him out for 12. In South Africa, playing for England under Hammond he could do nothing right; in pitiful sequence he faltered, but Hammond kept faith in him and at his last opportunity Edrich scored a double-century.

It is sometimes better to be born lucky than exceptionally gifted. I doubt if dispassionate criticism would rank that Edrich has ever been the superior of Ernest Tyldesley as a thoroughbred batsman. Yet consider the manner in which the paths of these two cricketers diverged in the direction of Test match renown: in 1921 Tyldesley played against the devastating Gregory and MacDonald and like Hendren and others he was overwhelmed, and was not given another chance until the fourth game of the rubber, at Manchester, where he scored a most brilliant 78 not out. He was therefore allowed to remain in the England XI for the Oval engagement, the last of the rubber, and he scored 39. Not until 1926 did he again attract the attention of a Selection Committee and in this summer all the denseness of perception and all the prejudice in the world could not possibly ignore his quality; for in 1926 he scored 1128 runs in nine consecutive innings from the end of June, averaging 141.

So he was chosen for England in the Test match at Manchester, where it would have needed courage, as well as stupidity, to keep him out of the game; he scored 81 at the one and only chance that came his way. But he was dropped, all the same, for the next and final Test of 1926. He was chosen to go to Australia in 1928–29 under the captaincy of A. P. F. Chapman. He played in one Test match, scoring 31 and 21. In South Africa in 1927–28 he had contributed to Test match history, with 520 runs, average 65.

The people in the North of England frequently have reason to suppose that a player at Lord's stands a far better chance of receiving invitations into the best company than the player whose appearances at Lord's are few and intermittent. But this is a digression which is not intended as a belittlement of Edrich as an England cricketer; I was led to it by contemplating how his career has been shaped by that combination of skill, toughness of character and good fortune which appeals to the instincts and fellow-feeling of the 'little man' of these days. There is nothing exclusive about Edrich's cricket, nothing esoteric of technique, nothing much too strange and good for human nature's daily food. When first he played for Middlesex and England he bowled fast; and here again was an appeal to the average man, for he bowled as boys and men bowl on any common or village green, if their intent is to bowl fast at all. He slung or hurled the ball at the wicket as fast as he could make it go even at risk of breaking his back. The energy of his action carried him sprawling half-way down the pitch, as though drawn in the draught caused by his velocity. I expected to see dust and newspapers eddying in the air whenever he bowled fast—like the tremendous atmospheric disturbance which happens on a railway station platform as an express thunders through. At the close of any day which had seen Edrich bowling to the end, I expected that the groundsman would find trouser buttons on the wicket and torn boot laces. A 'fighting' batsman, conquering not only the actual odds in the field, but conquering himself also by sheer grit and guts; a fast bowler spectacular and primeval; and a slip fieldsman who by agility and liveliness of mind could add inches to his stature—what other attributes of sport, making for recognition and affection from the crowd, could any cricketer desire? To crown all in the general esteem, he emerges from professionalism and becomes amateur and captain of Middlesex county. He is another truly representative cricketer, representative of our times and our changed social structure and sanctions.

He revealed his character and craftsmanship fully during the Australian rubber of 1946–47. For a while, until Hutton, Washbrook and Compton ran into some semblance of true form, he was the backbone in Test matches of the England innings; not only did he render it vertebrate, but he almost supplied the red corpuscles alone. On an infamous pitch at Brisbane he played an innings of quite tormented obstinacy; the ricochet of fast bowling was dangerous to every part of his person from big toe upward to the third frontal convolution of the cerebellum. The ball seemed attracted to his vitals as though magnetically, but he did not flinch, did not budge from the defensive zone of the wicket; it was an innings of noble if painful adhesiveness. We could almost see him torn from the crease, but by ligaments of his own tenacity he was held there. At Sydney and at Melbourne he again batted bravely more or less single-handed. At Melbourne he received a blow on the knee-cap from a terrific hit while he was fielding close to the wicket in a leg-trap. The impact of ball and bone could be heard all round the vast enclosure. It was necessary to carry him from the field; most of us imagined he would be out of action at least a fortnight. But next morning he opened the England attack, hurling himself into his work with the physical abandon of a body projected through entirely non-resistant space. He does not understand the meaning of a compromise with over-powering odds; he certainly seems able by will power to laugh or to ignore ordinary mortal wounds. In 1954, at Lord's, he was knocked out by Tyson, of Northamptonshire; a rising ball of unseen projectory hit him in the face, under the cheek-bone. He fell as though slain. Again he was led from the field—this time, surely, to the hospital for a month. Next morning he continued his innings at the first opportunity and from the first ball sent to or at him, by Tyson, he was bruised again, trying a vicious hook.

He is not tall, but there is enough in his frame of muscular strength. Dauntless war service for his country in the air caused him to thrive on ordinary challenges to nerve and stoutness of heart. By means of his attributes of character he has directed a professional skill of no common order into the ways and channels of high distinction. He became one of the most prolific scorers in 1947, that glorious summer of sunshine when English bowling was in a lowly state. Day after day the crowds at Lord's basked and revelled as Edrich and Compton helped themselves to centuries, neither in much danger of losing his wicket except through eccentric running by Compton. One day, Compton, having been the main cause of three run-outs in the Middlesex innings, and having next day received some censure from the newspapers in consequence, came to me and asked: 'But am I so bad between the wickets?' 'You are not exactly good, are you?' I said. 'But,' he responded, with a charming air of a culprit justifying himself, 'I don't know—I run myself out as often as anybody else.' Edrich and Compton at the wicket at Lord's, throughout the summer, not perhaps Mars and Jupiter in conjunction, but the image will serve an illuminative purpose, up to a point. It was a contrast of powerful, experienced, opportunist purpose—while the going was good—and art effortless and apparently unaware of its power at all, except power to play light-heartedly and venture from time to time beyond the limits of known science. Edrich's cricket has always had the concern, not to say anxiety, of middle age in it; Compton's mastery is easy and young and was not obtained by scorning delights and living laboriously; he was touched by the grace of genius in his cradle. Edrich, even at his most punitive—and he has many times bludgeoned bowling to a shambled condition—must needs watch closely and keep his head down and obey common sense. He has few equals at keen-eyed scrutiny, nose over the ball. Once on a time he could drive straight with majesty of swing and balance. He seems nowadays sometimes to make strokes not accurately timed; or he sends them with extra-ordinary precision straight to the fieldsman. But whether in form or out of form, Edrich needs, as bowlers say, to be 'got out'. He does not put himself forward as a likely accessory after the act of his own destruction. Very properly the crowd know him as 'Bill', exactly as the crowd very properly call Compton 'Denis'.

ALEC BEDSER

ALEC BEDSER at his best was undoubtedly a great bowler; always and for as long as he lives he will be a big man, big in physical size and weight, big of heart and friendliness. He had the kind of presence that overtopped even men not at all short of inches. His, in fact, was a formidable presence—on the field of play. As I watched him at the beginning of a match preparing to bowl, measuring his short run by half-a-dozen or so strides, then a leap, rolling up the sleeve of his right arm, a ham of an arm, muscled like the ancient blacksmith's—as I watched him going through these preparatory motions grimly, frowning a little, I always felt relieved that it was from the safe cover of the pavilion that I was indeed watching him. I have seen Bradman himself going in to bat, after Bedser had tasted quick blood, and there has been on Bradman's face an even more than ordinary look of tight-lipped determination.

Off the field, in his England or Surrey blazer, Alec was as gentle-mannered as the next Sunday school superintendent. His eyes, frank as the new boy's, looked you in the face, not aggressively but because of a natural openness of mind. At bottom he is a shy man, but not without a shrewdness not hardened by sophistication. On a sea voyage he and brother Eric always helped as ushers at Sunday morning church-service. Not town or country bred, but urban, Alec came of good stock. His father, now beyond seventy years old, is a fine vintage character of the sort going out of fashion. He taught his boys to play cricket the simple and the thorough way—practice, practice, practice. The straight bat. The good steady length. I asked father Bedser if he had been a bowler himself. 'Yes', he replied, adding with a twinkle— 'a seamer.' But in father Bedser's youth all bowlers had to make do throughout the longest innings of the other side, with the same ball. We must always bear this fact in mind as we compare bowlers who have skilfully used the seam. Heavens!— suppose Sydney Barnes had been offered more than one new ball within three hours or so. But usually he found one and the same ball good enough.

Here I must hasten to say that Bedser, though he got much of his destructive power from the seam and the 'shine', was certainly not a 'new ball' bowler in a restrictive way, not dependent on a 'new ball'. The basis of his attack was classical. He pitched an accurate length, just short enough to worry a forward stroke, and not short enough ever to encourage a long-lengthed on-side stroke. His pace from the ground came mainly from his powerful and concentrated action. Along his shortish run he strode rather heavily, as though going uphill. As the left arm pointed on high, the right made a sharp diagonal, and then the right arm swung a cartwheel, the left going down in perfect accord after the batsman had glimpsed the propulsive left side and shoulder. The action was suddenly made rhythmical. But it was a rhythm carrying a weighty and explosive harmony.

'To bowl well,' he once said to me, 'you have to *think*.' (The italic was in his voice!) He spent much time experimenting with the seam, and at last could pitch the ball between middle and leg and whip it across, keeping it well inside the batsman's danger-zone. The Sydney Barnes ball. The best of all tricks in the bowlers' armoury, whether the turn is occasioned by spin or seam-control. There is no safe stroke to play against a ball 'leaving' the bat. Other seamers have imagined they were getting themselves into the Bedser class by perfecting the inswinger. Bedser certainly gathered many wickets with his inswinger, aided by the leg-trap field. But I doubt if today I'd be ranking him as a fast-medium bowler comparable to Maurice Tate if his best ball had '*come into*' the batsman, and not gone the other way.

I have found him a most likeably modest cricketer, even given to pessimism. 'No good anybody bowling on this wicket today. Too slow.' Invariably he would express some such doubts at the beginning of a match. At Brisbane, in December, 1950, he was particularly gloomy about his chances on what he described as an 'unfair' wicket. Then he went forth and took the wickets of Arthur Morris, Neil Harvey, Lindsey Hassett and 'Bill' Johnstone for 45, in some 16 overs. And the wicket really was a beauty—for batsmen. This year of 1950 was crucial for Alec. In the English summer he had not bowled with luck against the West Indies—the victorious West Indies side containing Worrell, Weekes, Walcott, Stollmeyer and Rae. He did not play at Manchester in the first Test. At Lord's he took 3 for 60 and 1 for 80. At Nottingham, where Worrell and Weekes scored 283 together for the fourth wicket, in a West Indies total of 558, Bedser emerged with 5 wickets for 127 and none for 35, but his record in the five Tests of 1950 was only 11 wickets at 34·27 each. 'His arm's getting lower every day.' Already people were saying it. In 1946–47, Bedser had bowled for the first time in Australia. He was then submitted in tropical heat to the labours of a 'stock' bowler. In the five Tests he wheeled down 246 overs 3 balls for 876 runs, 16 wickets, 54·75 each!

So we can see how much in the balance Alec found himself in Australia in 1950, after his dubious performances against the West Indies. At first the fates were apparently set on a rapid and decisive eclipse of him. He began the tour ill of health. Then on the eve of the first Test match, he was thrashed (mainly by Keith Miller for New South Wales *v.* M.C.C.) to the extent of 1 for 127 in 24 overs. In the nick of time, with his future as an England bowler swaying insecurely, he asserted his character and, consequently, his technical mastery. Never did he look back as England's first line of her attack until, after Brisbane 1954, he was dropped from the England XI, dropped to his mute astonishment, an astonishment sad to behold. Only once more did he receive an invitation to bowl for England— against South Africa in 1955. Well, he could (if he had thought of it) have chanted '*Nunc Dimittis*', even after Hutton had dropped the pilot. He had taken 200 wickets in Tests (he took 236 in all); he had taken 100 against Australia. He had rooted out the failing link in Bradman's great chain. He bowled Bradman for 0 at Adelaide in 1947. And here, in England in 1948, he harried the great man sorely, getting him out in four consecutive Test innings, an achievement of itself enough to guarantee any bowler's posterity.

In praising this famous bowler we do not often enough remember (though Alan Ross has reminded us) that Bedser for long had to work for England on a lonely trail. He had no Statham, no Trueman, no Lock or Laker, to help him at the other end. And it was in a vulnerable England XI, a losing England XI, that he staked his claim to greatness, and to the attention of the game's historians for ever. I imagine that his 'finest hour' came to him at Nottingham in June 1953. Australia won the toss, and in showery weather which made the ball hard to grip even in a hand as capacious as Bedser's, Australia were sitting pretty with 243 for 4 at lunch on the second day. Bedser then crashed through the Australian innings like a 'bull-dozer'. Hutton cleverly nursed Bedser so that with a new ball, he took, in three spells, one for 7, two for 5 and four—all bowled—for 2. Australia were all out for 249. Bedser in this rubber took 39 wickets at 17·48 runs each, which was the largest 'bag' in international games until Laker helped himself to 46 v. Australia in 1956.

In June 1946, the Hon. George Lyttleton wrote to James Agate (dramatic critic of *The Sunday Times*) as follows: 'I can't see the English bowlers troubling Hassett and Co. much. Bedser, the Press with one accord, compare with Tate, I shouldn't go higher than Kermode. Has there ever been a Test match bowler with a *clumsy* action?' (Kermode was an Australian brought to Lancashire by A. C. MacLaren round about 1904. He was fast-medium and shaped with a peg-top kind of heavy muscularity.) Tate's action, like Alec's was not exactly as musical as Mozart, or if it comes to that, as Johannes Brahms. But it served. Like Bedser, Maurice got his annihilating energy from a swing of body and late propulsion of his shoulders. With Alec and Maurice it was a case of 'handsome is as handsome does'. I can do no greater honour to Alec, or to Maurice, than to link them with S. F. Barnes—an immortal trinity, each of the same order.

T. E. BAILEY

SOME cricketers are born to greatness. Trevor Bailey achieved it. For though he is an athlete by nature, his performances do not come easily. He conquers by tremendous effort and deliberation of aim. When he runs to bowl, he seems crooked in his approach; and the leap at the wicket, as Bailey releases the ball, is as strenuous and determined as the leap of a man at a bus that is nearly leaving him behind.

In the Test matches of the English summer of 1953 he frustrated Australia at least twice by a bat as completely locked as the door of a safe deposit. Yet Bailey is truly aggressive as a batsman and loves to attack any bowler. No batsman in England commands a better cover-drive. He really enjoys tribulation and apparently attracts pain to him as the sparks fly upward. (No cricketer has oftener than Bailey suffered bruises, sprains, concussions, abrasions.) The humour of it all is that he thrives on adversity and suffering. He has, whether he knows it or not, a genius for the histrionic attitude. When at Lord's, in the second Test match of the 1953 rubber, he made a mistake at long last, and saw himself irretrievably being caught, he clutched his forehead, tottered at the crease, the living and agonised picture of misery and self-disgust.

Bailey is a wonderful fieldsman. He has made catches bordering on the marvellous. But, here again he doesn't attain perfection of eye and agility with ease. There is usually a terrific convulsion of every nerve, sinew and bone. The catch is the swift, unexpected result of a spasm, or even an eruption of Bailey's vehement opportunism, and his violent intention to 'do the enemy down'. Most times, as he holds the 'catch of the season', he falls writhing to the earth. If ever a ball rises from the pitch abruptly and raps his hand, the injured member is withdrawn with a speed that suggests that the fingers of Bailey are each cells of conscious pain. If a batsman in with Bailey calls for a ridiculous run, Bailey's 'No!' calls up visions of Roman imperial purple.

He was born in December 1923 and at Dulwich College entered the lists of the finest boy cricketers of the 1940s. In 1941 he headed the Dulwich batting lists with 851 runs, average, 121·57. For Cambridge University in 1947 he scored 60 not out against Oxford University, and took 3 wickets for 112: in 1948 his contribution to the University match was 55 and 18, with five wickets for 110. He began to play for Essex in 1946. In 1947 he headed the county's batting averages, and was second in the bowling order. In 1949 he scored 1,000 runs and took 100 wickets. In 1952 he improved on this with 1,513 runs and 130 wickets. At Old Trafford he made that gallant stand with Godfrey Evans against the West Indians, after England had lost 5 for 88. Bailey scored 82 not out, and in the next innings he was run out for 33. Injury prevented him from taking part in this rubber as a whole.

He was chosen to go to Australia with F. R. Brown's team, and in the first Test match at Brisbane he took 3 wickets for 28 and then 4 for 22. At Melbourne, in the second Test, he took 4 for 40 and 2 for 47. He also caught Hassett off Brown from a great square-cut, an incredible piece of fieldsmanship, flat on the ground, and when it was accomplished, Bailey lay prone for a while.

It is no small thing to be a Trevor Bailey in a world of anonymous mediocrity. More power to his elbow—so long as it doesn't get put out, or dislocated.

BRIAN STATHAM

D URING the 'Golden Age' of Lancashire cricket, which was not of the period of Hornby and Barlow long ago, or even coincident with the high noon of A. C. MacLaren, but a burgeoning of a later day—between 1925 and 1930—the county XI could put into the field at least eight England Test players: Makepeace, Hallows, Watson, Ernest Tyldesley, Hopwood, Iddon, Richard Tyldesley, and Duckworth—with McDonald, an Australian, and one of the royal-blooded fast bowlers of all time, thrown in. Paynter had to wait until he was nearly 30 to find a place.

FIRST PRINCIPLES

Today, three Lancastrians remain at Old Trafford privileged to wear England colours—Statham, Pullar and Higgs; and, of course, the greatest of these is Statham. I mentioned his fine art parenthetically a few days ago, in an article in *The Guardian*; but Statham is not to be discussed on any occasion by the way, at any rate, not by me. I count him among the truly *classic* fast bowlers; for he commands the classic first principles; accuracy, heart, flight, and motion.

It's curious to recall that on his early appearances in cricket, his action could not satisfy *aesthetically* the purists, not, let it be emphasised, on any grounds of legality—no fast bowler has had an arm action as absolutely scrupulous as Statham's—but because he did not throw himself sideways, left shoulder pointing straight down the wicket, into attack. There was a hint of a full front detectable by the batsman. But this was a narrow view; Statham's run to bowl, loose and economical, his wheel of the arm, and his swing of body—here is the very rhythm and music of fast bowling.

I do not overlook Trueman, as I place Statham first of fast bowlers of the post 1946 years. Or Tyson. Trueman, compared with Statham, is as the thunderclap to the lightning. Trueman assaults, Statham penetrates, by light rays of velocity. Tyson was a brief quickly-spent hurricane. He bowled as fast in the Tests in Australia —1954–55—as, possibly, the legendary Kortright. The Australians could scarcely pick up their bats before Tyson's pace went 'through them'. His bowling complement on that tour was Statham and, at the time, I ventured to forecast that in the long run Statham would enjoy the more durable mastership of the two, because of his reserves of energy and his wider range of artifice.

I once asked J. T. Tyldesley, speaking of Kortright, 'What did he do with the ball?' 'He bowled it fast,' replied J. T. T. 'I know that,' I said, rather impatiently, 'but what did he "do"—did he swing, or come back?' 'No,' replied J. T. T., 'he was just fast—no time for anything else to happen.' So with Tyson: sheer, blinding speed.

I fancy that Statham learned something when watching Lindwall in Australia—Lindwall, in my opinion, the finest, most resourceful of fast bowlers of the last half-century. Lockwood at his best might have survived comparison with Lindwall on all pitches. But Lockwood was inconsistent, unpredictable, for long periods an inactive volcano.

Statham adds to his pace niceties of variation of direction and propulsion. He uses the seam subtly, not advertising its immediate function. Best of all, he keeps the batsman *playing*. 'I *never* let 'em rest,' said, and still says, S. F. Barnes. Statham is not, like Trueman, at all 'furious' (using the term in good-natured Yorkshire). If he misses the stumps by an inch, or sees a catch put to grass, he doesn't glare, or throw up his hands to high heaven, or go deeply into the umpire's upbringing, mentality or eyesight. He simply accepts frustration with a shrug, or a resigned look. Maybe his best trick is the ball which does its 'bend' slightly but acutely *off the pitch*.

CARRIED BURDEN

He is one of the few fast bowlers in cricket's history who has also carried the burden of captaincy. The dual job and responsibility are supremely testing to stamina, judgment, vigilance and capacity for self-examination. In a difficult passage in the history of county cricket, Statham is doing a splendid joint service, leading embryonic talent wisely and encouragingly. Last summer, when he became 36 years old on June 17, he took 102 wickets at 14·50 each, third in the bowling averages of the country. He is the best fast bowler extant at the present time.

Old Trafford, I am sure, doesn't take him for granted. He is part of Lancashire County cricket history for ever.

TONY LOCK

T ONY LOCK, of the balding brow on which the sun gleams, making it look not genial (like most bald pates), but as hostile as the rest of him. He is, I am told, a friendly approachable man really, off the field and at home, and on Sundays. In his flannels, at Kennington Oval, especially during the years of 1952 and 1958, he always seemed in my eyes a fellow of infinite antagonism, ready to get you out of the way, back to the pavilion almost before you had taken guard at the wicket, or knew exactly where you were. If he didn't happen to be bowling when you were taking your first ball, as likely as anything he'd catch you out at close short-leg, a pick-pocket of a catch, bare-faced daylight robbery.

Not quite as tall as he looks, Tony Lock of the rather stiff high shoulders, is the finest, cleverest, left-arm spin bowler ever to play for Surrey. He bowls frequently with his sleeves down—another feature in his appearance which frankly should cause misgivings in the minds of batsmen. During the period of Surrey's continuous championship supremacy—1952–58—Lock could pitch a ball at just over medium-pace on the leg-stump and threaten the off at a raspish speed from the ground. Often he was, as they say, unplayable. It was his good fortune, of course, to play at the Oval at a time when the turf there was of a nature calculated to conspire with spin.

A cricketer—or any other craftsman or artist—should take care to choose a favourable environment or soil for the blossoming of his talents. If Lock had arrived at the Oval in, say, 1930, with all his of present great dowry of gifts, we should have heard little of him, not much more than we heard of his famous namesake 'Bert' Lock, cleverest and wisest of our groundsmen, and himself, once upon a time, a skilful spinner of the ball, but doomed to twist his fingers in vain on pitches rolled and doped to stupefaction; though in Sam Apted's reign the Oval turf could be fast in dry weather, and treacherous after rain and sun. On an Oval 'sticky' pitch before 1914 'Razor' Smith, right-arm spinner, off and leg, was a terror to the greatest batsmen of the day, all of them more accustomed to spin than batsmen of 1963. In 1910, Smith took 247 wickets, average 13·05. Lock has so far twice taken 200 wickets in one and the same season—212 at 12·02 in 1957, and 216 at 14·39 in 1955. He owed much to Bert. In fact, Surrey may fairly be said to have won the championship seven years consecutively because of Surridge's leadership, 'Jim' Laker, and a joint Lock coincidence of circumstances.

Lock should be a first choice for any team for which he is qualified to play, so long as he is physically fit, with eyes to see. He is one of those rare cricketers who are 'always in the game', whatever he chances to be doing, bowling, fielding, batting. And he is no superfluity with the bat. I have seen Tony Lock defending, on a bowler's wicket with the scientific straight bat of a Hutton. And he has fine forcing strokes. Like his great colleague Laker, he could, given the time and need, have made a useful name as a batsman. He is a character, to be seen and picked out at once. In the field, near the wicket, he is a living embodiment of tense acquisitiveness, the clutching hands, squatting under the batsman's very nose, a body-snatcher, a picker-up of really good strokes or lightning lucky snicks off the edge. All come alike to him. I have seen him hold quite sinful catches, catches which were not there until his rapid hungry eyesight created them. Such a fieldsman has the power to win a match himself even if he bowls not a ball or scores not a run. He will appeal for a leg-before-wicket when he is bowling (and when he isn't) with a concentratedly passionate 'H'zat!'—leaping in the air quite vindictively. I have known people who haven't liked Lock's perpetual show of high-voltaged aggression. For my part, I'd like to see more of it from our day-by-day and too much routined county cricketers. 'The rigour of the game', so long as the rules are observed. Tony had to face a crisis a few years ago, the worst of all crises for any bowler. His action became 'suspect'. He was 'called' in first-class cricket. I refer to this incident or period in Lock's career, best forgotten, to emphasize the man's character and determination; for he set himself arduously to amend this occasionally dubious quick last-minute movement of the arm. Many great spin bowlers have found themselves unselfconsciously giving a flick, an 'extra' flick, to lend to the ball a final decisive vitality. The fault might easily befall any quickish spinner, as much to his dismay as anybody else's. Lock's bowling was on the whole too skilful, is too skilful yet, to suffer a general indictment, merely on the evidence of recurrent lapses from strict conformity. By all means let us have fair play. But the tendency at the present moment is to stiffen legality, so that it hinders a bowler's legitimate freedom.

After all, considering cricket, and especially bowling, as art, the fact that matters most is the technical product, the quality of the ball which comes to the batsman to be played. When Ernest Jones was the fastest of Australian bowlers in the late 'nineties, his action also aroused umpires' suspicions for a while. He was attacking fiercely one day at Sydney in a match between New South Wales and South Australia. When M. A. Noble arrived at the wicket, captain of N.S.W., he received a ball which came back at lightning speed on a flawless wicket, just missing the leg-stump. At the over's end, Noble went down the pitch to talk to the other batsman, a young colt of promise. 'Say, son,' asked Noble, 'don't you think Jones is "chucking" one or two?' 'Yes, sir,' replied the young colt, 'I think he is. But don't say anything about it. They might take him off.' The young colt was Victor Trumper. No batsman of Tony Lock's time has for a moment wished that Lock should be kept on. He has seldom sent down a ball that hasn't been willed to destroy, willed with all his heart, soul and nerve. He exults and he suffers. He rejoices openly at a conquest. He expresses disgust if luck betrays him, if a poor stroke frustrates a great ball. He throws back his head; he silently relieves himself by all sorts of lettered words not actually spoken; at any rate, not overheard by the distant spectators. Dull cricket is not to be seen when Lock is on the job. Into the most drifting match he will put a vehement purpose.

At the beginning of the present season of 1963 he had taken 2,092 wickets in top-class cricket, average 18·01 each. No other bowler playing regularly today in county cricket has taken more. His bag in Test matches is 164, average 24·45. Thrice he has done the 'hat-trick'. Against Kent, at Blackheath in 1956, he took all ten wickets in an innings for 54. In Tests against Australia his rewards have not been extravagant—some 31 wickets at round about 36 runs each. Figures often do no more than send out indications of high-class ability. I have watched Lock, 'on his day' (and on his, or his Surrey namesake's wicket), bowl the unplayable left-arm spinner's ball—quick to the leg-stump, the low flight disallowing any positive movement by the batsman to the pitch of it; then it has turned quicker than thought across to the off, always threatening the stumps, always demanding a stroke of some sort. Charles Parker, of Gloucestershire, shared this secret amongst left-hand spinners of our time, so did Hedley Verity. Nobody else. Today, at the age of 34 last month, Lock is still the only left-arm spinner who can be mentioned without some blasphemy in the context of the names of Parker and Verity. Playing for Western Australia last Australian season, his form of attack was unique, a survival, apparently, from a bygone classical age. We have heard much lately lamenting the decline of leg-spin. A just lamentation, too! But slow left-hand spin is the more classical of these two orders of the bowlers' arts, coming down from Peel (to go no farther back) and Briggs, and Rhodes, and Blythe, inherited by Parker, Verity and—is he at the moment the last of the great and fascinating line?—Tony Lock. The curving flight, the left-arm swoop, the supple fingers, the spin off the earth away from the bat, wicket-keeper and slips alert and gleefully avaricious! Is this beautiful skilful sort of spin destined to go out with Lock? The very thought of such a loss to cricket should make every lover of the game pray for more and more power to Tony's elbow.

COLIN COWDREY

AT first sight, when he is batting in full swing, Colin Cowdrey is a typical Kentish cricketer fit for all the tents and bunting of a Canterbury Festival. But he is subject to moods in which his strokes become inhibited. Now his bat seems leaded; he is temporarily a constipated Cowdrey. Under the influence of strange inhibitions his play might well perplex a Kentish Royal Commission set up to investigate him—a Commission composed of, say, K. L. Hutchings, A. P. Day, A. P. F. Chapman and B. H. Valentine. These great and gallant Kent amateurs could easily get to wondering if Colin had not at birth been crossed with some strain alien to the country whose insignia is the White Horse, and whose motto is 'Invicta'. Cowdrey, in fact, wasn't born in Kent. He first saw the light of day in a part of the world as far distant from the cliffs of Dover as Bangalore, where his father was a tea planter. And from age five and a half to thirteen he went to school at a 'Prep' in Surrey, coached in cricket by the Headmaster. He was thirteen when Kent and Tonbridge School claimed him and set him on his right way.

At his best he is, of course, an All-England and Kentish thorough-bred. At his best he would remain well within a sunlit Maidstone picture even if Frank Woolley were batting at the other end. For my part, I don't object to the vagaries of his batsmanship—to those enigmatic periods of self doubt, though I would rather he remained perpetually masterful and sure of enjoying himself. Maybe—for he has a sly sense of humour—he does enjoy, even if he can't explain, his occasional caprices, uncertain as an April afternoon. I am all in favour of a cricketer who avoids standardisation. The great appeal of Colin's batting is that you can never be quite sure whether it is about to thrill and delight you or cast you into a doldrum of inquiry and frustration.

His free and fully realised innings exceed in number those which suffer some sort of short circuiting. On his day there are few cricketers of our time better worth watching, as he unlooses his strokes, easily, rhythmically, with power hidden. I can never think of him and not see again his batting at Sydney in November 1954. Not yet twenty-two years old, he came to this great cricket field, the Valhalla on earth of Victor Trumper and Charles Macartney, and was not over-whelmed but actually scored two centuries in one and the same engagement *v.* New South Wales. A few weeks later, in the Test match at Melbourne, he scored one of the greatest centuries in all Test cricket—102 out of an 'all out' total of 191. He had only just reached his twenty-second year, and this wonderful innings began during a terrible ordeal for him. Keith Miller bowled at his most demoniacally improvisatory, on an ill-behaved pitch. Edrich and May were out for 21, and soon Hutton and Compton were back in the pavilion—England 41 for 4. Colin put his bat to the ball, his body over, sometimes behind it. For four hours he mingled defence and offence perfectly. This was a veteran's serene spirit and technique. Bill O'Reilly went so far as to maintain that this was the finest innings he had ever seen in a Test match. It was Cowdrey's finest hour. In three consecutive matches introducing him to the atmosphere of Test matches—Test matches in Australia at that!—Cowdrey was called on to face the music of the following situations and scores: 11 for 3, 147 for 3, 58 for 3, 55 for 3, and 21 for 2. This Melbourne century of 102, out of England's all-out total of 191, could have been achieved only by a cricketer born with extraordinary gifts for the game in him. (And how often in Test matches has one batsman scored so large a proportion of a team's one innings aggregate as 102 out of 191?)

I first saw Cowdrey at the wicket at Lord's in 1950, when he scored 31 and 97 for Tonbridge School *v.* Clifton. As soon as he began his first innings he drove past cover. And I had a vision again of the young Hammond. Cowdrey looked like Hammond, as he plastered the offside Clifton fieldsmen. A few years ago he was not physically as substantial as he is today, and his build, as well as his cricket, recalled the incomparable 'Wally'. Cowdrey, within a few months of his thirty-first birthday, still counts among the swiftest snapper-ups of catches near the wicket. It is astonishingly diverting and delightful, the way his rotundity can swiftly become resilient and swoopingly and dartingly active. He was endowed by nature with the ball-players eyesight and muscular reactions. When he is in the right vein his batsmanship is indeed batsmanship—not merely to be dubbed 'batting'. There is majesty in his driving to both sides of the wicket. He can bend down and cut late with a charming intimacy of touch. Indeed, the main appeal of his presence at the wicket is of a most likeable personality. If he hits a bowler for four fours in an over he commits the assault with an air of the utmost friendliness to the bowler. There are, as we have seen, days on which, as a batsman, he seems to get the sulks. At Lords' in 1956, *v.* Australia, he exasperated his best friends by three hours of the most sullen strokelessness imaginable—he was closeted three hours for 27. Yet a few months earlier I had written of him in this way—'Not since A. C. MacLaren and R. E. Foster has a young English amateur batsman come to Sydney and straightway attained to Cowdrey's power and reputation. He scored two hundreds in the game of his baptism to a great cricket field . . . he has something of the muscle and blood of Kenneth Hutchings. . . . He is a thoroughbred likely to go even beyond the scope of Peter May.' Has he fulfilled this promise of his burgeoning apprenticeship to great cricket?

Against Australia—the proper and consistent means of assessing a Test cricketer, temperamentally and technically—Cowdrey before last winter had scored 1,122 runs, average 33, with two centuries, once not out and five scores ranging from 79 to 93. Against the West Indies attack at its most challenging (in Cowdrey's time) he averaged 54·55 for 491 runs, in ten innings, once not out. Up to and the 1961 rubber *v.* Australia, Colin's record in Test cricket as a batsman is: 88 innings, four not out, highest score 160, total—3,411, average 40·60. Woolley himself didn't perform (statistically) as well as this, with a Test average of 36·07 for 3,283 runs in 98 innings. And, as a young county player of 1963 said to me the other day, 'Could

Woolley have been really all that good—why, look at his average.'

Averages! I would no sooner try to settle the class of breeding of a batsman from the number of runs he has scored in an innings than I would try to settle the difference between, say, Kenneth Tynan and Hazlitt as dramatic critics by counting the words written by each in a column. I have seen batsmanship by Cowdrey that had a pedigree quality, fit for a place in a cricketers' Debrett's. But he is incalculable yet. A curious feature in Cowdrey's batting a few years ago was that in the middle of an innings, after he had apparently solved all the problems in the bowling and had got it in his mercy, he would lapse into an anonymous inactivity. It was possibly a psychological trouble. He is a modest man and probably he couldn't at once believe he was as good a player as the score-board announced.

Should he take part in the opening of an England innings? He himself has confessed that he doesn't like to go in first. In heaven's name why? Once on a time every county captain who could bat at all opened an innings. As captain he was supposed to *lead*, to set an example to his side. County captains went in first from W. G. Grace onwards—MacLaren, A. O. Jones, H. K. Foster, P. F. Warner, C. B. Fry, F. L. Fane. If they didn't 'open' for England, the reason was that none was good enough to play for England, or that England possessed two first-wicket openers on a sort of ninety-nine years lease. All the above-named opened for their counties, most times. During the tour of the M.C.C. (England) team of the West Indies of 1959–60, Cowdrey went in first against the terrifying fast new-ball attacking Hall and Watson. How did he cope with it? Magnificently. In ten innings he scored 491 runs, average 54·55—thus: 30, 16 not out, 18, 5, 114 and 97 (same match), 65, 27, 119, 0. He hooked the lightning bumping bowling with courage, power and a sabre brilliance. He was subject to physical hurt and didn't flinch. It is, of course, not wise to ask an artist to do something he, for some reason (maybe superstitious), doesn't like. Obviously, as far as technique and concentration and courage go, Cowdrey has as many qualifications to 'open' for England as anybody else.

He is beyond argument a batsman out of the top drawer. It has been said that, as a captain, he is inclined to act defensively in his handling of a crucial situation. For my part, I don't like to question, from the viewpoint of a Press Box or a pavilion, any cricket captain's way of planning or executing a 'move'. Only the man 'in the middle' is in a position to know what is strategically in the wind. I am concerned in this article with Colin Cowdrey only or mainly as a cricketer of Kent and England. I would also like, just in a sentence, to dwell on Cowdrey as a man, a true sportsman, and blessed with charming unselfconscious manners. His cricket tells the truth about him, tells us that he is a man of good humour and taste, companionable yet a fine opponent, chivalrous yet not weakly compromising, sensible but not incapable of flights of fancy and fluctuations of temperament. He is the ideal and happy cricketer of Kent and All-England.

KEITH MILLER

KEITH MILLER, an Australian through and through, obviously an Australian at first sight, though not at the first sound of his voice, for he speaks English as it is pronounced, say, in Streatham. His appearance, the physical shape of him, is pervasive presence—he is pure eternal Australian, sun-saturated, absolutely 'dinkum'. See him in flannels, his wrinkled brow glistening with sweat, and surely you'll agree that he should inspire a sculptor to make an image of him to be erected in some public square in Canberra, there to stand down the ages as *'Australia in excelsis'*. I commend the idea to Prime Minister 'Bob' Menzies.

I could have sworn that he was a 'Sydney-sider', born near Randwick's racecourse. As a fact, he first saw the light of day in Melbourne, and so I suppose we must call him a Victorian. But he came in good time to live in Sydney, where Bondi beach, Dee Why, Elizabeth Street and—of course—Randwick, acclimatised him, expelled all decorum and released any inhibitions acquired while dwelling in the elegant city of the Yarra. I have always thought Melbourne is Australia in a top hat and a starched wing-collar. Sydney is inclined to be raffish, uncollared, racy, even indifferent to manners that get in the way of natural impulse. The solidity of Melbourne, social and economic, has somehow been hinted at by most of her greatest cricketers—the sane, down to earth Warwick Armstrong, Woodfull, Ponsford, Hassett, McDonald, Ian Johnston, to name a few. Neil Harvey, a brilliant deviation from type, gravitated, like Miller, and as inevitably as needle to pole, to Sydney. If we come to reflect on the matter, most of Australia's spectacular cricketers have been nurtured in New South Wales and tanned by the Sydney heat and the Sydney 'Southerly buster'—Trumper,

Macartney, Bradman, Kippax, Andrews, Mailey, Jack Gregory, Archie Jackson, Johnny Taylor, Bertie Oldfield, McCabe, O'Reilly, O'Neill . . . Miller fits into the Sydney scene every inch of him. Merely to get a glimpse of him prompts me to see, with my mind's eye, Randwick, Castlereagh Street, 'Ushers' and the Domain and the long bar in the Australian hotel and the lovely sweep of the green oval of the Sydney cricket ground. ' 'Ow yer gow-in', Keith?' they hail him; ' 'E's dinkum, too right, 'e is'. In our time no Australian has vied with Miller for first place as a national hero and symbol.

Miller, nearly six foot tall, knows the almost forgotten secret these days of *panache*. Loose of limb with good shoulders, he is alluring in the eyes of the ladies who sit in the Sheridan stand at Sydney. In the Test match *v.* England at Sydney in January 1951, Hutton and Simpson were well-rooted and the score 128 for 1. England had lost at Brisbane and Melbourne; the rubber was now at stake. Before this third Test, England had prayed to win the toss. 'Let us only bat first on a good wicket', they had said. Well, England was, on this hot scorching afternoon at Sydney, batting first. And Hutton and Simpson seemed impregnable. The Australians were waiting without much hope for the new ball. Ten minutes from tea, Miller had strayed from the slips to the outfield. He stood in front of the Sheridan stand. He was communing between one ball and the next with the ladies. Then Hassett, Australia's captain, called on him to send down a few overs, merely to mark-time, till the interval and to give the other perspiring bowlers a rest. Miller reluctantly took the old ball, and at a deceptive medium pace relaxed like a fast bowler formally swinging his arm in the nets, he got rid of Hutton and Compton in an over, suddenly, from a short run, delivering streaked lightning. Immediately after tea he had Simpson caught at short leg. In twenty-eight balls he took 3 for 5, and by sheer improvisation he won the rubber for Australia.

He was, in fact, a great artist in improvisation. When he bowled, he often ran to the crease from different places and always did he attack along a shortish distance. He couldn't bear to waste time. If a ball was played defensively from him he would clap his hands at the fielder retrieving the stroke, eager to 'get on with it'. At an inning's beginning his pace and bounce from the pitch were terrific and as though combustible. Certain England batsmen feared him even more palpitatingly than they feared Lindwall. He was 'at them' so abruptly, swinging round after his few impatient paces, his shoulders generating a last-second propulsive energy. 'If Keith had never gone in for batting', Cyril Washbrook one day told me, 'he would have been the most dangerous fast bowler ever'. He was quite dangerous enough. At Melbourne, he came close to equalling S. F. Barnes's wonder-bowling there, in December, 1911, when the Master took four wickets before lunch for one run, in five overs. Miller, at Melbourne in December, 1954, bowled throughout the ninety minutes before lunch, and took 3 wickets for 5 runs in 9 overs, despite a suspect knee. But when the mood to action visited Keith he was not conscious of physical impediments.

He was incalculable. Only mediocrity is always at its best. One day we would see Miller's bat trenchant and powerful, driving with a conquering swing, upright and free. Next day he might dismay us by pushing forward full stretch, groping at a good length ball, apprehensively groping. In 1945 he was the living embodiment of the game's and of London's resurrection from the ruin and the graveyard of the war. He came to Lord's, fresh from intrepid feats of battle in the air, and playing for the Dominions against England, enchanted the watching rationed English crowd by batsmanship glorious and visionary. He hit seven sixes and added 124 to a night before's score of 61—in ninety minutes. An imperious drive off Eric Hollies landed on the roof of the broadcaster's box, but for which obstacle the ball would have cleared the pavilion, even as Albert Trott's gigantic hit had cleared it years previously.

Incalculable and unpredictable. One day he is in the slips interrupting conversation by a sudden leap or thrilling dive to take a sinful catch. Next day he is at cover, his mind wandering or pondering the 'odds' or the 'weights' and an easy chance, possibly from Washbrook in a Test, goes almost unnoticed by Keith, who hardly unfolds his arms. He is a law and lawless to himself. In fighting mood he could hurl a 'bumper' with the jubilant ferocity of a 'Digger' at Gallipoli throwing a hand grenade. In some other mood of his own fancy, he might go on to bowl like a middle-aged gentleman playing with young folk on the sands, rolling along donkey-drops square-arm. During the course of F. R. Brown's England team's campaign in Australia in 1950–51 Miller promised on the eve of the third Test match at Sydney to play for me a dazzling innings tomorrow—'if we win the toss. And if we lose it, when we bat I'll give you something to write about'. Then, against an England XI with an attack reduced by injuries to Bedser, Brown and Warr, he batted five hours for 99 in scourging sun. In this same Australian summer of 1950–51 Victoria's spinner, Iverson, was a sore thorn in the sides of England's batsmen. On Sunday night as I was dining in Usher's Hotel, Keith dropped in and while we talked he asked 'Why don't your chaps get into Jack Iverson and beat the hell out of him?' I replied that it was easy for him to talk but it was 'our chaps', not Miller, who had to cope with Iverson. 'But New South Wales are playing Victoria next week', responded Keith, 'come along and I'll show you.' Show me he did: he flayed Iverson's attack, went down on the left knee and pulled off-breaks out of sight. Miller was not boasting as he spoke of Iverson's bowling and what should be done with it. In fact he was a great admirer of Iverson. But it is not in his mind or nature to understand submission to any obstacle or any antagonism. The stronger the odds in front of him the greater his relish of the game—game of cricket or game of life.

His technique as bowler or batsman could not be described as classic. The energy in him galvanised him to action which could not take the form of Lindwall's smooth poise and balance. Miller was the romantic, sometimes even the eccentric. With the new ball he could rap the batsman's gloves, even threaten the breastbone, from a good length. He could swing away very late at a pace which seemed to accelerate cruelly after the ball had pitched. I fancy his fastest ball was one of the fastest in all cricket's history. As a batsman he delighted the most critical eye whenever he was on the attack. Defensively, he prodded most gingerly. A certain great Australian batsman, now dead, once startled me by saying of Keith as a batsman—'He knows nothing about it really'. In other words, Miller plays by intuition, making up all his strokes as he goes along. Certainly he never played as though cricket were a problem for mathematicians or a duty for the consideration of moralists. If he lost his wicket to an absolutely crude stroke, he would just shrug his shoulders, but without contrition. In his Test match career, short and sweet, he scored for Australia 2,958 runs, average 36·97 and took 170 wickets, average 22·97, proof of rare all-round powers, seldom surpassed. Yet when we think of Miller now, we don't dwell too much on his skill or on his performances. It is the man, the Australian, the personality of him, that we remember. This summing-up may seem trite enough, but it's true. He was a virtuoso. Possibly he didn't consciously *present* himself. He was natural Keith when he tossed back his mane of hair, or when, if a bowler stopped a return from him and made aim as though to run him out, he would put forth an admonitory hand at the aforesaid bowler. He was himself one morning in a Test match at Sydney—he had just passed through the gates on his way to the wicket to bat v. England when a small schoolboy ran after him, for his autograph. The gatekeeper, scandalised, went immediately in pursuit of the schoolboy. Miller waved the gatekeeper away, handed his bat to the schoolboy to hold while he signed the autograph book. Meanwhile sixty thousand people waited. Imagine the small boy's ecstasy. Not only was he getting Keith's autograph; he was holding his bat while, in his eyes, all Sydney, looked on. Keith was simply doing the natural thing; he could no more act unkindly to a schoolboy than he could be discourteous enough not to admire a pretty girl. At Lord's, on the Saturday evening of June 23rd, 1956, he had scored 30 and looked good for a century when he was caught at the wicket off a truly grand ball from Trueman. He at once raised his bat as a salute to Trueman. Another quite natural gesture of a cricketer who, with all his recurrent tantrums, was a chivalrous opponent.

When I was a resident in Sydney, Keith for a while lived in the same block of flats as myself—in Crick Avenue, King's Cross, the Montmartre—or shall we say the Soho—of Sydney. He would come up to my room and ask if I would play the gramophone for him. 'What record, Keith?' Always he would ask for a piano concerto. Sometimes I would say, 'Why not a symphony this time?' No; it had to be a piano concerto. I imagine that he has scored hundreds of his runs and taken many, many wickets to the accompaniment, supplied mentally by himself, of the 'Emperor' concerto. The right music to go with his cricket at its greatest! Or perhaps something 'hotter'— say, 'Johnny and the Hurricanes'.

RICHIE BENAUD

AT the beginning of June 1961, before the first Test match between England and Australia, Norman O'Neill playing under Richie Benaud against Sussex injured a knee while fielding, and was obliged to retire. At first the damage threatened to remove for some lengthy period this brilliant young cricketer from the Australian team. The news of O'Neill's and Australia's misfortune upset me so much that I wrote at once to Benaud hoping that O'Neill would quickly be fit again. I was as much concerned about the loss, even for a while, to the game of an artist as I was about this threat to Australia's chances of victory in the rubber.

The reply of Benaud to my letter was true to his character and to the character of most Australians. He thanked me for my sympathy but finished by saying: 'I'm not worrying unduly. I think that you'll find we'll be there when the chips are down.' And so, at the decisive moment in the rubber, they indeed were there. At Old Trafford, where the rubber's issue was settled, England were winning easily on the fifth afternoon, 150 for 1 wicket, Dexter riding the storm and only 106 needed now in as many minutes. Moreover, the Australian attack seemed pretty bankrupt: Davidson weary, Mackay physically handicapped. Benaud actually called for a breathing space, and drinks were brought into action, under a hot Manchester sun. (In 1934, two Australians were afflicted by sunstroke at Manchester during a Test Match.) With the afternoon apparently lost for Australia, Benaud became a vessel of plenary inspiration. He bowled round the wicket and pitched his spin on the places on the pitch worn by Trueman's footmarks at the other end. As every cricketer and history knows, the trick came off. But it is not generally realised, even yet, how cleverly, how artfully, Benaud played it. He clean bowled the obstructive Subba Row the last ball, or thereabouts, before tea— with a full-toss. He knew well enough that, an interval due, Subba Row would take no risk, offer no stroke, to a good ball. When Dexter was racing ahead, and defeat stared Australia in the face, Benaud said to himself 'We can't possibly save this match but we *could* win it!'

He has been called a 'lucky' captain of cricket. The truth is that he, at his career's beginning, had to suffer hard blows to his confidence. At the age of twenty-one he played in his first Test match *v.* West Indies at Sydney in January, 1952. He bowled only four overs, three balls and took Valentine's wicket for fourteen, of which number Valentine's share was exactly none. And he scored 3 and 19. His baptism to Test cricket in this country, in 1953, was scarcely memorable—three matches, five innings, 15 runs, average 3; sixty-eight overs and two wickets for 174. He, supposedly a leg-spin bowler, failed to use the dusty wicket at Lord's when Willie Watson and Bailey retrieved a lost cause for England by hours of superbly dour defence. A famous player that afternoon was emphatic that Benaud never would reach top-class as a leg-spinner. 'He's a roller.' 'Give him time,' I said. For I had seen young Benaud, months before this forlorn afternoon for him at Lord's—I had seen him in the nets at Sydney. Moreover, Arthur Mailey was putting faith in his potentiality as a back-of-the-hand spinner. But Benaud again disappointed his prophets during Hutton's and Tyson's triumphant invasion of

Australia in 1954–55. He bowled 116 overs and 7 balls in the Tests for 377 runs and 10 wickets. And in nine completed innings he scored merely 148. For Australia in the West Indies, in 1955, he opened out his promise as a bowler, with 18 Test wickets, average 27.

None the less he was still on the doorstep of International achievement as recently as 1956, when he came to England for the second time. Another failure now could easily have seen the last of him amongst the Top People. He was nearing his twenty-sixth birthday. An Australian Test cricketer is usually established by this time of his life; in fact, many of them have looked towards retirement from the International scene by then—whatever Clarrie Grimmett may say to the contrary. Even in 1956, despite a resonant prelude to the season to the tune of an innings of 160 *v.* Worcestershire, Richie for a while still could not raise himself above the level of the team's subsidiary resources. He was useful week by week, but in the first of the summer's Tests, at Nottingham, which had no result, he was not particularly useful. He scored 17, and bowled (in England's second innings only) 18 overs, and took none for 41. Between this and the second and Lord's Test he played in one match, scored 7 and 15 *v.* Northamptonshire; and his one wicket cost 91. Conceivably he might not have been chosen for the Lord's Test if the Australian reserves had been stronger.

On the fourth morning of this match Australia, in a second innings, had lost six wickets for 115 and were only 229 ahead. On the evening before a morning on which Richie was destined to deal England a more or less death blow (with bat not ball), I met him for the first time at a dinner given by the most generous of hosts—John Arlott. We scarcely spoke. Benaud was not yet the confident Benaud of today. But there was a 'something' about him which impressed me, a suggestion of latent and alluring personality. The impression was strong enough to urge me to write an article, to appear before the game was resumed next morning, in which I risked a forecast. . . . 'Before we are much older Benaud will do something forcibly to demonstrate his natural and unmistakable gifts'. Well, on this fourth morning, in a ticklish moment for Australia, with the day fresh and Trueman after blood with 4 wickets already rendering him even more than usually voracious—(4 for 38)—Benaud arrived at the ground almost late and had to rush into action at once, pads buckled breathlessly. Immediately he attacked, risking a long-armed drive. Also he hooked Trueman for six—and Trueman was the first of thousands to applaud the stroke. Benaud trusted to his eye daringly. In two hours twenty minutes he scored 97, swinging clean round the wheel of the game in the one engagement of the rubber won by Australia. This innings, maybe, marked the turn of his career.

I have gone into these statistics of Benaud's cricket to show how little indeed, 'luck' has had to do with his development and progress. He, like any other man ever to do anything really well, had to be tested, not only in skill but in patience, philosophy and persistence. The only unmistakable good stroke from fortune to bless his onward course was at poor Ian Craig's expense, when this cricketer and captain of bright promise fell ill, and the Australian leadership passed from him to Benaud. With the swift resolution of something approaching genius, Richie grasped the chance. He directed Australia to victory in the rubber of 1958–59, in Australia. Seldom since then has he looked back. The entire world of cricket knows how he and Frank Worrell, by joint and imaginative agreement, saw to it that the Tests between Australia and the West Indies in 1960–61 produced some of the greatest and most thrilling and memorable cricket of our or any other time.

Richie, as befits an Australian and Sydney-sider, understands the value of realism. This good-looking captain of Australian cricket, with his frank eyes, and pleasant smile, scarcely fits at first sight into the general picture of an Australian skipper—think of dour immovable Armstrong, the lynx-eyed Herbert Collins, the shrewd watchful Sir Donald. But Benaud is not wholly the cavalier batsman and the speculative leg-spinner (all leg-spinners must necessarily be speculative!). He knows that the time to be there is 'when the chips are down'.

His precious contribution to the game has been, of course, not his flair as a cricket captain; not even his ability to steer an XI to victory in a rubber in England, with a bowling team fairly to be called one of the weakest ever, Benaud himself an incapacitated member of it for weeks. No; Benaud has so far enriched cricket best by his leg-spin. This beautiful and difficult art, and any kind of spin if it comes to that, has been discouraged by legislation which has aided and abetted seam bowling. Any healthy, bodily fit, even brainless, young man can readily learn to swing his arm holding the ball's seam in his fingers the right way up. To master spin from the back of the hand, spin involving turn of the wrist and flick of fingers right to left—here is an art or craft calling for years of practice, and beautiful is it to watch a great leg-spinner, to follow the ball's seductive flight (or it might easily pitch half-way!) as it lures the batsmen forward, then drops on the earth; and it whips away or, the 'googly', comes back! Nothing mechanical here. Leg-spin insists on constant careful manipulation from its exponents—and constant concentration of mind.

So you see, this 'lucky' Benaud has not only fought through preliminary set-backs of form. While opposing them he also learned and mastered one of cricket's most skilful and enchanting arts, leg-spin with changeful flight that asks questions in the air.

NEIL HARVEY

BROADLY there are two sorts or classes of batsmen. There is the batsman whose merit is measured exactly and totally by the score-board. If the score-board were not standing there, his presence at the wicket would scarcely be noticed by the crowd. Let him compile (that is the word) less than twenty runs and his visit to the wicket has been anonymous, not to say invisible. And should he mass two thousand runs in a season, average 52·17, we usually have little more than the scorer's word for it.

The other sort of batsman would hold our attention if all the scorers and the scoring boards in the world were to go on strike. He plays in a style that is beyond statistical assessment. Neil Harvey is such a batsman; he is an artist. You will no more arrive at a complete idea of his cricket by adding up the runs he makes than you will realise the quality of Mozart's music if you add up all the crotchets and quavers. Recently there has been much talk about the need to 'brighten' the game. Cricket captains at a season's beginning have spoken of this need, and of their determination to look to it, like so many political candidates in an election address. Neil Harvey has never, in all his career, needed any sort of propaganda to stir him to 'brightness'. Always he has performed, or tried to perform, strokes. His bat has been a stroke-maker all the time exactly as Yehudi Menuhin's violin has all the time been a music-maker. Naturally and inevitably enough, Harvey has on many occasions lost his wicket attempting a stroke. But I doubt if he has, once his career, cut out his finest strokes out of fear of attempting them. And in his career of almost persistent brilliance, taking the true sportsman's chance, he has made more than 5,000 runs in Test matches, averaging round bout 50 an innings—wonderful consistency on the part of a cricketer who has played less by calculation than by joyous impulse.

He, of course, is a master technician. No swashbuckling batsman could possibly achieve a Test match average of half-a-century over a longish period if he lacked knowledge of fundamentals and did not defend, at the sight of a dangerous ball, over the line. But Harvey's temperament would not be denied, even by the sight of a dangerous ball, if his team were in a strong position, or if the situation called for attack. I have heard critics complain that Harvey is too frequently 'careless'. Maybe; in fact, I know no batsman who has so frequently as Harvey got himself out to strokes which even his best friends have called 'silly'. As a fact, Harvey has seldom lost his wicket to a technically bad stroke; he has lost it, more often than not, to the wrong technically *right* stroke. In other words he has fallen because of an error of judgment—not an error of technique or style. At Old Trafford in 1956 (Laker's Test match), Harvey undoubtedly was guilty of one of the most shockingly wrong and ungrammatical strokes ever perpetrated by a well-bred batsman. Laker, in this Australian holocaust, removed Harvey twice for noughts; and the second of them was quite staggeringly the consequence of a cross-batted, cross-eyed pull at a full-toss. Harvey drooped his head in shame; and I liked him for a revelation of honesty.

A cavalier on swift feet? His sword a lance? He has been known to put on heavy armour. At Sydney, in 1954–55, Australia were being overwhelmed by the Tyson typhoon. On the fifth day Australia wanted only 151 to win, eight wickets in hand. Then the storm broke, the typhoon levelled the Australia innings to the earth. No Australian batsman, except Harvey, was strong enough, able enough, to withstand Tyson's hurricane, backed up by the gale force of Statham. Harvey, for four hours and more, put the straightest bat to the deadly ball. But at the sight of a ball in the slightest loose he cut, glanced or hooked with a brilliance which suggested that he and his bat were making the forked blinding lightning of the storm. That dire morning for Australia, Harvey scored 92. At Leeds, in 1956, he also disciplined himself superbly for the Cause, and in four-and-a-half hours fought a stubborn rearguard—in vain. Yet, for all his dour defence, his cricket remained good to see, beautifully poised, quietly throbbing with reserve power. It is easy for your Hutton, your Lawry, your Pullar, to stay at the crease for hours resisting temptation to hit the ball. It is not so easy for a Harvey to exercise self-control to the verge of austerity. The man born rich finds it painful to practise economy. Harvey was born with runs, strokes, lovely strokes, as a kind of inheritance. He has not so much *made* or *earned* his thousands of runs: he has spent them generously, to the enrichment of cricket.

Yet, in his very first Test match, against England in 1948 at Leeds, he was called on to bat, the first time for Australia, at a moment of incipient crisis for Australia. England, in first, had scored 496. On the third morning Hassett and Bradman succumbed to red-headed, magnificently Lancastrian Dick Pollard. Australia were 68 for 3 when Neil (aged nineteen) joined Keith Miller. In an hour-and-a-half he and Miller plundered 121 by glorious defiance and attack. Harvey reached a century. And it is said that after he had played a few overs at the beginning of his debut as a Test match batsman, the England bowlers having been inspired by Bradman's downfall—that in this challenging hour, he went down the wicket between overs and said to Miller: 'Don't help yourself to *ALL* the runs, Keith. Save a few for me.'

He is really a modest little man, quiet but with a twinkle in his eye. Also he is a big man—large of nature. He could easily have taken umbrage when Richie Benaud and not Harvey was chosen as Australia's cricket captain. But Neil became Benaud's great help, the eminence (not grey!) in the modest background. He has served Australian cricket handsomely. And just as handsomely has he served it by his experienced guidance out of the public eye. He is a remarkable example of maturity and youthful shyness. He has, as they say, 'an old head'. And a young heart. His batting, though it can put the best bowlers to the sword, with fours all over the field, is not at all brutal or excessive of power. He charms runs out of the attack. On dancing feet he goes to meet them, and he lures them to ruin by the hypnotism of his bat's movements. These movements are willowy. Harvey's bat has never looked like a bludgeon. It is all curves and rapier-thrusts. He is not, as even the fascinating Norman O'Neill is, a batsman too dependent on the leverage of the lower grip on the bat. And if he traffics hazardly to balls swinging away on the offside— drawn to the new ball's red light as a pretty moth to the flame— well, he can't help it. He was born that way. Moreover, by playing cricket as God and nature intended that he should play, he has long since joined the ranks not only of cricket's artist-batsmen but of those who have piled up fortunes in runs and centuries.

I am writing this chapter as though it were a tribute to a departing Old Master, a farewell. Harvey has adorned cricket for more than a dozen years. He follows in, and adds lustre to, the bright tradition established by Trumper, Kippax, McCabe, Archie Jackson. I don't mention Macartney in the context of Harvey, because Macartney was a ferocious batsman. Harvey, as we have agreed, was never that—his cricket delighted and hurt not. He didn't ever assault bowlers, never rubbed their noses in the dust. He lured them, allured them, to destruction. They got intoxicated with the champagne of a Harvey innings, joining in the universal chorus to him, '*For*—he's a jolly good fellow!' The Pied Piper of Australian cricket! He is not tall, but he is built like a cricketer, swift and weightless. And he is modest. His batting is, for all its glories, modest. Gentleman Harvey—no true lover of the game can think of him without pleasure and gratitude. I have not mentioned his fielding so far. As a cover point, in his younger days, he was of a piece with his batsmanship, rapid, comprehensive, graceful and electrical. It is because of cricketers of the thoroughbred order of Harvey that I have spent half-a-lifetime writing about the game, sometimes mixing it up with the higher art which has given Mozart to the world, and Schubert. Which is saying a lot of any sport, and game!

GARFIELD SOBERS

THE wonderful Gary Sobers, most easily masterful of batsmen, delights at one and the same time artists and statisticians, stroking the ball with a bat apparently itself alive, sensitive and powerful in turn. Also a cricketer who can use the new ball dangerously and, again, with an appeal to the watcher's love of rhythm, effortless of motion; for Sobers, when he runs to bowl, is relaxed until the swing over the left arm, then the accumulation of energy is a quite musical crescendo.

His all-round performance in the England *v.* Rest of the World match at Lord's must count amongst the most distinguished of all batsman-bowler achievements. He has done everything a cricketer can hopefully envisage: seven thousand runs in Test matches, 200 wickets—the greatest of all bowlers, Sidney Barnes had to be content, for want of opportunity, with 189. And Sobers can be two contrasted bowlers, a 'seamer' of guile, not mechanical, and a 'back of the hand' spinner of leg-breaks and 'googlies'.

UNDER A SPELL

At Lord's last week, while Illingworth and Knott resisted the Rest of the World attack more or less untroubled from half-past eleven to lunch, I said to myself, 'Gary could get Illingworth out in a few balls, if he bowled his slow spin,' which he did, as soon as he tried, at once putting the gallant obstinate workmanship of Illingworth under a spell.

Is Sobers the 'greatest' of all all-round cricketers even? This is an uncritical and rather vain question. Performance, in any calling of life, is related to environment, to the material pressures which, to some extent, 'condition' even genius. Maybe Sobers could have coped with the terrible 'sticky' wickets which Victor Trumper conquered triumphantly in 1902, against some of the finest spinners in cricket's history. But we cannot measure genius with genius; you cannot try to place a Mozart above a Beethoven, a Bach above a Schubert. Each is an *absolute*. It is only mediocrity that we can put into the scales, pricing So-and-So sixpence or so more saleable than—Never Mind.

A test of a great all-round cricketer is this: would he be picked to play in a Test match for his batting *only*, or for his bowling *only* (good fielding, of course, taken for granted)? Sobers, as a bowler, does not day-by-day 'run through' a side. He has, for all the cricket he takes part in, never approached Woolley's all-round excellencies of 1921–22–23, when in consecutive summers, he scored 2,101 runs, with 167 wickets, 2,022, with 163 wickets, and 2,091, with 101 wickets. And for all my admiration of Sobers as batsman, I do not rank him more technically accomplished, or more aesthetically satisfying, than Woolley was over many years. As I say, we should not attempt to weigh genius in the balance—but I didn't start it. The cry has long since been heard, 'Gary the greatest ever.' Let us be grateful to enjoy and admire him for what he is, as cricketer and purveyor of delight.

MOST DANGEROUS

If we could match him in a single wicket game what would be the odds on him to beat Keith Mller, Wally Hammond, Aubrey Faulkner? Would he be selected for representative cricket purely as a bowler? Keith Miller certainly would; I am not at all certain that Keith Miller was not the most dangerous all-round cricketer of our 'modern' times.

We cannot drag into this argument of comparative values W. G.

Grace, who, in his career, scored 54,904 runs and took 2,876 wickets. As a bowler, he exploited highly tossed slow balls. He placed a fieldsman at deep fine-leg, then sent the batsman an inviting ball to leg—inviting him to hit the ball into the said long-leg fieldsman's hands. One day, a University young batsman declined to fall into this obvious booby trap. He simply patted down the tempting full-tosses for safe singles to leg, whereat Grace cried out: 'Young feller, if you keep on doin' that, I'll take myself off.'

Then there was George Hirst's all-round magnificence in 1906—2,385 runs and 208 wickets. He was asked, at the close of the season, if he thought the dual feat would ever be equalled. He replied: 'Whoever does equal it will be tired.' Would Hirst be chosen for a Test match purely as batsman or bowler? I doubt it; he inexplicably failed, except on one famous occasion, to do himself justice in Test matches.

It is a fascinating question—Sobers or Hammond, both miraculous slip fieldsmen, both dangerous bowlers with a new ball; but Hammond seldom put his heart into his bowling. At the pinch, at Adelaide in 1937, v. Australia, he took five for 57, on a flawless wicket, with no 'atmosphere' to help him, as helped Sobers at Lord's. And Hammond's victims included Bradman, caught and bowled 212. It was during this match that I asked 'Bill' Voce which was the best ball to bowl at Bradman; and woefully he answered: 'There's no ruddy best ball to bowl at the Don.'

CLOSE INSPECTION

At Lord's in 1957, I stood in the Long Room watching Sobers batting. With me was S. F. Barnes, in his 85th year. After close inspection of Sobers, Barnes said: 'He likes flicking at the offside ball. I think I could get him out.' 'How?' I inquired. 'I'd pitch him one on his leg stump, going away.' Then, to 'draw' him, I asked, 'and what about Bradman?' He replied, unhesitatingly: 'I'd have to bowl my best to get him out' but the implication was that he could have.

But this Sobers is, in many ways, beyond compare. I fancy that, with aid of, say, Procter and a wicket-keeper, he could himself defeat the England XI on view the other day at Lord's. Not one player in that England XI could have got a place in the Rest of the World XI, which is a solemn or ironical thought.

THE CORONATION TESTS

ENGLAND v. AUSTRALIA, 1953

FIRST TEST (FIRST DAY)

THE first Test match began under a sulky sky, and when Morris and Hole walked out to bat there were anxious expressions on the faces of both. I was reminded of the way Hobbs and Sutcliffe would begin an England innings, as though going somewhere for the day, probably making arrangements about what they would be doing at half-past three. The wicket was dead easy, so much so that as soon as the new ball's polish had waned the bowling had little relation to what it was when it left the bowler's fingers: it was indeed like bowling into a void.

None the less I did not like the marks made so early in the morning on the pitch's surface; they hinted of a certain looseness of texture. We shall see. For the time being there was little prospect that any batsman would get out, except by his own consent or from absence of mind. Hole was clean bowled, it is true, by the first ball of Bedser's second over, an inswinger of generous length, nearly a half-volley, which Hole tried confidently to drive to the off: but his head moved upward instead of downward.

He had contrived to emerge alive from the game's first over, also by Bedser, and bowled with such beauty of science to the short-leg field that a complete book of the geometry of inswinging might have been written by deduction from the angles described by the strokes made to the fielders, and made by reflex action on the part of the rather agitated Hole, whose bad luck it was to find himself batting in his first Test match in England in a position not suitable to his free and stylish order of play.

HASSETT'S COMPOSURE

The crowd naturally emitted joyful sounds as disaster at once assailed Australia's innings. Hassett, looking very tiny and compact, joined Morris, and immediately made the crease his lair, from which he declined to come out for nearly an hour, though you could feel his sharp, shrewd gleam of inspection and suspicion as he played each ball in the middle of a straight bat. Morris also assumed an aspect of composure and durability, though he at times encouraged hope in the bowler by his movements over the line of flight, the feet shuffling and the bat seemingly making contact at a right, that is to say a wrong, angle.

The scoring was imperceptible and there was menace for England in Morris's and Hassett's deliberate austerity of method. No truly loose ball escaped, and it is really a compliment to England's attack and fielding that at the end of the first hour Australia's total was only 28: Morris 19, Hassett 9.

But the excitement and expectation stimulated by Bedser's quick success, and by the excellence of his opening overs dwindled to a sense of disappointment, if not disillusionment. It was as though an alarm clock had gone off too soon and had been promptly smothered, so that we could sleep until the proper Test match hour of waking up. Wardle pitched a pretty length over after over: there was little else for him to do in the circumstances, though frankly I was not enlivened or uplifted to see him brought without delay to the service of a partially defensive policy. Apart from Bedser with the new ball, the England attack was too obliged to labour largely on hope: a drizzling rain added to the batsmen's pleasure, or rather to the decrease of their responsibilities: for there was no sign that anybody on the field was experiencing the throb of pleasure.

After fifty minutes of anonymity and self-concealment, Hassett drove Bailey straight for four: he had earlier in time and space cut Wardle late and brilliantly to the boundary. He also drove a half-volley from Bailey to the off for four: and Morris lashed Bedser round to fine leg viciously, a stroke of considerable vindictiveness.

LUNCHTIME QUESTIONS

Sawdust debased the lovely green of Trent Bridge, and towels were brought from the pavilion to wipe the ball. Ten minutes before lunch play ceased until a quarter-past two: Australia 54 for one, the crowd getting moist, hungry, thirsty, and impatient. During the interval the question was asked if England had not made a mistake to leave Statham out of the team so that the tail-end batting might be strengthened; a great Test batsman of yesteryear emphatically stated his opinion that a middling good all-rounder is no sure substitute at Trent Bridge for a faster and more accurate bowler.

From lunch until twenty minutes to four, when rain again cleared the field, Australia in some 85 minutes added 69, and now the score was 123 for one, and not since the passing of Hole had anybody not incurably optimistic looked for the fall of another wicket. Not a ball was seen of a kind calculated to give concern to an expert cricketer.

Morris and Hassett grimly took good fortune by the hand, not gaily or with reciprocation but in the way that economical men use bequests to consolidate capital. The cricket, in fact, reflected the dull sky like a mirror that needed cleaning.

A fine hit from time to time told us that Morris and Hassett were cultured batsmen who if they had been taking part in an engagement not made known to the public under the name of a Test match, would have given delight to everybody present, themselves included. Gaps appeared in the England field even if neither Morris nor Hassett embarked positively on an offensive action. The fielding, let it be gratefully said, was first class in the various positions established, if not co-ordinated.

It cannot be said that Morris and Hassett made the most of their chances to score while the bowlers were incommoded by a ball greasy as wet soap. On the sluggish turf a batsman was at liberty to play back or forward with time to spare.

A quarter of an hour after the game was resumed after the tea interval, Morris yet again succumbed while going across his stumps to a magnificently spirited ball from Bedser, the new ball which on such a day and pitch is as the spirit and breath of life to all bowlers. Morris and Hassett increased Australia's total by 122, and while they were doing so the performance of two Bruckner symphonies might easily have seemed touched with an unusual brevity.

The great moment of the day was the downfall of Harvey, brilliantly caught at short leg by Compton, who held a swift glance enforced on Harvey by another red-hot ball swinging across the pads. Compton dived delightfully to the chance and as he caught his prize, a bird of dazzling plumage, he threw up the ball, the picture of a happy cricketer.

Bedser strove hard to remove Miller or Hassett after Harvey departed, so that Benaud, Davidson, and the more uncertain section of Australia's batsmen might be got at while the ball was new. He had bowled 23 overs, eleven maidens, for 21 runs and three wickets when Hutton rather mysteriously took him off.

Wardle came on for Bedser, while Miller was obviously ill at ease. Hassett, now the spinal column of the Australian innings, proceeded calmly on his way, admirably composed and correct, experience in his every stroke, with footwork so instinctive and charming that if the wicket had been sprinkled with snow the marks made by his movements would have been as pretty as a bird's on a lawn early on a winter morning.

Miller was so much out of touch that Bailey, aspiring if not persistently impressive, confounded him twice in an over, nearly getting him leg before and caught at the wicket. Miller, on the defence in a poor light, hungry for singles, presented a strangely forlorn and manacled sight: a drive by him for four, off Wardle and from the back foot to the off, was the sign of a chafed spirit. Still he attended to the call of duty: Australia could not afford to lose another mature wicket at this stage, as the evening's gloom deepened and encircled us.

Just after six o'clock the umpires decided that the light, which in Sydney could well have presaged revolutions and reversals in high heaven, was scarcely fit for further play and an indeterminate day ended, to pass into memory and soon into oblivion except that the connoisseur of technique may wish to cherish for the while the precise and fine art of Hassett's innings and the superb new-ball attack of the indispensable Bedser.

AUSTRALIA

First Innings

A. R. Morris, lbw, b Bedser	67
G. B. Hole, b Bedser	0
A. L. Hassett, not out	67
R. N. Harvey, c Compton, b Bedser	0
K. R. Miller, not out	19
Extras (b 2, lb 1, nb 1)	4
	—
Total (3 wickets)	157

To bat: Benaud, Davidson, Lindwall, Tallon, Hill, Johnston.

FALL OF WICKETS

1	2	3
2	124	128

BOWLING ANALYSIS (to date)

	O.	M.	R.	W.		O.	M.	R.	W.
Bedser	25	12	26	3	Wardle	29	14	34	0
Bailey	28	7	55	0	Tattersall	10	1	38	0

Bedser one no-ball.

ENGLAND: Hutton, Kenyon, Simpson, Compton, Graveney, May, Bailey, Evans, Wardle, Bedser, Tattersall.

ENGLAND *v*. AUSTRALIA

FIRST TEST (SECOND DAY)

NOTTINGHAM, FRIDAY

The first Test match took a sudden and feverish turn after lunch on an afternoon of improving visibility at Trent Bridge. During the morning the play was as slow and inert as the pitch itself, and the pitch was as alive and responsive as a doormat that had been out in the porch all night in the rain. Then before the taste of the cheese had left our palates the game was galvanized.

The crowd rose from the dead. Six Australian wickets down in three-quarters of an hour, then, in startlingly swift sequence, three of England's best batsmen overwhelmed. Events were electrical: the Australians were desperate to retrieve their dubious state. The rapid contrast between the morning's indecision and the afternoon's climax, a climax without crescendo, baffled composed and coherent description. These lines are written instinctively, to be read much in the same way.

At lunch Australia's score stood menacingly at 243 for four wickets, and three-quarters of an hour after lunch Australia were all out for 249. Bedser took four wickets for two runs, and put into the new ball tremendous vitality and all the arts of which he is master. The Australian opposition, once Hassett had gone, was pathetically frail: none of the others could make even a show of resource against quick late swing. Bats were thrust out as though in fearful supplication: I have never before known an innings collapse so suddenly, so incompetently, so shockingly as this. I do not decry great bowling: Bedser deserved the challenge of informed technique. Hassett, alone of the casualties, was defeated with the dignity which comes when the very good needs make place for the very best.

CLEAVING THE AIR

And Benaud fell to a superb catch by Evans. The others, Davidson, Tallon, Lindwall, and Hill were either empirical or agricultural; hypnotized or goaded to naïve cleavings of the air. Lindwall put his bat to a wide ball from Bailey as though he, of all men, had never seen fast bowling before.

Throughout the period from half-past eleven to lunch I could not feel that Hassett and Miller were playing the kind of cricket which fortune in the long run encourages or approves. The day was moist, damp and unpleasant when Hassett and Miller proceeded with Australia's innings, the score 157 for three. A towel was needed to

147

dry the ball. On the soporific turf a Test match batsman could not reasonably have hoped to find conditions so easy and amenable as this for the purpose of making quick runs. The new ball would not be at Bedser's or Bailey's service until just before lunch: meanwhile Tattersall, Wardle, and Bailey had to be content with as much accuracy as their fingers could connive on slippery leather.

But both Hassett and Miller remained more or less content with checked strokes: even a loose ball received polite inspection. Miller, though much surer of himself than during the gloom of yesterday evening, appeared for once in a lifetime to believe firmly that discretion is the better part of valour. He looked a great cricketer rather than a great batsman as he tossed his hair back and twiddled his bat before resuming his guard. So well and purposefully did he defend, so comfortably did he force the ball for singles and twos, that at any moment I expected from him the onslaught the occasion and Australia's position demanded.

Hassett at one end of the wicket was the image of permanence, a small cricketer sometimes apparently concealing himself behind a very broad bat. Once when he went down on his knee to hook Bailey the stumps seemed almost to rise above him.

In an hour between half-past eleven and half-past twelve Australia scored 36—Hassett 15 and Miller 21. At this stage Bedser, handicapped by a damp old ball, was obliged to labour as diligently as Bailey, who for more than an hour attacked steadily and like a cricketer of heart. In the grey atmosphere the green light on the scoreboard pointing to the players' names was as a will-o'-the-wisp flickering in a marsh. The boundary was so far away, so the batsmen gave us to understand, that the Ordnance Survey was needed to locate it.

A pull off a long hop from Wardle, and a full toss in the same over, enabled Hassett to arrive at a most estimable century after he had been on view six hours or getting on that way: something in the nature of a time-machine is necessary for a proper measurement of an innings as durable as this of Hassett's, for it was achieved by durability of mind as well as of skill, a metaphysical affair almost. But the value of it to Australia is not to be measured by any economical reckoning, and a whole textbook might have been compiled from it, with pictures and diagrams to scale, done by an engraver with the finest point. Hassett is easily the most organized of all the batsmen in the present Australian team: he might do worse than open an academy for some of his colleagues.

BAILEY'S RUNNING CATCH

A quarter of an hour before lunch Miller essayed a bold pull from Wardle, and Bailey held an extremely difficult running catch near square leg. Miller had a moment earlier driven Tattersall in the air to the pavilion for four. Unnatural constraint has a way of provoking revengeful reactions. Miller's fatal stroke was injudicious with the interval at hand: perhaps the imminence of the new ball inspired him to sudden belligerency. He had certainly behaved pacifically enough in the presence of the old ball. In an hour and three-quarters today Hassett and Miller scored only eighty: the use of the towel was possibly not absolutely necessary.

The new ball might have been an atomic bomb of cricket. The Australian innings not only crashed at a speed that probably turned the dressing-room into a scurry and panic of pads put on wrong legs with buckles complicated and obstinate: also the England innings began in ruin against a fiery, vehement Lindwall. Kenyon, Simpson, and Compton were removed for 17 all told. Compton marvellously if voraciously caught by Morris at fifth, sixth, or eleventh slip—I could not count them all. And Compton's stroke was not too bad, at that.

Graveney came to the wicket with a chasm yawning before him deep as the one into which Australia had fallen. On the other edge of it stood Hutton, as strong, tranquil, and apparently as deeply rooted as an oak tree in a storm, and not more likely to be struck by lightning. For an hour and more Lindwall attacked brilliantly and beautifully: when he trapped Simpson leg before he clapped his hands and applauded himself. Greatness had entered the match like a visitation. Here was the finest fast bowler of our times at his most determined.

We had just seen the finest seam bowler of our time touched with inspiration. And here was Hutton defending in a searching hour, letting us look at science based on canons established years ago by the greatest of Trent Bridge's classical batsmen, Arthur Shrewsbury.

But a clever ball from Hill, moving from middle to off, confounded Hutton and nearly finished him. Lindwall bowled fast, on the whole all out, but from time to time he insinuated into his attack a slower ball and at least one inswinger. Usually he causes the swing to go the other and more perilous way. After tea Hill beat Graveney and nearly bowled him with another quasi leg-spinner from the back of the hand. It is hard to believe that Hill can really spin from leg at his quickish pace on Trent Bridge in damp weather.

THE ONLY 'BUMPER'

Lindwall sent a 'bumper' at Graveney which collided with the batsman's back, whereat the Trent Bridge crowd, including those who have not forgotten Larwood, howled out execration. This was Lindwall's only 'bumper' in a sustained and glorious exhibition of his art.

A back square cut by Hutton, off Hill, was noble in its timed power. Then, in the same over, a chorus of appeal for leg before went out against Hutton, and when it was dismissed the crowd again howled wrathfully, then exulted as Hutton again smote Hill to the off, another imperial blow. At last we were witnessing a Test match inflammatory to the passions: and there are no inhibitions about the Trent Bridge multitudes. Another magnificent catch ended Graveney's brave innings, played with a veteran tranquillity: Benaud caught him off Hill close in on the leg side at the second attempt as he stumbled.

England 76 for 4, a vast improvement on 17 for 3: but we were not out of the wood yet. Much depended on May, next man in. Hutton, of course, we were taking for granted: he was not only putting to the ball a bat that might well have drawn eyesight and experience from him, so instinctively did it frustrate good balls, but also he was quick to see the loose ones and punish them severely. Some of his strokes to the off, square, and to the right hand of cover, were as brilliant as they were handsome and powerful. It was a quite un-Huttonesque flash to the slips from Davidson that was his undoing, a strange lapse in the circumstances, with England still in questionable position at the evening's turning to gloom.

The time of day was half-past five when Benaud caught Hutton after nearly missing the chance, and the joy of the Australians to see Hutton falter so much out of character was open, unashamed, and justifiable. England 82 for five, and now there were two ends for the bowlers to threaten.

The wicket, though quicker now, was in no way responsible for the afternoon's extraordinary display of bad or unprincipled strokes. Some imp of mischief came into the game, tempted by the long hours of mechanical rotation yesterday and this morning. Perhaps one way of explaining the batting failures would be to say that the atmosphere was suitable to a new-ball attack, and that the fielding was first class.

And, of course, it was while the ball was new that the batsman ran into trouble. May, in spite of an error of judgment against Hill,

ayed well enough if anxiously—an off-drive by him from Davidson
as a beauty—until at five minutes to six he was caught at the wicket,
st flicking a ball from Hill which I am sure was turned from leg
y spin. A moment after he had left us bad light brought the day to
1 end, with England, after all, precariously situated.

AUSTRALIA
First Innings

A. R. Morris, lbw, b Bedser	67
G. B. Hole, b Bedser	0
A. L. Hassett, b Bedser	115
R. N. Harvey, c Compton, b Bedser	0
K. R. Miller, c Bailey, b Wardle	55
R. Benaud, c Evans, b Bailey	3
A. K. Davidson, b Bedser	4
D. Tallon, b Bedser	0
R. R. Lindwall, c Evans, b Bailey	0
J. C. Hill, b Bedser	0
W. A. Johnston, not out	0
Extras (b 2, lb 2, nb 1)	5
Total	249

FALL OF WICKETS

1	2	3	4	5	6	7	8	9
2	124	128	237	244	244	246	247	248

BOWLING

	O.	M.	R.	W.		O.	M.	R.	W.
Bedser	38.3	16	55	7	Wardle	33	16	55	1
Bailey	44	14	75	2	Tattersall	23	5	59	0

ENGLAND
First Innings

L. Hutton, c Benaud, b Davidson	43
D. J. Kenyon, c Hill, b Lindwall	8
R. T. Simpson, lbw, b Lindwall	0
D. C. S. Compton, c Morris, b Lindwall	0
T. W. Graveney, c Benaud, b Hill	22
P. B. H. May, c Tallon, b Hill	9
T. E. Bailey, not out	2
T. G. Evans, not out	0
Extras (b 5, lb 3)	8
Total (6 wkts)	92

To bat: Wardle, Bedser (A. V.), Tattersall.

FALL OF WICKETS

1	2	3	4	5	6
17	17	17	76	82	92

BOWLING (to date)

	O.	M.	R.	W.		O.	M.	R.	W.
Lindwall	12	1	35	3	Hill	14	7	24	2
Johnston	8	3	14	0	Davidson	8	4	11	1

FIRST TEST (THIRD DAY)

NOTTINGHAM, SATURDAY

The wicket was entirely docile when England, 92 for six, continued with Bailey and Evans against Lindwall and Johnston on a sunless morning. No vitality was put into the old ball: even Lindwall could be played from the pitch with reasonable comfort: and the left hand of Johnston came over like an artificial limb.

Yet little effort was made either by Bailey or Evans to score precious runs while circumstances favoured safe hits down the line of flight. It was hard to understand this show of dilatoriness, known nowadays as science in batsmanship, while every over was bringing us nearer to the moment when the new ball would be available to recharge the Lindwall dynamo. It was as though Bailey and Evans were two condemned men declining to eat a hearty breakfast on the morning of an execution.

When at last Evans let fly with his bat he chose to experiment with a slashed off-drive at a spacious out-swinger from Davidson: and when Bailey succumbed leg before to Hill not more than 38 runs had increased, or substantiated, England's total in eighty minutes: now Hassett could ask for the new ball which he at once handed to Lindwall. I must praise the extraordinary bounce obtained from the easy pitch by Davidson, whose left-arm action is free, loose, yet strong and determined.

From the rejuvenated Lindwall's first over with the new ball Wardle snicked thrice to the value, in the scorebook, of seven, all skimming to leg, and it is not certain yet to what part of the field Wardle intended them to go. Tattersall was, according to his custom against Australia, obstinate for a while in that awkward, angular way which is the source of irritation to all bowlers at the end of any team innings: and Wardle did his best to hit a four or two and also was instrumental in proving to us that the Australians' fielding can on occasions miss a catch at leg-slip. England were all out just before lunch, 105 in arrears.

AUSTRALIA IN AGAIN

When Australia batted again, Morris immediately attacked Bailey with the decision and easefully directed power of a great batsman so much in form and sure of himself that he can think of human error and fallibility only by close abstract thought. He cut for four, pulled with a sweep of grandeur for four, and drove for three to the off, running into the stroke gracefully. But Hole played over nearly a yorker from Bedser and Hassett received a ball from Bedser that rose up alarmingly and ungeometrically, so that though he countered it with a technically correct bat he sent a catch to short leg.

A ravenous roar of the crowd at Hassett's ball had scarcely died in the afternoon's veiled sky than Harvey was most brilliantly caught at leg not far from the bat, which hooked a rising ball from Bedser, a stroke as electrical and clever as the catch itself. This was wretched luck for Harvey, and wonderful fielding by Graveney. None except a great batsman could have made the stroke at all.

Miller, in next, appeared set at all costs on removing Bedser from England's attack, temporarily at any rate, if not permanently. For obviously while the wicket was in its present state Bedser was England's only positively dangerous wicket-taker. Hutton shrewdly maintained a close, intimidating field for Miller who, rather more buccaneering than Australia's position really called for, drove a full toss from Bedser clean into Kenyon's hands at mid-on. Miller nowadays gives the impression of a rather disorganized cricketer: yesterday he was all for modern science, when a little freedom of will might have been permissible; today he went to an irrational extreme. And I wonder if Bedser did not send him a full toss deliberately; he does not usually bowl full tosses.

Attacking like a man inspired by success and devotion to his team, Bedser utterly defeated and confounded Benaud's leg stump, a glorious inswinger which left poor Benaud in a vague state, mentally and physically, so that apparently somebody had to tell him by word of mouth that he was out.

Australia were now 173 in front and five wickets down. Morris still in command and Bedser still bowling his heart away. He had taken all these wickets for 20-odd runs. There was an enchanting contrast between the cricket at one end of the pitch and the other while Morris was batting and Bedser bowling. Mastery and distinction, then labour or empiricism. The others were so many capable stooges or supers. At a quarter to four Bedser was obliged to rest himself, after an hour and a half of as finely sustained bowling as this grand old ground of Trent Bridge has ever witnessed. He played a lone hand, but it was directed by what a strong arm.

As a fact it was Tattersall, who took Bedser's place, who advanced England to a point from which victory might be seen from a sort of Pisgah height, not, let us hope and pray, as a mirage. He pitched a nicely flighted off-break and Morris for the first time in an innings of isolated splendour fatally faltered. Davidson showed sensible fight until Graveney caught him at long-on from a splendid drive, even if it was risked against the spin. By means of two admirable catches by Graveney he served his side to the value of many runs in a situation where they were at a premium for both and all opponents.

MAGNIFICENT CATCHING

The England catching was really astonishing: Australia had reason to suppose that some imp of misfortune was dogging them. Tallon swung a ponderous bat to Tattersall, and the ball soared high and away beyond square leg to the on, but Simpson chased it and held one-handed the catch of a season, if not of a lifetime. And it was taken with an ease that was entirely deceiving.

So to tea with the match surely within England's reach though not yet within her grasp—Australia only 211 to the advantage, only two wickets in reserve. It was all very exciting to see, but frankly the cricket, apart from catches, sadly lacked Test match class. Bedser and Morris alone attained the expected stature and told of the proper pedigree. Lindwall, after making at least two splendid hits, was also caught from a towering blow of violent disregard.

I have never before seen in Test cricket between England and Australia so many signs of atavism to Saturday afternoon's cricket as on this misty Saturday afternoon at Trent Bridge. No reasonable account can be made of Australia's poor total. Only Morris and Hassett were out in a manner not injurious to a Test match batsman's dignity, knowledge, experience, and common sense. It was the innings of a team suddenly bereft of purpose. When I remember the deliberate, opportunist, and often handsome or brilliant cricket of Bradman, Ponsford, Woodfull, Kippax, and McCabe I am inclined to wonder what has recently happened to Australian batsmanship, psychologically and technically.

An all-out score of 123 would be considered mediocre on a wicket definitely a bowler's. I am not disparaging the attack of England, especially that of Bedser; I am directing my criticism, in cricket values, against Australia.

ENGLAND'S RISING ODDS

After Lindwall had bowled four balls in England's second innings which needed to get 229 for victory, an appeal against the light was lodged, and the game interrupted for nearly a quarter of an hour. All afternoon there had been periods justifying such an appeal by the Australians. Lindwall's first ball crashed into Hutton's pads and another and more audible appeal was dismissed with a promptitude which synchronized with the verdict of the crowd packed in all places in the ground.

At the resumption Kenyon somehow emerged intact from a terrifying over of Lindwall's of perfect length, the pace just missing the edge of a bat drawn into the danger zone as though by some irresistible fascination. Next over Kenyon glanced a four to leg off Lindwall, or at any rate the ball flashed in that direction, by a stroke apparently intuitive. Then he drove Lindwall to the off for three with commendable firmness and the Australian attack began to look worried.

Hill came on for Johnston and began with a capacious wide. Next he sent Kenyon a long-hop which was summarily sent to the boundary; next ball, a full toss, Kenyon lifted to mid-on and was out, a foolish gift to Australia, who obviously needed encouragement just now. From the fifth ball of this same over of Hill's, Simpson had reason for gratitude that he was not caught at slip from a hopeless snick. Such strokes might well have suggested a doubtful wicket to the uninitiated onlooker: but it was still more than good enough for good batsmen, a very comfortable wicket on which Lindwall, expecting one or more overs, was not as difficult to time as on Friday evening.

With Hutton still in possession the odds are now definitely in England's favour.

AUSTRALIA

First Innings		Second Innings	
A. R. Morris, lbw, b Bedser	67	b Tattersall	60
G. B. Hole, b Bedser	0	b Bedser	5
A. L. Hassett, b Bedser	115	c Hutton, b Bedser	5
R. N. Harvey, c Compton, b Bedser	0	c Graveney, b Bedser	2
K. R. Miller, c Bailey, b Wardle	55	c Kenyon, b Bedser	5
R. Benaud, c Evans, b Bailey	3	b Bedser	0
A. K. Davisdon, b Bedser	4	c Graveney, b Tattersall	6
D. Tallon, b Bedser	0	c Simpson, b Tattersall	15
R. R. Lindwall, c Evans, b Bailey	0	c Tattersall, b Bedser	12
J. C. Hill, b Bedser	0	c Tattersall, b Bedser	4
W. A. Johnston, not out	0	not out	4
Extras (b 2, lb 2, nb 1)	5	Extras (lb 5)	5
Total	249	Total	123

CARDUS IN THE COVERS

FALL OF WICKETS

First Innings

1	2	3	4	5	6	7	8	9
2	124	128	237	244	244	246	247	248

BOWLING ANALYSIS

First Innings

	O.	M.	R.	W.		O.	M.	R.	W.
Bedser	38·3	16	55	7	Wardle	33	16	55	1
Bailey	44	14	75	2	Tattersall	23	5	59	0

FALL OF WICKETS

Second Innings

1	2	3	4	5	6	7	8	9
28	44	50	64	68	81	92	106	115

BOWLING ANALYSIS

Second Innings

	O.	M.	R.	W.		O.	M.	R.	W.
Bedser	17·2	7	44	7	Wardle	12	3	24	0
Bailey	5	1	28	0	Tattersall	5	0	22	3

ENGLAND

First Innings		Second Innings	
L. Hutton, c Benaud, b Davidson	43	not out	10
D. J. Kenyon, c Hill, b Lindwall	8	c Hassett, b Hill	16
R. T. Simpson, lbw, b Lindwall	0	not out	8
D. C. S. Compton, c Morris, b Lindwall	0		
T. W. Graveney, c Benaud, b Hill	22		
P. B. H. May, c Tallon, b Hill	9		
T. E. Bailey, lbw, b Hill	13		
T. G. Evans, c Tallon, b Davidson	8		
J. W. Wardle, not out	29		
A. V. Bedser, lbw, b Lindwall	2		
R. Tattersall, b Lindwall	2		
Extras (b 5, lb 3)	8	Extras (b 1, lb 4, w 1, nb 2)	8
Total	144	Total (1 wkt)	42

FALL OF WICKETS

First Innings

1	2	3	4	5	6	7	8	9
17	17	17	76	82	92	107	121	136

BOWLING ANALYSIS

First Innings

	O.	M.	R.	W.		O.	M.	R.	W.
Lindwall	20·4	2	57	5	Hill	19	8	35	3
Johnston	18	7	22	0	Davidson	15	7	22	2

FALL OF WICKET

Second Innings

$$\frac{1}{26}$$

BOWLING ANALYSIS

Second Innings

	O.	M.	R.	W.		O.	M.	R.	W.
Lindwall	9	4	18	0	Hill	3	0	11	1
Johnston	5	2	5	0					

NO PLAY ON THE FOURTH DAY BECAUSE OF RAIN.

FIRST TEST (FIFTH DAY)

NOTTINGHAM, TUESDAY

Not until half-past four was play in the first Test match proceeded with, and only after several examinations of the wicket, much manual labour by the groundsmen, with rollers, sawdust, mats, and probably blotting paper and warming-pans. There was also a certain amount of argument between the two captains.

When play began, two hours remained for cricket, and then England could scarcely hope to score 90 runs an hour to obtain victory, but there was just a bare chance that Australia in the time might take nine wickets. Hassett began his attack with Johnston and Hill; the ground to begin with was too soft and greasy for Lindwall. Five successive maiden overs were wheeled up until Simpson cut Hill for four.

But England obviously were not intent on runs; the onus to force the game miraculously to a decision was on Australia. After all, it was Australia, not England, who wanted to play at all so late in the day on a piece of sodden turf with something perhaps to gain and nothing to lose; meanwhile we had all missed our trains and paid our hotel bills, ready to depart from Nottingham hours ago.

SPIN—OR FANTASY

After sixteen runs in nearly half an hour Hassett asked Benaud to

bowl instead of Hill; most of us would have expected to see Davidson trying to get pace out of a sluggish earth not at all suitable to leg
breaks. Probably Hassett's view was that in the conditions wickets
could be got only by flight through the air or spin, actual or a
fantasy in the mind of batsmen. A lovely cover drive by Hutton, off
Benaud, temporarily transformed a formal, not to say dutiful
occasion, with cricket and personal art.

At five minutes past five, Lindwall came into action, running carefully so as not to slip and strain a limb, content with a pace a little
above fast medium. Hardly a ball behaved contrary to logical
conclusion drawn from the ball's aerial progress. The match was now
going on and being continued simply because there was no legal way
of stopping it. Even Lindwall could get the ball to rise no higher
than the stumps, and neither Hutton nor Simpson attempted a stroke
unless it invited polite and safe treatment.

A four by Hutton through the slips was not really a good stroke
until it reached the boundary. Then Johnston beat Simpson, the
first ball of the evening to come from the pitch with the speed that
positively stimulates the interest of fieldsmen in the slips. Another
beautiful cover drive by Hutton, off Lindwall, provoked applause
from the not very large crowd, and for a while prevented us hearing
the adjacent broadcast commentator speaking his piece like an old
recitation. There was not much more, in the circumstances, for him
to say. The wonder was that he could be interested in saying it at all.

In an hour 38 runs were registered on the books of the scorers,
who had nothing else to do and so were much in the same situation
as the players and the rest of us. It was all a waste of time and leisure.
Yet the Australians performed several superb bits of fielding; a
pick-up by Morris was brilliant. Hutton batted as easily as a great
pianist rehearsing, running over the keyboard of his strokes at half-
pressure, so to say, as though as much for his own study and self-
scrutiny as for any other purpose. At the wicket's other end Simpson
conscientiously defended and was satisfied to frustrate the Australians, who, after all, brought on themselves the superfluous postlude
to the match. Still, it was only right and it was certainly cricket that
the game was not given up prematurely, when most of us had
counted it 'washed out'.

A STRANGE SIGHT

A strange sight at ten minutes to six was Lindwall's field near the
wicket, no slip and four short-legs. With not more than forty

minutes left for play, Davidson came on for Lindwall; he might as well have been Hassett for what point the change of bowling had now. Hutton received cheers as he reached 50; and subsequent proceedings interested me, or many people else, no more.

The drawn match, though a disappointment, has had its valuable uses. England should go into the second Test match at Lord's next week with a moral ascendancy, as they say, and that, against Australia, will be a change and an asset.

AUSTRALIA

First Innings		Second Innings	
A. R. Morris, lbw, b Bedser	67	b Tattersall	60
G. B. Hole, b Bedser	0	b Bedser	5
A. L. Hassett, b Bedser	115	c Hutton, b Bedser	5
R. N. Harvey, c Compton, b Bedser	0	c Graveney, b Bedser	2
K. R. Miller, c Bailey, b Wardle	55	c Kenyon, b Bedser	5
R. Benaud, c Evans, b Bailey	3	b Bedser	0
A. K. Davidson, b Bedser	4	c Graveney, b Tattersall	6
D. Tallon, b Bedser	0	c Simpson, b Tattersall	15
R. R. Lindwall, c Evans, b Bailey	0	c Tattersall, b Bedser	12
J. C. Hill, b Bedser	0	c Tattersall, b Bedser	4
W. A. Johnston, not out	0	not out	4
Extras (b 2, lb 2, nb 1)	5	Extras (lb 5)	5
Total	249	Total	123

FALL OF WICKETS

First Innings

1	2	3	4	5	6	7	8	9
2	124	128	237	244	244	246	247	248

BOWLING ANALYSIS

First Innings

	O.	M.	R.	W.		O.	M.	R.	W.
Bedser	38·3	16	55	7	Wardle	33	16	55	1
Bailey	44	14	75	2	Tattersall	23	5	59	0

FALL OF WICKETS

Second Innings

1	2	3	4	5	6	7	8	9
28	44	50	64	68	81	92	106	115

BOWLING ANALYSIS

Second Innings

	O.	M.	R.	W.		O.	M.	R.	W.
Bedser	17·2	7	44	7	Wardle	12	3	24	0
Bailey	5	1	28	0	Tattersall	5	0	22	3

ENGLAND

First Innings			Second Innings	
L. Hutton, c Benaud, b Davidson	43		not out	60
D. J. Kenyon, c Hill, b Lindwall	8		c Hassett, b Hill	16
R. T. Simpson, lbw, b Lindwall	0		not out	28
D. C. S. Compton, c Morris, b Lindwall	0			
T. W. Graveney, c Benaud, b Hill	22			
P. B. H. May, c Tallon, b Hill	9			
T. E. Bailey, lbw, b Hill	13			
T. G. Evans, c Tallon, b Davidson	8			
J. W. Wardle, not out	29			
A. V. Bedser, lbw, b Lindwall	2			
R. Tattersall, b Lindwall	2			
Extras (b 5, lb 3)	8		Extras (b 8, lb 4, w 2, nb 2)	16
Total	144		Total (1 wkt)	120

FALL OF WICKETS

First Innings

1	2	3	4	5	6	7	8	9
17	17	17	76	82	92	107	121	136

BOWLING ANALYSIS

First Innings

	O.	M.	R.	W.		O.	M.	R.	W.
Lindwall	20·4	2	57	5	Hill	19	8	35	3
Johnston	18	7	22	0	Davidson	15	7	22	2

FALL OF WICKETS

Second Innings

1
26

BOWLING ANALYSIS

Second Innings

	O.	M.	R.	W.		O.	M.	R.	W.
Lindwall	16	4	37	0	Benaud	5	0	15	0
Johnston	18	9	14	0	Davidson	5	1	7	0
Hill	12	3	26	1	Morris	2	0	5	0

Umpires: H. Elliott and D. Davies.

ENGLAND v. AUSTRALIA, 1953

SECOND TEST (FIRST DAY)

O N a wicket which nearly all day resembled a batsman's processional carpet Australia up to tea time had little trouble in laying the foundation of a great score. Then Hassett, not out a century, was taken with cramp and obliged to retire to the pavilion. The way was open for England to get at the younger and less accomplished batsmen.

The crowd, subdued since noon and not naturally jubilant, soon found consolation in the ten minutes before six o'clock and the five minutes after. In those fifteen minutes, in which there were ten deliveries, Wardle took the wickets of Hole, Benaud and Miller—Miller, who, the ball before, had pulled him prodigiously into the grand stand for six. Australia 180 for one at tea, and now Australia 240 for five. A narrow and unhoped for escape!

When the players went into the field the morning was warm, with sunshine imminent. The crowd packed its thousands into Lord's and the camera and newsreel men got to work on a high scaffold that defaced the side of the pavilion near the green bank. The time seems at hand when a Test match will resemble a film studio and an England eleven might conceivably be strengthened by the inclusion of Michael Wilding and Stewart Granger.

UNCERTAIN START

The stand of Hassett and Morris for Australia's first wicket amounted to 65, but it might have ended for next to nothing. In his opening over Bedser beat Hassett on the off-side, and Hassett then touched Statham to the leg-side, where Evans endeavoured to make a catch out of a ghost of a chance. Statham's next ball, a short embryonic 'bumper', was crudely clumped or 'hoicked' by Hassett over his shoulder to fall safely, but unbeautifully, well in front of long-leg. Then Morris played Bedser with the edge of his bat; altogether the Australian innings was long-emerging from a sort of rough sketch of competent and not confident batsmanship.

Brown came on for Bedser, the ball still 'new', and he obtained a pace from the pitch livelier than that of Statham, to whom Hassett played back more than once with a leisure that caused me to think of an appointment punctually, not to say impatiently, kept. A leg glance by Hassett, when he was 22, just eluded Compton at short-leg in Bailey's first over. Bailey, like all the other quick England bowlers, excepting Brown, was too short in length; Australian batsmen like to play from the back foot and should be drawn forward.

GLUED THERE

The England attack afforded no convincing reason to explain the sense of anxiety prevailing hereabout in the Australian innings; it was an anxiety born within the minds of Hassett and Morris. Still they both remained adhesively at the wicket until nearly one o'clock. Hassett especially seeming as though glued there, so that I received the curious illusion of watching a batsman attached to the crease by some sticky stuff; error pulled him away and self-preservation pulled him back.

He is a deceptive little craftsman, and today the inability of the England bowlers and fieldsmen to get him quickly caught in the region of short-leg suggested a magnet straining to attract a needle, placed a little too far away. Hassett's sore wrist obviously troubled him; frequently he appeared to use the force of one hand. He gives thought to his every movement, takes no ball for granted, and because of his intelligence he is constantly interesting to the student of the game. Sometimes he cuts charmingly, telling us as he does so to take care not to miss the sparkle. He is a small batsman in inches who enjoys a long innings, and his cricket, like his face, is humorously inexpressive, yet obviously indicative of the essence of him. A witty man without epigrams, so to say.

Morris, in spite of a few fine hits and conditions entirely after a batsman's heart, did not threaten to root himself to the ground like a plant in the sumptuous sun. He was stumped, the ball glancing from his pad, and Evans as quick to the opportunity as one monkey chasing another.

As soon as Harvey came in, he leapt down the pitch to drive Bailey defensively on feet so light that he might have had wings or no weight in him at all.

ATTACK WITHOUT VARIETY

After lunch a brilliant ball from Statham flashed near Hassett's blade on the offside; for a few overs Statham considerably improved on his form of the morning. But the attack needed variety. Hutton did not bring on Wardle until three o'clock; his policy was, I gathered, to keep the runs down until a new ball became available as the gorgeous afternoon spent its heat. Harvey, not sure of himself to begin with, checked his strokes, and once or twice fumbled them; and Hassett, when his score stood at 55, sent a very sharp low slashed chance to Hutton at second-slip; had it been taken, as well it might have been and brilliantly so, Australia's second wicket—would have fallen at 106.

After a great pull by Hassett off Bailey, Hassett was beaten by Bailey: the cricket strangely vacillated between dour competence and uneasy insecurity. There was no continuous appeal to the connoisseur's insistence, for the purposes of a Test match between England and Australia, on a certain distinction of style and technique. A lovely off-drive by Harvey came as a welcome flavour of blue blood and aristocracy; Debrett after the Board of Trade returns. A straight drive by Harvey, off Wardle, the bat cracking and flashing simultaneously, thrilled the imagination like lightning and thunder announcing a storm coming to make a sad mess of England's steady but not over-sophisticated attack.

ALMOST BORING

The bowling made no excessive demands on the batsmen's experience or intellect; only a good eye and an incapacity to suffer boredom was needed to play it on the lazy comfortable turf.

Leg-spin is necessary on such an occasion as this, both as a means of getting on with the game and as a means of quickening the interest of those of us who do not watch cricket with our eyes always on the scoreboard. Wright, of Kent, whether he is taking wickets or not, enlivens the imagination; it is tedious to look at seam-bowling, actual or potential, hour after hour; and when the ball has lost its shine, to look at any seam-bowler is as unsatisfactory as watching a workman using a blunt tool or a pianist practising on a 'dummy' keyboard. At half-past three Australia were 153 for one and now, surely, Compton's spin would have had its uses and provided some relief, practical, comical, or other.

At five minutes to four, when Australia were 167 for one, Bedser attacked again with the new ball, blessed symbol of contemporary and rotatory efficiency in cricket. He at once found again an edge on Hassett's bat: but I must say that if Hassett did play with the edge he apparently played with the middle of it. Harvey reached his 50 in some two and a half hours: the threatened storm had not broken yet, but the flicker of his occasional beautiful hits was not the flicker of harmless summer lightning.

HARVEY GOES

At tea, the Australian position was ominous for England: 180 for one. The attack seemed content to wait the new ball. I cannot describe Hutton's captaincy exactly as Macchiavellian, nor was it openly aggressive. He seldom placed a close intimidating field. At last, after tea, Harvey succumbed leg before, a mistake of timing on his part as he played a short decisive push against Bedser.

Miller was given a no-ball from Bedser to open his score, and he drove it convulsively and high to the straight off, where it fell amongst a fraternity of pigeons. Then by an exquisite late-cut Hassett arrived at his hundred, after roughly four and a half hours of cricket so nicely fashioned that the watchmaker's eye was required to detect a loose screw or loose end here and there. Hassett now left the field with cramp in the legs, an affliction more likely, I should have thought, to visit the bowlers.

So Hole joined Miller, and the new ball and the new faces at the wicket clearly renewed hope and vitality in Bedser, who on the whole had not bowled many overs positively menacing, though, of course, he was perseveringly steady. Much the same may be said of Statham.

Brown at any rate always suggested he was trying by will-power to get wickets and not relying entirely on the mechanics of the bowler's trade. All his overs spoke of a dogged sullen determination; but he, too, was inclined to pitch too short a length. Once or twice he turned a leg-break by authentic spin. He sent a slower-flighted ball to Hole, and the hit that went rather weakly over his head emphasized what the England attack generally wanted in the way of intelligence and sense of humour.

The trouble with Test matches these days is not only that they are frequently dull; they are as frequently pompous. The Australian stroke play was not so versatile or ubiquitous to challenge the England fielding; but it was as watchful and accurate as the opportunity allowed.

Under the blue sky Lord's made a handsome picture; the crowd in many colours, the trees at the nursery end rich and still of foliage, the pigeons absorbed in their own way of enjoying a perfect June afternoon, oblivious of cricketers unless the ball definitely threatened them with physical hurt, oblivious of the crowd, oblivious of all humanity and human conduct.

A LITTLE SPIN

Wardle, when he bowled again, caused a ball or two definitely to spin in no merely decorative way. I imagine that if the weather remains hot and dry, a leg-spinner will look for some sympathetic collaboration from this Lord's wicket on Monday or Tuesday. England must be thankful that Ring is not the incomparable and fabulous Grimmett.

I had no sooner written that foregoing sentence than Hole was caught at slip from a really sharp spinner from Wardle. England were emerging from a situation which at tea hinted of a terrible lot of wrath to come. None the less, Australia's position at close of play, if not impregnable by any means, is not one which England will get round without immense effort and strain. Some truly beautiful hits by Davidson after six o'clock reminded us that Australia's innings is not over and done with yet.

AUSTRALIA
First Innings

A. L. Hassett, retired hurt	101
A. R. Morris, st Evans, b Bedser	30
R. N. Harvey, lbw, b Bedser	59
K. R. Miller, b Wardle	25
G. B. Hole, c Compton, b Wardle	13
R. Benaud, lbw, b Wardle	0
A. K. Davidson, not out	17
D. Ring, not out	10
Extras (b 4, lb 4)	8
	—
Total (5 wickets)	263

To bat: Langley, Lindwall, Johnston.

FALL OF WICKETS

1	2	3	4	5
65	190	225	229	240

BOWLING ANALYSIS (to date)

	O.	M.	R.	W.		O.	M.	R.	W.
Bedser	30	5	77	2	Bailey	16	2	55	0
Statham	19	3	35	0	Wardle	17	5	42	3
Brown	22	6	46	0					

ENGLAND: Hutton, Kenyon, Graveney, Compton, Watson, Bailey, Brown, Evans, Wardle, Bedser, Statham.

SECOND TEST (SECOND DAY)

LORDS, FRIDAY

In spite of an early loss in England's innings a resonant retaliatory blow has been struck at Australia today by Hutton and Graveney in a stand which, so to say, has put our batsmanship back on the gold standard. Fine strokes were plentiful: technique went hand in hand with style. Graveney has at last come to full flower; this indeed was Test-match batsmanship not to be estimated by the accountancy of the scoreboard.

While a natural and welcome satisfaction at England's present position should be encouraged, while it lasts, optimism must be tempered by the possibility that our batsmen may have to play a fourth innings on a dry Lord's wicket after four days' wear and tear. This is, or should be, a sobering thought. And a new ball will be at Lindwall's disposal first thing tomorrow.

In hot sunshine the crowd baked at Lord's even before the match was resumed. Moreover, if I am not mistaken, the earth baked: Wardle, bowling to the pavilion end, made more than one ball spin quickly, and from one of them Hassett was missed at first slip by Compton off a stroke involuntary enough to tell us that the wicket might easily deteriorate to dustiness. We can only, as patriots, hope that the Lord's wicket behaves as sometimes it has behaved in the past and achieves a sudden if unexpected reformation in conduct, much as the renowned and revered Charles Peace would from time to time put on a clerical collar and go to church.

CATCHES AND MISSES

After Ring fell to Wardle, leg before, Hassett continued his innings. After his good fortune against Wardle's waspish away-from-the-bat spin, he succumbed, hopelessly overwhelmed, by a brute of a ball from Bedser, a spiteful, kicking, good-length ball, to which Hassett could retaliate only by reflex-action, which got him caught near the gully by Bailey, who held his chance tumbling. It was a welcome sight, this visible and dynamic piece of fieldsmanship in the England team: for frankly there was more than one slow runner among them.

Inexplicably, Hutton missed Lindwall at short leg chest high, also he missed Davidson at cover low down; and each chance was of the sort he most times holds as a matter of course. A sharp blow on the left arm earlier in the day may possibly have left his mind a little unsettled. Davidson was also missed when his score was not more than eighteen, this time at mid-off from Wardle. Wardle himself endeavoured to leap and grasp the high return, then Bedser, behind him, was rather late, intellectually and physically.

The present Australians do not include in their ranks a Bradman, a Ponsford, a Woodfull; but they are not so vulnerable as batsmen that England can afford to give more than one innings to any of them, excepting possibly—and he is such a good fellow—W. A. Johnston.

DAVIDSON FULL OF PROMISE

Davidson played a curiously contrasted innings. When he defended, he suggested the seriousness of a student who has not yet graduated; then suddenly and at intervals, he drove with a speed, ease, brilliance and upright pose that delighted the eye and thrilled the senses. Nobody in the match so far has shown us strokes as handsome and as spontaneously created as Davidson's. Yet, his cricket for the most part was that of a young man still at school and willing to learn from the two most austere of masters, trial and error. Throughout the summer, I have formed the opinion that Davidson is the best of Australia's contemporary aspirants; he shows more cricket sense than Benaud and Hole, though he is naturally a stroke-player he keeps his head down to the line of the good and problematic ball. He will, I think, go a long way, and so will much of the bowling delivered at him. In time he will develop short-armed hits and cope with the leg-side. Even if he never becomes a master of leg-side strokes he need not despair; the incomparable Hammond found mastery in such a limitation.

GIVEN TO IRONY

A clever and pretty one-handed catch at short-leg by Watson not only accounted for Langley but restored the temper of the crowd, a portion of which seemed inclined to irony at England's fielding, not realising with proper philosophy that missed catches at cricket do not necessarily signify inept fielding but merely the way of the world, with its ups and downs. None the less, England's work in the field rather sadly wanted singleness of purpose and initiative. Hutton apparently wavered between an offence aimed at a speedy wreckage of the Australian rearguard and a canny defence aimed at keeping the runs down. I actually saw Davidson batting to Wardle with not a fieldsman at or adjacent to short-leg.

Australia's innings closed at twenty minutes past two, and a superb one-handed deep field catch by Statham ended it; he took the ball with astonishing looseness and confidence of limb, under the eyes of the pavilion. The question before us now was twofold; would Australia's total prove a handful of runs too many, and would the wicket disintegrate in any dangerous way. This message is being written as the afternoon unfolds itself, while what is to come is still unsure. Yet I risk the opinion that England will do prodigiously well to win the match, unless some gentle rain falls soon and binds the turf.

Bedser, as usual, was responsible for the capture of most of the Australian wickets; but Wardle was really the 'key' bowler. And Brown's analysis is quite libellous.

CHARGED ATMOSPHERE

From Lindwall's first over, at the nursery end, Hutton drove with supreme and tranquil mastery to the off for three; and Kenyon made a confident forcing hit to the on for two. The cheers of the multitude, greeting these strokes, were like the greetings roared at the relief of a beleaguered army. In Lindwall's next over a ball flashed upward, found some part of Kenyon's bat near the handle, and Davidson, at leg-slip, seized an obviously triumphant catch. For the first time in the match, the atmosphere became electrical; the loss of another wicket now, especially Hutton's would surely see England in a relentless grip.

Miller, attacking from the pavilion end, was the living image of abandoned vehemence and hostility undisciplined, for he sent down some unruly stuff, with more than one shell that could not explode because there was nothing in it more combustible than his own impulse and swagger. If Lindwall was beautifully classical in method, Miller was neo-Romantic, decadent, eccentric. He was quickly taken off, Johnston bowling in his place.

COOL GRAVENEY

Graveney opened his innings cool as a veteran, drove Johnston straight for four with a lovely pendulum swing, and in the same over placed him square for another boundary which possessed the leisure of good breeding. Very quickly did the England ship appear to steer clear of the rocks sighted when Kenyon's wicket fell. Momentarily, at any rate, the wicket was not doing anything untoward; but it is a wicket more likely to collaborate with spin than pace. A stroke of Hutton from Lindwall, off his toes, to the on for four not only honoured Lord's on this June day but all the traditions of stylish and blood-royal batsmanship; the timing was perfect, the balance and poise of his body a delight.

Towards half-past three, with England 45 for one, Lindwall

rested, and Ring came on with leg-spin; at the other end Johnston changed from pace to medium left-hand spin. It is lucky for England indeed that today Grimmett is in Australia and O'Rielly is one of my colleagues in the press box. Three short legs and a first slip reinforced Johnston's bowling; but, so far as I could see, no positively dangerous spin. Later, perhaps, Hassett will put him on at the end from which Wardle found some actual or potential help from the pitch. Ring's leg-breaks spun very slightly after they had left his hand.

The batting since Kenyon departed has certainly cleared the air for England for the moment. But no student of cricket will commit himself to more optimism than this, except to hope that he is not mistaken in thinking that Australia lacks the right bowlers for the pace and texture of the wicket. Hassett invited Benaud to bowl instead of Ring, looking for the spinner to take the measure of it.

SOME FINE BATTING

Graveney played well enough to look well in a picture which framed Hutton's masterfully composed canvas. He pulled Ring spaciously to the over-populated Tavern: his was the best batting seen in an England eleven for contrasted style as well as for runs, in recent summers.

After tea Hassett entrusted his attack to the only leg-spinners at his service. Benaud looked more likely than Ring to get a wicket, and twice his low-flighted spin beat Graveney, striking his pads. Ring's length and direction needed precision. Either Ramadhin or Valentine, or both, would have revelled in the conditions and the opportunity. Benaud fell to the earth after leaping high to catch and bowl Graveney from a drive that reached the sight screen, and in the same over, Graveney, with two late cuts, passed his fifty amid tumultuous applause.

Now Miller bowled again, above medium pace, not fast, with three slips but no short leg. He inserted a bumper and acknowledged the crowd's howls of derision by raising his arms on high. He suggested a sort of fallen Lucifer.

The batting by this time was, as they say, entirely on top, better still, it satisfied the taste of the connoisseurs. At last Hassett put Johnston on from Wardle's end, with two slips and a short leg, a case of optimism or pure conjecture; for truly the Australian attack on a wicket not suited to Lindwall suggested a condition of perspiring embarrassment. Splendid fielding was its most substantial asset.

It was a refreshing change to look upon an England innings again, and believe one's eyes and know that it actually was being played in a cricket field, the boundary close at hand and not as impenetrable as the stone walls of a prison. A fast full toss and another tame bumper merely emphasized Miller's impotence; I would have described him as a shorn Samson had he not thrown his brown hair out of his eyes as jauntily as ever.

HARD LABOUR

Lindwall came into action for the second time at half past five when England were 145 for one. This was only his eighth over and it was eminently respectable throughout, inviting the application of a virtuously straight bat. Johnston could not root out the spot which yesterday conspired with the fingers of Wardle. There seemed no reason why Hutton or Graveney should ever get out, except that an innings of the most skilful and watchful batsman is bound and destined to come to an end sooner or later. Memory has to grope back a long way to recall an Australian attack condemned as severely and surely as this one to hard labour in the heat of a long afternoon.

Hutton and Graveney have so far batted together for nearly three hours and a half, scoring 168; it probably appeared longer than that to the Australians.

AUSTRALIA
First Innings

A. L. Hassett, c Bailey, b Bedser	104
A. R. Morris, st Evans, b Bedser	30
R. N. Harvey, lbw, b Bedser	59
K. R. Miller, b Wardle	25
G. B. Hole, c Compton, b Wardle	13
R. Benaud, lbw, b Wardle	0
A. K. Davidson, c Statham, b Bedser	76
D. Ring, lbw, b Wardle	18
R. R. Lindwall, b Statham	9
G. R. Langley, c Watson, b Bedser	1
W. A. Johnston, not out	3
Extras (b 4, lb 4)	8
Total	346

FALL OF WICKETS

1	2	3	4	5	6	7	8	9
65	190	225	229	240	280	291	330	331

BOWLING ANALYSIS

	O.	M.	R.	W.		O.	M.	R.	W.
Bedser	42.4	8	105	5	Bailey	16	2	55	0
Statham	28	7	48	1	Wardle	29	8	77	4
Brown	25	7	53	0					

ENGLAND

First Innings

L. Hutton, not out	83
D. Kenyon, c Davidson, b Lindwall	3
T. W. Graveney, not out	78
Extras (b 8, nb 5)	13
	—
Total (one wicket)	177

To bat: Compton, Watson, Bailey, Brown, Evans, Wardle, Bedser, Statham.

FALL OF WICKET

$$\frac{1}{9}$$

BOWLING ANALYSIS (to date)

	O.	M.	R.	W.		O.	M.	R.	W.
Lindwall	11	2	30	1	Ring	10	1	30	0
Miller	8	2	16	0	Benaud	11	3	30	0
Johnston	22	7	49	0	Davidson	4	0	9	0

SECOND TEST (THIRD DAY)

LORD'S, SATURDAY

At lunch today England's score was 287 for three. Not only that, the Australians presented the appearance of a team a little bereft of ideas. The match was almost in England's hands. At all costs and with every effort they needed to avoid a hard task in the fourth innings.

After lunch seven wickets were lost by England for 85. The wheel of events swung us from optimism, not to say complacency, to disillusionment.

The miscarriages in the England innings occurred in swift and cruel sequence. The removal of Hutton, the spinal column, was as much the consequence of an accident as a fall downstairs that puts a man on his back for a month. A ball lifted to his bat unexpectedly, and it came from the rather limp arm of Johnston, whose bowling was usually as genial and amenable as Johnston himself. The loss of Watson was definitely a gift to Australia from the ironical gods, as will be understood from a later passage in this report. Compton, on full and happy wing, was brought down by one of the few dangerous balls bowled all day by any Australian not named Lindwall.

England 200 for 2; England 301 for 5, and no batsman to come whose grasp does not most times exceed his reach.

ANYBODY'S GAME

Australia's second innings began with the game anybody's, swaying in a void. Pandemonium broke out when Hassett, beaten by Statham's speed, was caught at the wicket. Statham proceeded to hit Miller on the thigh and Miller hurled his bat yards away, a gesture supposedly of injured pride and annoyance, or of sheer devilment. He had obviously been sent in earlier than usual to keep Harvey from the dreaded new ball.

The sun streamed on the field, and the heat of it, we could easily imagine, was going into the battle. Bedser and Statham strained to force home the sudden advantage gained by the capture of Hassett's wicket, and Morris and Miller were equally strained. The boundary, near enough to the wicket this morning, was receding to a horizon. Miller put foolishness aside, watched the ball, played straight and sometimes forward with his own spasmodic lunge which it is hard to reconcile to his main air of panache. Morris pulled Statham to the mound stand grandly and ponderously; he suffered no indecision against Bedser and, all in all, there was menace for England in his smooth rhythm and latent power. A truly handsome straight drive off Bailey from the back foot told us the mood Miller was in at this crucial point; it was thoroughly controlled, but savage.

An old pessimist in the pavilion, a bishop maybe, said: 'Confound these Australians; they always fight their way out of a corner.' They were palpably in a corner at one o'clock today.

A magnificent pull for six from Wardle, Miller again, fell in the grandstand crowd, another proof of the superbly proportioned aggression and determination that are the sign of Miller at his best. At six o'clock Bedser tried his hand again; a wicket by England was a terribly urgent need, and a snick by Miller from him gave the crowd convulsions.

As the afternoon ached to the end, everybody tense and fearful, the typewriters clicking in the press box, with the unemotional agility of those who work them, a thrush sang somewhere in a garden overlooking Lord's. Miller's innings reached 50 at ten minutes past six and it was an innings that he and all of us could be proud of, for it proved his essential class and quality of nerve. All in all, it was a day much more pleasing to Australians than to us.

THE ATTACK ON HUTTON

At the beginning of the morning, in cooler weather, the air and atmosphere were more helpful to swing bowling than yesterday, but it was Lindwall's fourth delivery with the old ball that bowled Graveney, a yorker to the base of the stumps; Graveney's bat just touched it and he made a rather lazy stroke.

The new ball was taken as soon as Compton arrived at the wicket. Hutton sliced through the slips from Lindwall an involuntary four, then survived an appeal for a catch at the wicket (which is nearly more than I did). The downfall of Hutton at this point would, we all knew, be a disaster to England perhaps beyond power of remedy. The Australian fast attack strove desperately and spectacularly to remove him while the ball was shiny. Miller knocked his bat out of his hands, then sent him an incipient bumper, Miller gave the impression of a determined slinger rather than of a great fast bowler; an atrocious long hop, supposedly a quick leg break, was hit with proper contempt by Compton for four. But Compton needed to snick luckily and apprehensively at the sixth ball of Lindwall's first over. At noon tremendous cheering announced that Hutton, with a leg glance for four from Lindwall, had reached his century.

And suddenly the temperature of the match, and the temperature of the Australian bowling fell several degrees: Lindwall went out of action, and Johnston took his place at the nursery end, while Ring superseded (and I use the word advisedly and pointedly) at the other end.

The onslaught of Lindwall and Miller had been vehement but not always technically exacting. Too much short stuff to the off was banged down. I have seldom, if ever, before known an Australian attack which could be changed by good batsmen with a blunt instrument as quickly as this one at Hassett's command. Hassett, in fact, often needs to turn to Lindwall for the accuracy which usually is the only means by which stock bowlers keep their jobs and earn their livings. Compton hit another long hop, this time from Johnston, to the leg boundary; his innings began to emerge from the chrysalis.

Meanwhile all eyes were on Hutton at his most coolly masterful, with rare skill he safely coped with the one or two awkward balls from Miller which rose sharply hip high with intent to provide the adjacent leg fielders with catches. A noble sweeping pull by

England's captain actually lent dignity to a long-hop from Ring, a ball that had reason to be ashamed of itself until the great stroke had sent it to the boundary. Ring usually bowled a long hop or a full toss every over; good batsmen would have scored freely from him on a pitch as dusty as a country road.

THE FALL OF HUTTON

Miller tried his improvisations from the nursery end, and he at once beat Hutton, then seemed to appeal for leg before, or maybe he had recognized an acquaintance in the crowd. In the same over Hutton drove to the off and forced square with his wrists, strokes fit for McLaren and the cricketer's Parthenon. Both Hutton and Compton batted easefully and with pleasure; strokes sped over the field at will, roared home all the way. The Australian fielding was quick individually; but I could discern little sign of a policy in Hassett's control, either offensive or defensive, once the new ball waned. Of course, he could not be held responsible for bowling of irregular length.

The fall of Hutton, just before lunch, came like some arbitrary interference from the outside of visible events. A ball from Johnston lifted a little, and Hutton propelled it to forward short leg, where Hole seized the catch acrobatically as though not daring to drop it for dear life.

Between half-past eleven and lunch England scored 110, and the score now was beautifully and provokingly poised at 287 for three.

Sheer mishap ended Watson's innings. He hit Johnston high to leg for four, and in the same over drove freely and missed his aim. Langley thrust his pads out to save byes, quite helpless to touch the ball it bounced from them to the stumps, with Watson's foot outside the crease. A sinfull visitation of bad luck to a very fine cricketer.

Compton, apart from a dangerous swing at a wide offside full length from Davidson, was thoroughly organized, making strokes with time to spare, so that he was free to enjoy them like, and with, the rest of us. Benaud caused a leg break to turn from time to time; and even as I am writing this sentence, a very pretty leg break from Benaud has found the edge of Compton's bat, and Compton is departing to the pavilion, caught at first slip.

Any expert and experienced leg spinner would often have aroused hope and anticipation in the breast of slip fieldsmen on the Lord's wicket since yesterday noon, even before then. Benaud, next over after his dismissal of Compton, nearly caught and bowled Bailey for nothing. I stated in my message of last evening that Benaud was Australia's most potential spinner for this occasion and this turf. Benaud beat Brown, another lovely spinner, whereat Brown drove Benaud to the on for four, to the off for four, and cut him late for four in one and the same over. Benaud's length was not steady, he has probably not been trusted enough to bowl at long intervals. The fact is that on the few occasions when he found the right spot on which to drop his spin, he looked likely to get somebody · out.

TOO BRIGHT TOO EARLY

Lindwall returned to attack, for Benaud, and immediately Brown was caught from him on the leg side. England 328 for six; the morning's rosy dawn paling Lindwall's next ball clean bowled Evans. And now, with England's tail here, the Australian fast bowlers once more released themselves, full fury. Miller assailed Wardle with the fastest and most accurate over he has unleashed this summer so far. Twice he missed the stumps only because there are three of them, not four.

But it was a slow ball which trapped Bailey, who seemingly struck it or his bat to his boot; for he did not leave the wicket promptly, and Miller, having held a return catch, threw up the ball, then after it had fallen to the grass, kicked it like a footballer practising 'shooting-in' at a goal.

Lindwall now bowled Bedser all the way, ninth out at 341, England five runs behind on the first innings—Heavens, suppose it had been in the second and last of the match!

A magnificent drive to the off from Miller by Wardle put England statistically ahead, and the crowd roared jubilantly, ringing imaginary bells. Let us hope and pray that on Tuesday they won't be wringing their hands. I am sadly disappointed at the breakdown in England's innings this afternoon, just as the Australian attack wore a confused complexion, and I fear for the team that takes the last innings on this uncertain, deceptive Lord's wicket.

Statham, in last, wouldn't promptly get out. The fast bowlers were relieved and the Australian attack resumed the aspect of striving mediocrity. Wardle thumped Johnston to the Tavern, then to show democratic breadth of mind to the stately pavilion, and generally entertained the crowd until comprehensively bowled, leaving Statham unbeaten, as 'Wisden' will record to generations yet unborn. It is possible that the Australians permitted a little licence to England's last wicket to deprive England's bowlers of two intervals for rest, between innings and tea.

AUSTRALIA

First Innings		Second Innings	
A. L. Hassett, c Bailey, b Bedser	104	c Evans, b Statham	3
A. R. Morris, st Evans, b Bedser	30	not out	35
R. N. Harvey, lbw, b Bedser	59		
K. R. Miller, b Wardle	25	not out	58
G. B. Hole, c Compton, b Wardle	13		
R. Benaud, lbw, b Wardle	0		
A. K. Davidson, c Statham, b Bedser	76		
D. Ring, lbw, b Wardle	18		
R. R. Lindwall, b Statham	9		
G. R. Langley, c Watson, b Bedser	1		
W. A. Johnston, not out	3		
Extras (b 4, lb 4)	8		
Total	346	Total (1 wkt)	96

FALL OF WICKETS
First Innings

1	2	3	4	5	6	7	8	9
65	190	225	229	240	280	291	330	331

BOWLING ANALYSIS
First Innings

	O.	M.	R.	W.		O.	M.	R.	W.
Bedser	42·4	8	105	5	Bailey	16	2	55	0
Statham	28	7	48	1	Wardle	29	8	77	4
Brown	25	7	53	0					

FALL OF WICKET
Second Innings

$$\frac{1}{3}$$

BOWLING ANALYSIS
Second Innings

	O.	M.	R.	W.		O.	M.	R.	W.
Bedser	11	2	27	0	Brown	5	2	14	0
Statham	9	3	17	1	Bailey	6	1	23	0
Wardle	10	4	15	0					

ENGLAND v. AUSTRALIA

ENGLAND

First Innings

L. Hutton, c Hole, b Johnston	145
D. Kenyon, c Davidson, b Lindwall	3
T. W. Graveney, b Lindwall	78
D. C. S. Compton, c Hole, b Benaud	57
W. Watson, st Langley, b Johnston	4
T. E. Bailey, c and b Miller	2
F. R. Brown, c Langley, b Lindwall	22
T. G. Evans, b Lindwall	0
J. H. Wardle, b Davidson	23
A. V. Bedser, b Lindwall	1
J. B. Statham, not out	17
Extras (b 11, lb 1, w 1, nb 7)	20
	—
Total	372

FALL OF WICKETS

1	2	3	4	5	6	7	8	9
9	177	279	291	301	328	328	332	341

BOWLING ANALYSIS

	O.	M.	R.	W.		O.	M.	R.	W.
Lindwall	23	4	66	5	Ring	14	2	43	0
Miller	25	6	57	1	Benaud	19	4	70	1
Johnston	35	11	91	2	Davidson	10·5	2	25	1

SECOND TEST (FOURTH DAY)

LORD'S, MONDAY

Today has again dithered this way and that.

At lunch England might have had no appetite at all, for Australia were 209 for two, Miller and Harvey undefeated. At tea, with seven Australians out for 305, England though 279 to the bad, could here indulge the optimism of reasonable sportsmen. By truly glorious and Herculean driving, Lindwall added an additional weight to England's task, so that as much of faith as rare skill, patience, nerve, and endurance would be needed to sustain it, even granted that all the fortune in the world at once came in support of the effort.

Lindwall, flushed with conquest having overwhelmed Kenyon as though as a matter of course, broke England's back by fairly and vividly defeating Hutton. Given a miracle tomorrow—or rain— England could save themselves. Nothing less than a miracle could achieve the rescue; and miracles come by faith more than by skill or even good words.

SOFT THE ZEPHYR

When the fourth day began with a soft wind blowing in the blue
sky the situation of the match was exquisitely balanced; and the
crowd simmered nervously as they waited for the kettle to boil over.
Apparently the lid of the kettle was too loosely fixed; the steam could
get out and evaporate without risk of any Australian's getting scalded.

I have seldom before seen an attack as torpid and amiable as this
of England's in a crucial moment at the beginning of a day. The
game, and perhaps the rubber, might depend on the happenings of
the first half-hour: a quick dismissal of Morris and Miller would
swing the advantage the way of England once more. I prepared
myself for a passionate onslaught by Bedser and Statham.

But Brown, Statham, and Wardle bowled while Morris and Miller
settled down again on the leisurely couch of confidence they were
obliged to remove themselves from on Saturday evening. The England field was set pretty as a picture; the green sward was decora-
tively dotted by men in nice white flannels as though to tell the
crowd that they were really watching a pleasant cricket match in
June weather with the fielders arranged so as to keep the pattern of
appearances balanced and idyllic. No nasty, avaricious clutching
hands congested at the wicket disturbed the general equanimity.

Statham was quickly taken off for Wardle at the Pavilion end:
Bedser was not asked to go into action until the new ball was
available at a quarter to one. He then bowled four overs before lunch;
indeed, he bowled only these four overs in the first two hours of a
morning on which a Test match hung in a balance. Morris played
comfortable cricket and scored 53 in 45 minutes, while Miller scored
seven.

MILLER BEING GOOD

Miller disciplined himself in a way that I found as amusing as
admirable. He was like a naughty boy mightily pleased at his own
good behaviour. He combined in proportion his upright back foot
defensive and his far-reaching and not always elegant, forward
pushes. On the whole though, he looked now an organized batsman,
with as much of skill at his command as glamour. Morris, seemingly
assured of his century, gave the semblance of a chance to Hutton at
slip off Wardle. Morris was then 82; and a few moments later the
Australian innings was visited by the 'accident', or good fortune, for
which the England quietist policy had obviously, or not obviously,
been waiting.

Hutton put Compton on to try his spin at last, and Morris pulled him round to leg rather square, where Statham ran like a student of butterflies and marvellously overtook the ball and held it, though turning a somersault. Harvey, after being persuaded into a swift low glance off Bedser, a stroke which short leg nearly caught at the risk of a wounded hand, had the satisfaction of seeing Bedser retire to his sweater, and of seeing Wardle wheel his left arm again with the new ball.

At lunch Australia were 209 for two, Miller not out 93, and he had so far been on view in this innings for nearly four and a half hours, always good to watch and fascinating as much for what he suggested he was thinking of it all as for the highly principled batsmanship he showed to us. A short-armed forcing stroke to the on, from a really fine ball of Bedser—new ball at that—was in itself the sign of a cricketer richly gifted. Harvey could not discover touch yet again, and Bedser clean bowled him not long after lunch and after Miller had scored his century, his first in a Test match at Lord's of recognized and historical status.

JUST A CHANCE

Australia were 201 in front at the fall of Harvey's wicket, the third down. There was just a bare chance left for England, some will o' the wisp of hope—if Bedser or somebody else could rapidly crash through the supposedly dubious middle part of Australia's batting represented by Hole, Benaud, and others. Miller, he gave us to understand, was not for once in a way ready to risk a gambling throw; his innings was a very reformation of cricket, until at ten minutes to three he played out at Wardle, and was beaten and bowled, whereupon he picked up the bails, tossed them back to Evans, and departed, cheered out of sight by an admiring but relieved multitude. Miller's innings lasted some five hours: style and vivacity of temperament in slow motion, so to say.

Wardle lured Benaud forward and nearly had him stumped immediately. The match went into an unrelated key, from flat to sharp. The England attack revived when fortune's breeze veered a little; or like poor relations who look up in the world after coming into an unexpected legacy, the bowlers were persuaded by some success to take heed of respectable appearances.

Wardle pitched a clever length hereabout, and both Hole and Benaud lunged rather myopically forward. A poor stroke by Benaud, a catch to the on near the umpire off Bedser, accounted for Benaud, who though naturally gifted is not yet a Test match batsman by a long way. I fancy that the boy Craig would learn more, and advance quicker, than any of the young aspirants of the present Australian team.

BACK IN THE GAME

With five of the opposition out of the way for 248, England after all were back in the game; a state of affairs which supports the view that England's attack before lunch should have been far more determined and purposeful than it was. Davidson joined Hole, and we could be pretty sure that a good stand by them must settle the decision for good and all to an issue bound to suffer illogical fluctuations, for the reason that so few of the contestants were masterful enough to control, or reinsure against, the hazardous ups and downs of much embarrassing mediocrity.

Without a hint of impregnability Hole and Davidson played resolute cricket, and whenever a short ball came along they struck it well and hard, adding 48 priceless runs. Then, as the match was slipping from England's grasp irretrievably, a slower ball enticed Davidson to reach forward, whereupon Brown raised himself in the air and held a return catch. As I wrote the other day, England's bowlers should aim persistently at drawing all Australian batsmen from the back foot. There is not a bowler in English cricket today who is fast enough to pitch short to them.

The fall of Australian wickets after lunch stirred the crowd to huge delight, but an old pessimist on the pavilion, not a bishop this time, only a dean, said that the sooner Australia got out the more time would be left for them in which to win.

Hole, who was out to Brown just on tea, batted with the too much flushed complexion of young cricket that is not destined for a long innings, yet he made several hits worthy of Lord's and the radiant afternoon. And five minutes after tea Brown defeated Ring, whose innings, in contrast to Hole's, began in old age advancing to decrepitude.

I did not entirely enjoy seeing Brown and Wardle turning the ball now, even if the pace of the pitch was not quick. In fifteen balls Brown took three wickets for 8. This morning he had lumbered along, rolling his arm as industriously as hopefully. Lindwall drove Wardle for four high to the pavilion eluding straight deep, swung him for six on the on, and pulled him for four in the same over; he is a dangerous and quite beautiful driver who would rather score a century any day than take six wickets. England batsmen might possibly share this preference. He cut Wardle stylishly for four and by this time Wardle's feet must have felt numb and tired; for he had bowled and bowled nearly the day through.

In these days it seems quick bowlers are of little use on hard wickets except while the ball is new; once on a time the hotter the weather the more fast bowlers were seen in hot and ravenous action. The art and science of the game would enjoy a fresh lease if a new ball were available according to custom in MacLaren and Grace's period only at the beginning of an innings.

Lindwall smote Bedser for six into the Mound stand, a mighty and confident blow; his hitting, while Langley stopped the few balls he was called on to cope with, was responsible for the ninth-wicket stand of 54 in less than half an hour, a typical Australian rally of last-minute defiance and disdain, as much as though Lindwall were saying to us, 'Now win if you can.' He reached 50 in less than three-quarters of an hour, and there was judgment as well as physical power in his innings, which may well be estimated by Australia at twice its present score-book value.

MERCILESS AND EXULTANT

Not Miller, but Johnston bowled when England at twenty-five minutes to six began the long climb. But Lindwall, as though stimulated and not at all exhausted by his batting, attacked like a hound fresh from the leash, and soon removed the unfortunate and out-classed Kenyon, who lobbed an easy catch to the on side; then a few minutes afterwards Lindwall sent his most brilliant late out-swinger of lovely length to Hutton, not short but imperiously demanding a stroke as counter. Hutton had no choice but to play the ball, which found the bat's edge, whence it flashed to Hole. And Hole gripped a lightning catch in a way that was a compliment both to Lindwall and to Hutton.

Next, almost before Hutton could have unbuckled his pads, Langley avidly caught Graveney amid such a cluster of close fieldsmen, and to the accompaniment of so triumphant a noise from them, that Graveney seemed at a loss, and waited for the umpire's sentence. The Australians exulted greatly in the way I have known, and dreaded, boy and man, a lifetime. When Hutton got out, Lindwall ran down the wicket clapping hands, clearly having the afternoon of his life.

By dint of struggle and stress, Compton and Watson staved away for a while a terrible load of impending trouble; and the crowd went away quiet as lambs.

AUSTRALIA

First Innings		Second Innings	
A. L. Hassett, c Bailey, b Bedser	104	c Evans, b Statham	3
A. R. Morris, st Evans, b Bedser	30	c Statham, b Compton	89
R. N. Harvey, lbw, b Bedser	59	b Bedser	21
K. R. Miller, b Wardle	25	b Wardle	109
G. B. Hole, c Compton, b Wardle	13	lbw, b Brown	47
R. Benaud, lbw, b Wardle	0	c Graveney, b Bedser	5
A. K. Davidson, c Statham, b Bedser	76	c and b Brown	15
D. Ring, lbw, b Wardle	18	lbw, b Brown	7
R. R. Lindwall, b Statham	9	b Bedser	50
G. R. Langley, c Watson, b Bedser	1	b Brown	9
W. A. Johnston, not out	3	not out	0
Extras (b 4, lb 4)	8	Extras (b 8, lb 5)	13
Total	346	Total	368

FALL OF WICKETS

First Innings

1	2	3	4	5	6	7	8	9
65	190	225	229	240	280	291	330	331

BOWLING ANALYSIS

First Innings

	O.	M.	R.	W.		O.	M.	R.	W.
Bedser	42·4	8	105	5	Bailey	16	2	55	0
Statham	28	7	48	1	Wardle	29	8	77	4
Brown	25	7	53	0					

FALL OF WICKETS

Second Innings

1	2	3	4	5	6	7	8	9
3	168	227	235	248	296	305	308	362

BOWLING ANALYSIS

Second Innings

	O.	M.	R.	W.		O.	M.	R.	W.
Bedser	31·5	8	77	3	Brown	27	4	82	4
Statham	15	3	40	1	Bailey	10	4	24	0
Wardle	46	18	111	1	Compton	3	0	21	1

ENGLAND v. AUSTRALIA
ENGLAND

First Innings		Second Innings	
L. Hutton, c Hole, b Johnston	145	c Hole, b Lindwall	5
D. Kenyon, c Davidson, b Lindwall	3	c Hassett, b Lindwall	2
T. W. Graveney, b Lindwall	78	c Langley, b Johnston	2
D. C. S. Compton, c Hole, b Benaud	57	not out	5
W. Watson, st Langley, b Johnston	4	not out	3
T. E. Bailey, c and b Miller	2		
F. R. Brown, c Langley, b Lindwall	22		
T. G. Evans, b Lindwall	0		
J. W. Wardle, b Davidson	23		
A. V. Bedser, b Lindwall	1		
J. B. Statham, not out	17		
Extras (b 11, lb 1, w 1, nb 7)	20	Extras (w 1, nb 2)	3
Total	372	Total (3 wkts)	20

FALL OF WICKETS

First Innings

1	2	3	4	5	6	7	8	9
9	177	279	291	301	328	328	332	341

BOWLING ANALYSIS

First Innings

	O.	M.	R.	W.		O.	M.	R.	W.
Lindwall	23	4	66	5	Ring	14	2	43	0
Miller	25	6	57	1	Benaud	19	4	70	1
Johnston	35	11	91	2	Davidson	10.5	2	25	1

FALL OF WICKETS

Second Innings

1	2	3
6	10	12

BOWLING ANALYSIS

Second Innings

	O.	M.	R.	W.		O.	M.	R.	W.
Lindwall	5	1	7	2	Ring	3	1	2	0
Johnston	4	1	6	1	Miller	2	1	2	0

To bat: Bailey, Brown, Evans, Wardle, Bedser, Statham.

SECOND TEST (FIFTH DAY)

LORD'S, TUESDAY

In a terrific closing period this evening there was still a chance for Australia to win. As six o'clock approached a heroic match-saving stand by Watson and Bailey was broken. Soon after this mishap to England Bailey got out. Now, with less than half an hour to pass, Australia strove to capture four wickets. England 246 for six.

Panic gibbered on the ground when Evans was nearly stumped off Benaud. Brown sent the temperature to fever point by massive hell-for-leather drives, powerful and ponderous and brave. Evans stood his ground impertinently, aggressively. So all the alarums died away in the evening's lovely mellowing sunshine.

It had been an afternoon of intense strain. We could suffer no further tug on the nerves when Brown was out after 25 minutes past six, except to feel he should have survived, because plainly he wanted to stay in the fight to the last.

The result, I think, did justice to both teams; neither quite deserved to win, and Watson's and Bailey's stand was not made of the stuff of which lost causes are compounded. It was a stand of noble martyrdom, and at the end it was the martyrs who each had been crowned with a laurel wreath.

A MOST UNCONSCIONABLE TIME

The cricket before lunch was rather limp and indecisive and the quiet, attenuated crowd sat and waited for the end. Even the Australians seemed to be waiting, with all the rest of us. I was reminded of Jowett of Balliol on his death-bed. In the ante-room, a distinguished company was silently gathered together, resigned yet hoping. And towards midnight Jowett, who had been comatose—like this match this morning—wearily raised himself from his pillow and, turning to his nurse, said: 'Please tell those dear, kind people outside that I don't think I am going to do anything tonight.' He lived several hours longer, and the dear, kind people outside were at liberty politely to go home to bed. Likewise before lunch today we were free not unnecessarily to agitate ourselves.

Lindwall began bowling from the Nursery end at half-past eleven; compared with the Lindwall of Monday evening he could be likened to a volcano which having erupted was content to sleep a while. And just as villagers dwelling on mountain sides settle down again as soon as the lava has subsided, so did the England innings begin building itself up again.

Johnston, with left-arm swinging material, contributed to relaying the basement floor. No casual uninformed visitor to Lord's would have suspected that the Australians were actively engaged in winning the match. On the contrary, the bowlers might well have been a gang of slave labourers pressed into England's service, 'navvies', hod-carriers, all toilers under the sun.

The wicket was willing to collaborate, definitely if not hurriedly, with spin. When Ring came on his second ball was hit to leg by Watson, a long hop which would have made Grimmet shudder. Compton obtained three fours in a single over from Benaud, whose efforts at leg spin cost him 22 runs in eighteen balls. Poorer spin than Ring's can never before have been seen in a Test match. Ring apparently had no 'googly' for left-handed Watson, who, diffident and hedged round by mortality last evening, was now assured and upright, if occasionally still uncertain of the exact place in his bat of the blade's middle. Compton batted without an obvious worry, though, of course, the game's situation persuaded him into a care and charity which he would not have and could not have exercised against bowling of this amiable kind a few years ago.

In little more than an hour 53 runs rippled over the field, like background-music at a funeral service. Johnston crossed over to the Nursery (or Pigeons') end, and without fair warning, perhaps because he himself had not received due notice, a quicker ball from him kept a little low, trapping Compton leg before wicket. England 73 for four, as surely doomed in this match as could be said of any team in a world so ruled by uncertainty as that of cricket.

REVIVER FOR THE RELATIONS

Even so grave a relapse as this in the England innings did no obviously enliven the Australians, whom we could at this point think of only as a number of expectant relations affecting sympathy as the end apparently drew near, and also affecting to have no interest in the will and the bequests. True, Miller tried offspin, low-armed speed, and other devices presumably hostile. But Bailey and Watson remained undisturbedly in possession at lunch. England 114 for four: Watson an admirable 54, Bailey an obstinate ten which threatened to become as much a nuisance to Australia as a certain other and recent innings by him. He played forward, head down, with eyes peering like a man looking downstairs, searchingly but determinedly, for a burglar.

Oxygen, in the shape of the new ball, was administered at three o'clock, not to the allegedly expiring England innings but to the so-far frustrated Australian body-snatchers.

England here were 140 for four, with rather less than three and a quarter hours left for play. Watson, sound sometimes as a rock and truly straight of bat, with strong pulled drives for short stuff, was playing so coolly that it was beginning to be possible to encourage hope in our breasts that England might after all save themselves, for Bailey continued to defend in spite of a blow on the hand or arm from Lindwall. Watson naturally found Lindwall's pace disturbing to his poise and touch, yet he resolutely withstood the new ball's first fusillade, so that expectancy seemed ready to wait on our hope that England really would achieve a draw.

Miller sent a 'bumper' at Watson, who made the proper or fashionable genuflexion. And he nearly had Watson caught at the wicket when Watson was 74 at twenty-five minutes past three; but fortunately Watson missed his aim on the off side.

HASSETT GROWS IMPATIENT

At twenty minutes to four Lindwall went out of action; the only question which tormented me now was what he would be able to recapture of his true fire after tea. But Watson and Bailey, in spite of recurrent vicissitudes, seldom suggested a fatal error; and Australia's reserve bowling was palpably dependent on good luck and a batsman's miscalculation. Ten minutes before tea Lindwall was called back; clearly Hassett was getting troubled and unusually impatient.

A curious fact about Watson's batting was that he played the good balls with more certainty than he played the amorphous spin and slower stuff of the day. At tea Watson and Bailey remained obdurate and not out: England 183 for four.

It would be a poor compliment to Watson and Bailey to say that they batted better than the Australians bowled for the Australian bowling woefully lacked resource. This gallant stand really called for an ethical as much as a technical evaluation. It was a triumph of character, all the more to be extolled, because recently the middle part of an England innings has hinted of weakness of fibre and of skill alike.

As the day spent itself and the Australian attack came to wear a more and more debilitated look, some of us even wondered if a more realistic scrutiny of the Australian attack might not have encouraged England's batsmen to go all out for victory after lunch. But to say this much is perhaps to fall into sentimental idealism.

LAURELS

Watson was nearly caught near the wicket on Monday, and from time to time he missed his aim and more than once approached near to error. None the less, his cricket was always pleasing to the expert eye, while the essential stuff of it was of the soil of Yorkshire. He deserved to prevail, if only as recompense for his shabby fortune on Saturday.

Bailey, not less than Watson, must have this tribute. Frankly the sight of Bailey coming to bat for England fourth wicket down is not stimulating to pride or confidence; today his duty was to persist, to survive whether fit or not. By patience, a cricketer's instinct, and any amount of ability with a straight bat he won through not only the ordeal of his four hours' innings but to a permanent page in large print in the annals of games between England and Australia.

Just after five o'clock Watson brought hearts to many mouths by a sliced stroke from Davidson to the slips, providentially it went to ground well in front of the fieldsman, and indeed scarcely left it. To say the truth I was surprised that any ball bowled now could root out human fallibility in either Watson or Bailey. Inexplicably Lindwall did not go into action after tea. With an hour and a quarter to go, and six wickets to take, Australia needed to work much harder to win than England to escape. In fact, my impression all day has been of an exact and severe division of labour, very hard labour.

REMORSE

Bailey reached fifty in three hours 40 minutes, and Watson reached his century in five hours and a half. Then, at ten minutes to six, Watson gently but fatally touched a leg break to the slips and the four hours' vigil was over, with even yet time for Australia to snatch the prize. What a see-saw of a game, defying augury, upsetting the press box, where pages of copy had to be torn up and thrown away, especially as Bailey, just on six o'clock, drove mistakenly and, as he realized he was out, threw his head back, put a hand to his brow, the living image of remorse and self-disgust.

At the end of the match the thought occurred to me that the occasion's obsequies should really have been prepared not for England but for the Lord's wicket. It certainly 'did nothing' today; at any rate, the Australian bowlers had no power over it, in life or in death.

AUSTRALIA

First Innings		Second Innings	
A. L. Hassett, c Bailey, b Bedser	104	c Evans, b Statham	3
A. R. Morris, st Evans, b Bedser	30	c Statham, b Compton	89
R. N. Harvey, lbw, b Bedser	59	b Bedser	21
K. R. Miller, b Wardle	25	b Wardle	109
G. B. Hole, c Compton, b Wardle	13	lbw, b Brown	47
R. Benaud, lbw, b Wardle	0	c Graveney, b Bedser	5
A. K. Davidson, c Statham, b Bedser	76	c and b Brown	15
D. T. Ring, lbw, b Wardle	18	lbw, b Brown	7
R. R. Lindwall, b Statham	9	b Bedser	50
G. R. Langley, c Watson, b Bedser	1	b Brown	9
W. A. Johnston, not out	3	not out	0
Extras (b 4, lb 4)	8	Extras (b 8, lb 5)	13
Total	346		368

FALL OF WICKETS
First Innings

1	2	3	4	5	6	7	8	9
65	190	225	229	240	280	291	330	331

BOWLING ANALYSIS
First Innings

	O.	M.	R.	W.		O.	M.	R.	W.
Bedser	42·4	8	105	5	Bailey	16	2	55	0
Statham	28	7	48	1	Wardle	29	8	77	4
Brown	25	7	53	0					

FALL OF WICKETS
Second Innings

1	2	3	4	5	6	7	8	9
3	168	227	235	248	296	305	308	362

BOWLING ANALYSIS
Second Innings

	O.	M.	R.	W.		O.	M.	R.	W.
Bedser	31·5	8	77	3	Brown	27	4	82	4
Statham	15	3	40	1	Bailey	10	4	24	0
Wardle	46	18	111	1	Compton	3	0	21	1

ENGLAND v. AUSTRALIA
ENGLAND

First Innings		Second Innings	
L. Hutton, c Hole, b Johnston	145	c Hole, b Lindwall	5
D. Kenyon, c Davidson, b Lindwall	3	c Hassett, b Lindwall	2
T. W. Graveney, b Lindwall	78	c Langley, b Johnston	2
D. C. S. Compton, c Hole, b Benaud	57	lbw, b Johnston	33
W. Watson, st Langley, b Johnston	4	c Hole, b Ring	109
T. E. Bailey, c and b Miller	2	c Benaud, b Ring	71
F. R. Brown, c Langley, b Lindwall	22	c Hole, b Benaud	28
T. G. Evans, b Lindwall	0	not out	11
J. W. Wardle, b Davidson	23	not out	0
A. V. Bedser, b Lindwall	1		
J. B. Statham, not out	17		
Extras (b 11, lb 1, w 1, nb 7)	20	Extras (b 7, lb 6, w 2, nb 6)	21
Total	372	Total (7 wkts)	282

Did not bat: Bedser, Statham.

FALL OF WICKETS
First Innings

1	2	3	4	5	6	7	8	9
9	177	279	291	301	328	328	332	341

BOWLING ANALYSIS
First Innings

	O.	M.	R.	W.		O.	M.	R.	W.
Lindwall	23	4	66	5	Ring	14	2	43	0
Miller	25	6	57	1	Benaud	19	4	70	1
Johnston	35	11	91	2	Davidson	10·5	2	25	1

FALL OF WICKETS
Second Innings

1	2	3	4	5	6	7
6	10	12	73	236	246	282

BOWLING ANALYSIS
Second Innings

	O.	M.	R.	W.		O.	M.	R.	W.
Lindwall	19	3	26	2	Benaud	17	6	51	1
Johnston	29	10	70	2	Davidson	14	5	13	0
Ring	29	5	84	2	Hole	1	1	0	0
Miller	17	8	17	0					

Umpires: F. S. Lee and H. G. Baldwin.

ENGLAND *v.* AUSTRALIA

THIRD TEST (FIRST DAY)

AFTER the sunshine of Lord's we sat down today by the waters of Old Trafford and waited for cricket until a quarter to three. By the end of the day England had been unable to press home advantage quickly won.

A crippled attack to begin with was handicapped by injury or strain to Laker. To omit Trueman from the side seemed an invitation to trouble; for though Bailey is immensely willing and more than useful he scarcely fills the part of an England fast bowler, or controls a new ball with the accuracy which is a guarantee against wastefulness. Australia lost the wickets of Morris, Miller, and Hassett for 48 and the retrieving stand of Harvey and Hole did not begin so solidly that adequate reserves of England's bowling might not soon have found a weak spot in the defences.

Within a brief space of half an hour from the start of play, not to take a larger span of time as an example, I saw more second-class cricket than I have ever seen before in a Test match. Excepting Bedser, and a late cut and a late leg-glance by Hassett, both from Bedser, we might easily have been looking at any ordinary county game between Leicestershire and Northamptonshire; indeed the stroke-play of an Oldfield or the spin of a Tribe would surely have elevated the style and individuality of this occasion.

Morris played back while moving vaguely on his feet to a length ball from Bedser, and though he played on he deserved no other fate because he didn't, with his experience of Bedser behind him, go forward. Bedser with a strong wind encouraging him mentally—for no wind from any quarter of the compass could actually propel his vast frame—pitched the accurate length we expect from an England bowler; but it is an interesting fact that we don't particularly extol or mark out from average performance a pianist, say, merely if he plays the right notes.

MOIST AND LOVELY

The wicket was easy on the whole for batsmen accustomed to turf containing a little moisture; but the Australian batsmen seem to become psychologically affected nowadays if a cricket pitch is not as dry as Sahara without an oasis.

Hassett, after at least hinting of breeding, was bowled with his side's total 48, driving across good length from Bailey; and with no runs added, Miller struck or deflected a low ball from Bedser into his stumps. Bedser, by the way, had changed over to the Manchester end of the ground, with its grass so green that much more aesthetic pleasure was to be had from contemplating it than from a critical view of what was taking place on its historic surface.

Harvey, as soon as he came in, drove Bailey brilliantly near cover for four, flicked recklessly at a ball from Bailey rather too high for cutting, then might have been caught at the wicket off Bailey, again slashing by pure reflex-action at Bailey, who for all his ardour, is not as fast as Lockwood or even Lindwall.

The batting lacked tenacity of purpose and concentration. It was neither masterfully offensive in the Trumper-McCabe way, nor relentlessly watchful in the Noble, Collins, Woodful way. And, needless to add, it was not supremely resourceful in the Bradman way. Not only Bedser's attack but Bailey's, also, caused these Australians to go through physical adjustments which must have been as uncomfortable to themselves, as they were undignified to the eye of the discerning spectator. Hassett nearly fell over as he tried to cope with Bedser.

Hole cut Bedser late to the boundary, and Harvey, with a leg glance, brought into the afternoon some gleam of unusual personal fascination. All in all, when the tea interval arrived and Australia's score was 81 for three, we had witnessed nothing worth a man's while to write about. If the match at Lord's called for the cadence of Latimer, today's play, so far, had asked only for the succinct accurate prose of Bradshaw.

Criticism should seek reasons for its grievances, and always remember that it springs from Christian charity. The conditions this afternoon were not entirely after a batsman's heart. The new ball swung in the wind and came from the ground at different levels. But a Drobny or a Sedgman is expected to have a stylish and distinguished reply or counter to a tennis ball hit back to him and rising at swiftly changing angles. No ball today reared abruptly near the breast bone as years ago at Old Trafford. Cotter's great pace threatened the breast bone, not to say the cranium, of my hero R. H. Spooner, who when I was a boy scored a lovely fifty at Old Trafford in his first Test match against Australia.

After tea Laker, strapped up to alleviate his physical disability, stopped a drive off Harvey smartly at cover, a position in the field which once on a time demanded the swift diving agility of Hobbs, Andrews, and Spooner.

A TEA CHANGE

The Australian innings began at last to assume a planned shape; improvisation gave way to selection and deliberate ball-by-ball treatment, head down, with the bat reasonably sure of the whereabouts of its centre. What happened at tea, and what was put into it, I do not know; but now the cricket of both Harvey and Hole hinted of growing assurance and improving eyesight. Even yet Hole missed his aim at an off-side ball from Wardle in a dangerous manner which, if he had been, say, Ponsford or any other qualified Test player, might have occasioned some rising of eyebrows among connoisseur onlookers.

A shower of rain dispersed the cricketers just after five o'clock, whereat they were roundly abused by a spectator near the pavilion with his umbrella capaciously and obstructively up. All things considered the crowd was excellent in numbers and of exemplary patience and good nature. But there was little sense of an event, little or no atmosphere. When Australia's first wicket fell the applause sounded as tentative as that which is heard between movements at the performance of a new string quartet.

At twenty minutes past five, when the players returned to the field, sawdust was needed, and amid cheers a man with a bag emerged into the glare of publicity, and inadvertently emptied nearly the whole of it on the grass, an incident which cheered us all immensely.

A four from the edge of Harvey's bat off Bailey reminded us that we were still watching batsmen in whom technique has not yet run ahead of ordinary human fallibility. In the same over Harvey missed aim by such a margin that error couldn't get a look in. In England, at any rate, Harvey frequently seems to me a beautiful stroke player rather than a thoroughly organized and truly great batsman. A round of applause recognized the merits of a sustained and useful spell of bowling by Bailey; but the England attack, with Laker back again in the pavilion, was obviously short of resource.

REALITY OF GHOSTS

Trueman fielded for Laker on an afternoon very much like the occasion at Old Trafford half a century and more ago when Lockwood went on for the first time in the day to bowl fast on a drying ground, and sent the Australian innings crashing after Trumper had scored a century before lunch. The sky was the same, the alternations of cloud and sunshine the same. In the changeful light, ghosts could be seen, less spectral than the present living reality. A lovely easy straight drive by Harvey, off Wardle, caused this vision more and more to mingle with actuality; for Harvey can show us strokes which have the gleam of considerable ancient courtliness and charm. Hole's innings gradually settled down to a technical stability not recently a characteristic of his batting.

Another rainstorm broke the game's lame rhythm after six o'clock, and with not more than a quarter of an hour remaining the players returned to sounds from the crowd suspiciously ironical. Possibly for tactical reasons nobody really wanted to begin again at this time of day; the England bowlers would not relish the wet ball and no batsman enjoys taking guard afresh in an evening's declining, irretrievable minutes. The crowd, of course, does not go to cricket to consider moves of policy; they go, even to Test matches, for fun, but at Lord's the other day they found fun in abundance—which is more, possibly, than they did today.

Except for some hits by Harvey I saw no cricket at all; but I shall try to remember whether I am mistaken the moment I have done my duty and finished this report.

AUSTRALIA
First Innings

A. L. Hassett, b Bailey	26
A. R. Morris, b Bedser	1
K. R. Miller, b Bedser	17
R. N. Harvey, not out	60
G. B. Hole, not out	41
Extras (b 4, lb 1, nb 1)	6
	—
Total (3 wickets)	151

To bat: de Courcy, Davidson, Archer, Lindwall, Hill, Langley.

FALL OF WICKETS

1	2	3
15	48	48

BOWLING ANALYSIS

	O.	M.	R.	W.		O.	M.	R.	W.
Bedser	18	3	44	2	Wardle	14	4	42	0
Bailey	20	3	59	1					

ENGLAND: Hutton, Edrich, Graveney, Compton, Watson, Simpson, Bailey, Evans, Laker, Wardle, Bedser.

THIRD TEST (SECOND DAY)

OLD TRAFFORD, FRIDAY

Less than an hour and a half's cricket was possible at Old Trafford today and Australia added 70 runs to their total without further loss. Harvey's share was 45 and Hole's 25.

The rain showers postponed procedure until noon and then from the Olympian height of the press box we could look down on the green field and admire Hutton's far-flung battle line. A long-leg and a distant third-man protected the boundary against Harvey facing Bailey, who bowled with only one slip, a deepish mid-on, and two short-legs. For Hole, as he faced Bedser, a closer net was cast; but when Laker came on for Bailey only one slip and two short-legs stood within conversational range of Hole. Moreover Laker went into action over the wicket. All of which manifestations told us that Hutton was taking a realistic, not to say truthful, view of the soft dead turf and would not presume to practice deception on the Australians.

LIKE CHASING SOAP

The moist ball must have felt as elusive, even in Laker's strong fingers, as soap on a wet bathroom sink; two fours were driven from him in one and the same over by Hole and Harvey. The opportunity before the Australians to score easy runs was golden—and nothing else was golden in the chill morning under a dirty sky.

Another rainstorm emptied the playing ground shortly after half past twelve, when Australia's score was 178 for three, Harvey 81 not out. The conditions really were not fit, even if they were legally deemed so, for the exhibition of Test match talents. As one who once was a bowler, I am inclined to think that a greasy ball is definitely an unfair handicap to any bowler; a lifeless pitch is burden enough to his existence. Once on a time bowlers coping with slippery leather were consoled to know for certain that sooner or later, after the ground had dried, they would be as free to spin as yesterday they were doomed to toil. Whether this Old Trafford wicket will develop 'stickiness', given dry weather, I cannot say. If it does, then I fancy Australia's position is already formidable.

A pretty ball by Laker thoroughly beat Hole when he was 49; it lifted enough to promise amusement to come, granted a clearing of the threatening heavens. Harvey and Hole batted competently, but Hole needed more than two hours and a half to reach 50. The Australian batting rather lacked imagination hereabout, while the

194

ball was not only hard to grip but old; and the new one merely round the corner. The crowd sat in damp silence; the match was apparently rudderless, drifting nowhere or somewhere, and, like Tennyson's tide, though moving, seemed asleep. The new ball, taken just before lunch, apparently lost its polish as quickly as a woman's cheek loses rouge.

A great on-drive by Harvey brought his score to 101 in some three and a quarter hours. This morning, up to the interval, Harvey and Hole added 63 in roughly eighty minutes, and could hardly have made less, all things considered. It had been entertaining to watch Edrich who so far in the match had scarcely touched a ball, but between overs borrowed it momentarily to keep in touch with affairs, so to say.

During the lunch period I heard one or two criticisms in the crowd so drastic that I was forced to the view that in the press box we are all of us so many gentlemanly amateurs. A man who might easily have been Al Read himself delivered judgment in no un-certain voice. He said Bailey's bowling was 'shocking'. That's what it was. 'Shocking.' And 'though Lancashire are bad enough, I say though Lancashire are bad enough this lot are worse. I say this lot are worse. They've got better captains in the Salvation Army. I say they've got better captains in the Salvation Army.' He was enjoying his grievances with immensely Lancastrian relish. He added, as though by an afterthought, that what they needed 'out there' was 'This feller Bradman', but did not tell us to whom he was referring as 'they'. I especially liked his allusion to 'this' fellow Bradman; not, mark you, 'that' fellow. I regarded it as a great compliment to Bradman's omnipresence even among later generations.

The weather prevented cricket from lunch until a quarter to four and sections of the crowd greeted the players with the kind of noise which once was reserved for the villain in the old melodramas. But really the villain of the piece in this match has been the rain. And possibly the rain will behave even more villainously at Old Trafford before we are much older, with the wicket a willing conspirator. In a poor light Harvey and Hole continued their stand; nobody I suppose, dared appeal against it. A brave man will be needed in this Test match to obstruct the progress of it if rain is not falling with a persistency that conforms to the general and broadminded view of what Manchester regards as a wet day.

In a quarter of an hour the cricketers were again driven to shelter. Their comings and goings, out of the pavilion and back again, recalled the processional recurrences and reappearances of the stage armies which in ancient plays would march past a backstage window, the same faces in the same places in the file.

This time the rain came down heavily, with Australia's score menacingly looming at 221 for three. Evans' missed catch from Harvey may well go down in history with Tate's tragic blunder on this same ground in the 1902 Test match. It was as easy a chance as any wicket-keeper could wish to see and receive; and already it has cost England at least a hundred runs. The ironical fact about England's fateful missed catches in the present rubber to date is that they have mainly been the consequences of mistakes of our most reliable fieldsmen.

As the Al Read character in the crowd remarked; cricket is a funny game. I say cricket is a funny game.

AUSTRALIA
First Innings

A. L. Hassett, b Bailey	26
A. R. Morris, b Bedser	1
K. R. Miller, b Bedser	17
R. N. Harvey, not out	105
G. B. Hole, not out	6
Extras (b 4, lb 1, nb 1)	66
	—
Total (3 wickets)	221

To bat: de Courcy, Davidson, Archer, Lindwall, Hill, Langley.

FALL OF WICKETS

1	2	3
15	48	48

BOWLING ANALYSIS

	O.	M.	R.	W.		O.	M.	R.	W.
Bedser	27	5	60	2	Wardle	19	5	53	0
Bailey	26	4	83	1	Laker	8	1	19	0

England: Hutton, Edrich, Graveney, Compton, Watson, Simpson, Bailey, Evans, Laker, Wardle, Bedser.

THIRD TEST (THIRD DAY)

OLD TRAFFORD, SATURDAY

In a day of commonplace cricket, poorly related to Test match quality, England sought to emerge from a situation which at one time threatened grave trouble; for during the morning nobody could be sure of the subsequent behaviour of the pitch. Fortunately a heavy roller and a drying wind quietened the turf's incipient awkwardness. Following a dubious start, England's innings found comfortable waters; Hutton and Compton played together with assurance and leisure, until once more and yet again in this rubber a single change in the wind sent England into difficult currents.

In the afternoon's last quarter of an hour Hutton and Compton lost their wickets to an attack which on the surface had gradually lost positive hope, and was waiting for something to turn up.

THE STAND BROKEN

From Bedser's first ball of the day, following a tentative maiden over to Harvey by Laker, Hole was caught by Evans. Thus Australia's fourth wicket, which added 173, fell at ten minutes past twelve, with the score 221. The stand persisted through variable weather for 204 minutes, Greenwich time. Hole got out to an excitable slash at a ball which rose quite vivaciously on the offside.

De Courcy began his innings with a congested stroke from Bedser over fine leg's head, a stroke probably enforced on him; then he drove a half-volley off Laker square and powerfully, and also he swung round to pull Laker and, missing aim entirely, no doubt experienced the sensations of a man who, with all his energy tries to thrust himself through a non-resisting door. The sort of stroke that makes a cricketer feel apologetic if not silly. Some lovely hits by Harvey alternated with one or two gauche slices of the sort Harvey seems liable to commit in his longest innings. He fell at last to a very good catch at the wicket on the leg side from Bedser. Harvey of course owed Evans a death, for he should have been caught by him when his score was merely 4.

Bedser obtained a vitality out of the earth that I doubt if Hutton really wished to know was in it; also Laker caused an off-break to uncoil and spit upward at Davidson, whose instinctive effort to cope with the ball might have, or should have, got him also caught at the wicket. The sight of an angular off-spinning ball obviously presented to De Courcy and to Davidson problems nearly beyond the scope of their knowledge to solve, problems as much, I gathered, metaphysical as geometrical. Laker was looking dangerous indeed when, presumably because of his injury, he was rested for Wardle at one o'clock. Australia round about 270 for four. Davidson was twice thumped on the hand by Bedser's enlivened attack, so that he needed to go to the pavilion for repairs. An agitated and intended on-drive against Bedser by De Courcy towered over the slips; another stroke not exactly straight out of Debrett.

So spitefully was the turf behaving now that Hutton no doubt was feeling apprehensive that Hassett might declare Australia's innings at an end. Davidson, in despair as another spinner from Laker hovered before him, 'let fly' so forcibly that when his bat clove vacant air he collapsed as though the earth's foundations had given way; he was stumped semi-recumbent. Archer and Lindwall succumbed to slip catches, one to the hands of Edrich, who at once looked at the object in his grasp as though a cricket ball were some sort of precious stone hard to come by nowadays. The attempts of Australia's batsmen to score quick runs were not convincing; their bowlers might, perhaps, have made much more use of the wicket than this. De Courcy's useful innings was mainly notable for what the old-time evolutionists would have called its survival value; his cricket today suggested that it had been born under a bar sinister. Australia's innings ended at ten minutes to three, when Edrich, at first slip, held another catch with the floating poise of a ballet dancer taking an encore.

And now the question before us was whether the wicket would go to sleep or not, and whether or not Hassett, by not putting into force a declaration at, say, a quarter to one, had missed an opportunity. Today Australia lost seven wickets for 97 in just under two and a quarter hours, a waste of the dubious wicket surely from Hassett's point of view. And Hutton began England's innings so propitiously, and Lindwall so soon went out of action after bowling three not very alarming overs, that it really did look as though the wicket was indeed about to turn over, put out the light, and go to sleep, after reading a chapter or two in a tolerably exciting crime story.

Hutton helped himself to three runs from Lindwall's first ball; and after Edrich had withdrawn from a fast outswinger as if it had been David's javelin, Hutton forced Lindwall for four to the on, a glorious forearm thrust off his pads. The England innings promised to begin more or less securely, in spite of one or two spasmodic reactions by Edrich to Lindwall. But Hill came on for Lindwall, England's score 19; and Edrich sent a rolled leg-break, Hill's third ball, fatally to the slips. The length was just short enough to invite the safest back-stroke.

Graveney, after giving us the briefest glimpse of the quality in him which exasperatingly remains in chrysalis, lobbed Miller to mid-off, where De Courcy caught him, going down almost on his knees; the ball came to him so gently that he might well have held it one-handed lying prone. England's second wicket fell at 32. Miller's field contained two short legs, a close mid-on, and two slips, an arrangement or pattern indicating off-breaks and a quicker one that went away. On the whole neither Hill nor Miller gave evidence discernible from a distance of a positively dangerous attack, or drew as much aid from the pitch as Bedser, Wardle, and Laker had drawn only an hour or two since. Two full tosses in one over from Hill were dismissed from Hutton's proximity with contumely. I have seldom seen as many bad-length balls bowled by Australians as in this summer's Test matches; in Hassett's team Arthur Mailey would stand in danger of losing that capriciousness, which, when he was of Armstrong's forbidding machines, made him as ironic a contrast as the jester in 'King Lear'.

PROPHET IN HIS OWN COUNTRY

At tea England's score was fifty for two, both wickets lost mainly because of strokes that neither Edrich nor Graveney would wish to cherish and remember. During the interval the ground, though not insufferably crowded, appeared congested in its traffic and queues. Is it absolutely necessary, by the way, that gatekeepers at Old Trafford should maintain so suspicious a vigilance on ticket-holders or on any unfamiliar face in the sacred precincts? I propose to take my pass-port to Old Trafford on Monday with my latest photograph—myself, mind you, who was born and bred at Old Trafford. The crowd, good-natured, yet as plain-spoken as ever, clearly enjoyed the fine afternoon; sunshine was imminent any moment.

Lindwall bowled again after tea, and Compton, who has not been running himself or anybody else out lately, dashed for a short single, and if the throw-in had hit the stumps Hutton's wicket might have been lost. Then a ball from Hill jumped viciously, hitting Langley in or near the face; if asleep the wicket was not dreamless yet. But Australia lacked a truly masterful spinner. Or a bowler of the Bedser type. Whenever Lindwall is not taking wickets, this Aus-tralian attack frequently looks at a loss for ideas and resource. The loss to Hassett of Johnston is grievous.

A lovely square drive by Compton sent forth the willowy sound of a batsman settling down and in tune with himself. Hutton again batted with that sound of permanence which in Australian ears is probably becoming quite a psychologial obsession. At this point,

England 77 for two were not palpably engaged in a struggle harder than the one straining the Australian bowlers. Miller swung his arm optimistically; Lindwall could get little or no motive power from the pitch. In fact at five o'clock circumstances favoured some freedom of stroke play; here plainly was a situation England could scarcely have hoped for at lunch: a tamed pitch, more or less, a tamed attack more than less. There was no reason perceptible to the naked eye why England should not by close of play save the follow on, while the going was good, or better than at one time it had promised to be.

Miller tried what he could do from round the wicket, and Compton drove him for four to the on easily as if he were trying the balance of a new bat in a shop. When he was 27 and England 87 Davidson desperately hurled a short potential bumper to the leg side of Compton and Compton, hitting under it, sent the ball soaring to long leg, who, with our hearts rising to our mouths, waited for a catch; but the stroke landed over his head for six, as much I fancy to Compton's relief as to that of the rest of us. As handsome an off drive as Compton or anybody else has ever made wheeled the scoreboard to England's 100 for two; a moment later Hutton reached fifty almost by habit. At 109 the Australian attack was under the obligation to ask Harvey to bowl. A sort of bankruptcy seemed to be setting in.

I could not deduce from the placing of Harvey's field what stuffs he was bowling; it was set for any emergency, covering all ways of getting out, including hitting the ball twice. Still, he was permitted to deliver a maiden of unquestionable chastity. Though both Hutton and Compton played safely and well, many more runs could have been scored by both. So far this Test match has sadly wanted distinction of style, technique and personal fascination. Mediocrity has ruled supreme.

A quarter of an hour before close of play Compton and Hutton astonishingly got out, a mishap as serious to England as it was unexpected; for not a single Australian bowler could have foreseen it. England's position on paper at the end was scarcely secure but, unless the weather plays for Australia, we should not lose this match. Hutton was out to Lindwall leg before; Lindwall, brought back to bowl for the third time, proved his greatness at the pinch by dismissing our greatest batsman. But I do wish that Hutton would more frequently use his finest strokes as soon as the bowling waxes and wanes.

AUSTRALIA
First Innings

A. L. Hassett, b Bailey	26
A. R. Morris, b Bedser	1
K. R. Miller, b Bedser	17
R. N. Harvey, c Evans, b Bedser	122
G. B. Hole, c Evans, b Bedser	66
J. de Courcy, lbw, b Wardle	41
A. K. Davidson, st Evans, b Laker	15
R. G. Archer, c Compton, b Bedser	5
R. R. Lindwall, c Edrich, b Wardle	1
J. C. Hill, not out	8
G. R. Langley, c Edrich, b Wardle	8
Extras (b 6, lb 1, nb 1)	8
	—
Total	318

FALL OF WICKETS

1	2	3	4	5	6	7	8	9
15	48	48	221	256	285	290	291	302

BOWLING ANALYSIS

	O.	M.	R.	W.		O.	M.	R.	W.
Bedser	45	10	115	5	Wardle	28·3	10	70	3
Bailey	26	4	83	1	Laker	17	3	42	1

ENGLAND
First Innings

L. Hutton, lbw, b Lindwall	66
W. J. Edrich, c Hole, b Hill	6
T. W. Graveney, c de Courcy, b Miller	5
D. C. S. Compton, c Langley, b Archer	45
J. W. Wardle, not out	0
W. Watson, not out	0
Extras (lb 4)	4
	—
Total (4 wickets)	126

To bat: Simpson, Bailey, Evans, Laker and Bedser.

FALL OF WICKETS

1	2	3	4
19	32	126	126

BOWLING ANALYSIS

	O.	M.	R.	W.		O.	M.	R.	W.
Lindwall	9	3	19	1	Miller	16	9	19	1
Archer	11	6	10	1	Davidson	7	1	21	0
Hill	18	4	51	1	Harvey	3	2	2	0

RAIN PREVENTED A BALL BEING BOWLED ON THE MONDAY.

THIRD TEST (FIFTH DAY)

OLD TRAFFORD, TUESDAY

The final day's play, mainly abortive, was notable at the finish for a rather inglorious collapse by Australia in conditions favouring spin. It was by no means a case of batsmen surrendering themselves light-heartedly in the great cause of cheering us all up. No Australian really gave evidence of a command of the kind of skill needed to cope with a wicket encouraging to bowlers who know how to give a cricket ball flight and break.

The closing scene, with everybody in the crowd hoping to see Australia all out, was almost exciting and caused us to wonder how Australia would have fared had they lost the toss in weather not rainy for so long a time as it had been since Thursday.

Play was not possible until ten minutes past two, and the connection between the proceedings and those of far distant Saturday was difficult to establish. The cricket seemed merely formal and more or less decorative during a windy afternoon. Though England lost the wickets of Watson and Wardle, fifth and sixth out at 149, we could scarcely doubt that the follow-on would comfortably be saved on a wicket generally soft, even if now and again a ball rose unpleasantly. Watson drove Lindwall for a four and Bailey from time to time let us see a very good stroke; but on the whole he assumed his customary 'over my dead body' attitude against the Australians. Also he contrived to suffer pain, from a blow on the hand, though this time his expression of it was not as histrionic as usual.

LOITERING WITHOUT INTENT

The only sensible reason why the match was being persisted with at all, I take it, was for the entertainment of the crowd; yet few efforts to score were discernible until, as far as I was concerned, sheer weariness set in. Lindwall, for more than an hour, was clever and worth the while of our eyesight; and Hill caused his spin, potential or actual, to rear occasionally towards the batsmen's knuckles. The afternoon seemed a waste of time and of leisure. Failing miracles, the game had long since been dead beyond revival. Still Bailey went on and on, fighting the good fight; while Simpson, at the other end, was of course under an obligation to himself to prove his claims to a place in the England eleven.

When I entered the ground I watched the game for a while from an unpopulated gap between two stands near the pavilion, but a policeman, after eyeing me suspiciously, asked me to move on. A little later a chef, a very large one, adorned in his tall white hat, inspected the scene from the middle of a stand by the pavilion. But nobody moved him on. Perhaps the best thing the alien visitor to Old Trafford can do these days is to make a clean breast of it at once and give himself up.

After tea, the turf became increasingly livelier and Hill caused more than one ball to turn away from the bat, either by finger-spin or the roll of the hand; he deserved his wickets, but often his length was so short that stroke players of resource, subject to temptation like normal human beings, would have suffered hardship of self-denial not to thump a boundary each over. Evans infused some vigour and heartiness into the evening, one of his drives off Davidson going straight for six. The crowd apparently got an amount of enjoyment out of it all, tinctured with ironical laughter. Still, there was no lawful way of ending the match sooner. Why couldn't the police have moved it on?

WHERE WE CAME IN

When Australia batted again at half past five, Hassett and Morris came in first and Bedser bowled at Hassett. For a moment I experienced the dreadful illusion that the match was beginning again and we were all of us back once more to last Thursday morning. Two fours by Hassett in Bedser's opening over were reassuring, however. But the spin of Laker which quickly confounded and overwhelmed Morris, hinted at the fun we might, after all, have witnessed yesterday at Old Trafford had sun and wind not been interrupted by rain from half past eleven to close of play.

Hassett fell to a slip catch off Bedser, 50 minutes from half past six, Australia 12 for 2; and both Hassett and Morris had been well and truly beaten, on a pitch rapidly falling into decay and viciousness. Miller died the death with recklessness and high spirits, also with a dash of desperation. These Australians, taking them by and large, are naïve technicians on a turning turf.

Hole was easy game: the attack of Laker and Bedser was worthy of better opposition, say that of Hobbs and Sutcliffe or Bardsley and Macartney. Wardle came on for Bedser when Australia were 18 for four, Hutton no doubt thinking that fair division of labour should be observed in a general scramble or lust for cheap wickets. De Courcy smote Laker for six, a magnificent blow from a half-volley, then tried a hit into Stretford, and when he was out was down on the earth, helpless as a newly caught haddock.

Australia, 31 for five, a state of affairs which brought Harvey in number seven—and as quickly out, totally bowled by Wardle. Where in the circumstances was all the modern science of batsmanship we hear so much about, a science presumably unguessed by such as Trumper, MacLaren, and Tyldesley? Archer, another innocent abroad, was utterly at a loss to length and spin from Wardle.

The game ended in unmistakable sunshine. Indeed the weather had the last sardonic laugh.

AUSTRALIA

First Innings		Second Innings	
A. L. Hassett, b Bailey	26	c Bailey, b Bedser	8
A. R. Morris, b Bedser	1	c Hutton, b Laker	0
K. R. Miller, b Bedser	17	st Evans, b Laker	6
R. N. Harvey, c Evans, b Bedser	122	b Wardle	0
G. B. Hole, c Evans, b Bedser	66	c Evans, b Bedser	2
J. de Courcy, lbw, b Wardle	41	st Evans, b Wardle	8
A. K. Davidson, st Evans, b Laker	15	not out	4
R. G. Archer, c Compton, b Bedser	5	lbw, b Wardle	0
R. R. Lindwall, c Edrich, b Wardle	1	b Wardle	4
J. C. Hill, not out	8	not out	0
G. R. Langley, c Edrich, b Wardle	8		
Extras (b 6, lb 1, nb 1)	8	Extras (lb 3)	3
Total	318	Total (8 wkts)	35

FALL OF WICKETS

First Innings

1	2	3	4	5	6	7	8	9
15	48	48	221	256	285	290	291	302

BOWLING ANALYSIS

First Innings

	O.	M.	R.	W.		O.	M.	R.	W.
Bedser	45	10	115	5	Wardle	28·3	10	70	3
Bailey	26	4	83	1	Laker	17	3	42	1

FALL OF WICKETS

Second Innings

1	2	3	4	5	6	7	8
8	12	18	18	31	31	31	35

Did not bat: G. R. Langley

ENGLAND v. AUSTRALIA
BOWLING ANALYSIS
Second Innings

	O.	M.	R.	W.		O.	M.	R.	W.
Laker	9	5	11	2	Wardle	8	3	7	4
Bedser	4	1	14	2					

ENGLAND
First Innings

L. Hutton, lbw, b Lindwall	66
W. J. Edrich, c Hole, b Hill	6
T. W. Graveney, c de Courcy, b Miller	5
D. C. S. Compton, c Langley, b Archer	45
J. W. Wardle, b Lindwall	5
W. Watson, b Davidson	16
R. T. Simpson, c Langley, b Davidson	31
T. E. Bailey, c Hole, b Hill	27
T. G. Evans, not out	44
J. C. Laker, lbw, b Hill	5
A. V. Bedser, b Morris	10
Extras (b 8, lb 8)	16
	—
Total	276

FALL OF WICKETS

1	2	3	4	5	6	7	8	9
19	32	126	126	149	149	209	231	243

BOWLING ANALYSIS

	O.	M.	R.	W.		O.	M.	R.	W.
Lindwall	21	8	30	2	Davidson	20	4	60	2
Archer	15	8	12	1	Harvey	3	2	2	0
Hill	35	7	97	3	Hole	2	0	16	0
Miller	24	11	38	1	Morris	1	0	5	1

Umpires: D. Davies and H. Elliott.

O N a wicket mainly easy, or at any rate impersonal, England
has missed a chance regrettably. The dismissal of Hutton by
Lindwall, second ball, obviously depressed the spirit of the
England innings, so much so, that Edrich and Graveney immediately
allowed the Australian attack to get on top.

Even when Lindwall and the new ball were in abeyance, little was
done in the way of determined stroke play, on quick feet, to retrieve a
sinking situation. It was all rather reprehensible, and a sorry anticlimax after the encouragement our cricketers have given us in this
rubber to suppose that they are on the whole the better side of the
two and capable of regaining the Ashes. Today's poor batting,
poor of heart and consequently poor of technique, may well have
lost this crucial game already.

SAMIVEL WAS RIGHT?

It is alleged that Hassett won the toss and asked England to bat
first; I can make the statement in no bolder way because of the law
of libel. The morning threatened rain, so did the weather reports.
I can only suppose that Hassett's gamble was enforced on him by a
dread of Bedser and the new ball on a moist wicket in an atmosphere
likely to help swerve. The wicket, though not altogether trustworthy
to begin with, could scarcely be described as difficult or anything
like it. It was certainly not as awkward as England's batting. 'These
are awkward skates, Sam,' said Mr Winkle. 'It's an awkward gen'l-
man as is using them,' said Weller.

Hutton's sudden downfall from the second ball of the match
bowled by Lindwall certainly could not be blamed on the state of the
pitch, for he succumbed to a late-swinging 'yorker'. Hutton has on
other occasions been found fallible against a length well up to his
bat, but today he was out with an abruptness which took critical
observation and judgment off guard, so to say. In eloquent silence he
returned to the pavilion—and any suggestion of silence on the
Headingley cricket ground is almost a phenomenon in nature. The
accident to Hutton and possibly uncertainty of mind and outlook
in the England camp about the pitch, a psychological unease no
doubt aggravated by Hassett's invitation to England to take first

innings—these must charitably be mentioned to account for the deplorably irresolute batting which ensued for 100 minutes until lunch, in which time only 36 runs were scored and two more wickets lost in addition to Hutton's.

AURAL AID

Except for a straight drive from a half volley by Graveney and a sort of putt from a short ball off Lindwall, nothing hinting of a determined hit, or an attempted one was to be seen, or indeed to be expected. Constantly the ball was striking the pads, a sign admittedly of swing. The miscalculations in timing of Edrich and Graveney prompted one to think that they might have played with surer direction of bat if a small tinkling bell could have been put inside the ball. Edrich and Graveney were each nearly bowled and Graveney at 19 might well have been run out if Harvey for once in his lifetime had not thrown in crookedly.

At the end of the first hour England's score was 18 for one wicket. Batsmen ask for trouble if they acquiesce in circumstances that flatter bowlers and depress their own spirits. After 79 minutes of anxious, not to say agitated watchfulness and suspicion, Edrich missed a quick lowish one from Miller and was leg before. With 5 runs added, which made England's grand total 36, Compton turned an inswinger clean into Davidson's hand from the leg side close up, one of those impulsive strokes which even while he is making it causes a shock of apprehension throughout a batsman's system.

I have not seen a Test match innings begin as timidly and as dejectedly as this of England's. The glowering sky, the stolen gleams or excursions of sunshine, the subdued crowd, all seemed an objective presentation from the wan and flickering spirits and character of the cricket. The rhythm of the game, such as it was, could not achieve acceleration; a small boy held up the proceedings as he walked to his place in the seats behind the bowler's arm. There is apparently no room or space for sight screens at Headingley. Yet Yorkshire folk are not so big or as broad as all that.

At the fall of Edrich's wicket Miller reclined on the boundary at third man chatting to the crowd there. I entirely agree with his view of the match, expressed so gracefully and nonchalantly.

Two lovely strokes immediately after lunch, one a sweet off-drive, told us that Graveney's innings was more or less emerging from the caterpillar stage. He had before the interval promised to remember his innate skill when he glanced the fast bowling once or twice to leg.

Another off-drive by Graveney, powerful and easy off Miller, carried England's score to 50 for three in just under two hours.

If the pitch before lunch had even contained a penn'orth of real unpleasantness (which I doubt) it was manifestly easy enough at half-past two, when Miller and Lindwall strove in vain to persuade the ball to lift. Only by intense shoulder action did Archer compel a ball short of a length to rise at Watson, who in coping with it might have been caught brilliantly by Langley; Watson was then five and England 61 for three. I could discern no great variety of ideas in Australia's attack, no questions asked in the air, no sense of subtlety of craft. The Australian attack today was mainly muscular as soon as the new ball waned and Lindwall went out of action, though I swear I saw Miller bowl one pronounced 'tweaker', to use Mr Ian Peebles's delectable and recurrent term. Miller seemed to send down the kind of ball that comes into his head at the last minute or split second; and many times it takes a direction which puts geometry out of countenance and order.

The slightest deviation from the unexpected in the Australian bowling startled the batting into a kind of bankruptcy of resourcefulness. A 'bumper' from Archer, an easy four for Sutcliffe, put Graveney into the throes of spasmodic reflex action. A good hooker or cutter would have scored plentifully today. And Archer completely beat Graveney at 43; Graveney's cricket is shot through with strands of fine style and blemishes of ill-adjusted poise. Balls of the right height for cutting on the off-side and balls on the leg-side clamouring to be pulled or hooked went by unpunished. Several long-hops to leg from Archer escaped whipping by Watson, who needed only to take care of a deep fine leg. In any case the length of these balls called for a squarer stroke. In half an hour I counted at least six major errors of timing and footwork by Graveney and Watson. If an orchestra were to make mistakes as persistent and fundamental as these, we would find it no easy task to recognize even the 'William Tell' Overture. A wide full toss by Archer travelled rapidly for four byes; the next ball was an atrocious bouncer to Watson, who withdrew his presence from it. The crowd hooted, but McCabe would have cursed himself if he had not hooked it with time to spare to the boundary.

The quality of the cricket thereabouts was deplorable, and in a Test match almost offensive. But apparently common competitive interest is satisfied by the showing of the scoreboard. A connoisseur of technique is a spoil-sport.

NOT TIME ALONE YAWNS

After three hours England reached the aggregate of 85 for three and Graveney arrived at his 50 in something like this yawning gulf of time, whereat the crowd applauded jubilantly. Graveney so far had added three fours. On a day much the same as this one and on a pitch fairly identical Macartney scored a century before lunch (after Australia had lost a wicket for next to nothing, or nothing at all) against Tate, Macaulay, and Geary, to name only three superb bowlers then in their prime. But it is not decent to mention Macartney's name in association with the cricket seen so far today. Champagne and small beer do not mix.

At four o'clock a shower drove the players off the field and out of sight; for this relief much thanks. England 94 for three wickets in nearly 3½ hours.

After tea a new ball was hopefully taken and from Miller's first thrust with it Graveney slash-cut to Benaud in the slips and a fine catch was held at the second attempt, in spite of loss of balance on the earth. Graveney's variegated innings lasted three and three-quarter hours; it is possible to go to Madrid in that time. Towards five o'clock some ghostly applause greeted the arrival of England's score at 100, in 236 minutes, on a wicket since lunch as comfortable as a well-worn shoe.

Then Simpson retired, hit by Lindwall on the elbow, which made room for the gallant, histrionic Bailey. He at once declined to run a short single, sending Watson back with a declamatory 'No!' in a tone of voice that Mr. Donald Wolfit usually reserves for King Lear and the drowning and cracking of the world on the heath. Then he drove Miller stylishly forward for two. He is a character, and would be wise to reserve his film rights.

AS MANY WASTED AS SCORED

Watson's end was unfortunate. A very fast ball from Lindwall landed on his boot and sped thence to the wicket, moving only his leg bail, while he hopped in pain. His innings of 24 endured 2 hours and 43 minutes, no minute of it, I imagine, a source of enjoyment to himself or to anybody else not inveterately a Yorkshireman. Evans was nearly caught wide on the leg side by Langley before he had scored off Lindwall. Then poor Bailey was run out backing up to Evans. England were now 110 for six, with as many runs at least wasted through a reluctance to hit much loose stuff while the ball was old.

While Evans and Laker were together the bat sent out a sound more confident than any heard before all day. They lifted the score to 135, not without vicissitude, but with a welcome show of vigilance for the easy ball. So far England's innings has lasted some 5½ hours —and look at the score at the end of it all. Such cricket defies explanation and disperses the most charitable excuses.

ENGLAND
First Innings

L. Hutton, b Lindwall	0
W. J. Edrich, lbw, b Miller	10
T. W. Graveney, c Benaud, b Miller	55
D. C. S. Compton, c Davidson, b Lindwall	0
W. Watson, b Lindwall	24
R. T. Simpson, retired hurt	2
T. E. Bailey, run out	7
T. G. Evans, not out	18
J. C. Laker, c Lindwall, b Archer	10
G. A. R. Lock, not out	5
Extras (b 8, lb 3)	11
Total (7 wickets)	142

To bat: Bedser (A. V.).

FALL OF WICKETS

1	2	3	4	5	6	7
0	33	36	98	108	110	133

BOWLING ANALYSIS

	O.	M.	R.	W.		O.	M.	R.	W.
Lindwall	28	8	40	3	Archer	13	4	17	1
Miller	28	13	39	2	Benaud	8	1	12	0
Davidson	19	6	23	0					

AUSTRALIA: A. L. Hassett, A. R. Morris, K. R. Miller, R. N. Harvey, G. B. Hole, J. de Courcy, R. Benaud, A. K. Davidson, R. G. Archer, R. R. Lindwall, G. R. Langley.

FOURTH TEST (SECOND DAY)

LEEDS, FRIDAY

At one time today England's hopes of saving the match seemed spectral indeed. Australia went ahead with only three wickets down. And again in this rubber the wind changed for no perceptible reason. Things became level and nobody could confidently find the technical clue to it all, except in terms of revived England bowling and fielding, a new ball, and the instability of Australia's batting, especially when it is arriving at the middle of an innings. The England team achieved nothing less than resurrection.

During the stand between Harvey and Hole they looked fairly rudderless when Bedser was not in fresh action. The fall of Harvey no doubt came as an encouragement, even if he had not exactly played like a master. A spirited force in England's renewal was Bailey who, it now seems certain, thrives on adversity and like all the great martyrs enjoys his hairshirt and the slings and arrows. A last-wicket rally by Archer and Langley, though naturally aggravating to the crowd, merely added to the game's prospects of comporting itself capriciously and for our entertainment to the end. Both sides will need to work hard to win or to save themselves.

LONG AND INGLORIOUS

England's innings came to an end at twenty minutes past twelve with 25 runs added to yesterday's score in fifty minutes. It lasted in all nearly six and a half hours for 167. I cannot remember that any first innings has persisted as long and as ingloriously as this ever before in Test matches between England and Australia. Cricketers of the breed of MacLaren, Jackson, Trumper, Quaife, and Hayward, not to mention Woolley and Dipper, would have been ashamed to be associated with such doings.

Simpson, in spite of his bruised elbow, came forth to bat though he was unable later to field; and he played a stylish little innings until he reached across too far and touched an out-swinger from Lindwall, sending a difficult wide chance which Langley held with clever agility. Lock was assured and obstinate until he ventured beyond his territory as a batsman and tried his hand at a stroke.

Lindwall again bowled admirably, not at his fastest maybe, but intelligently and determinedly. None the less, Australia's attack was absurdly flattered throughout England's crocodile of an innings, even if Miller often gave Lindwall some mettlesome support.

IF LOOKS COULD KILL

A pretty hullaballoo occurred during Simpson's innings. The Australians clearly believed they had run him out while he was going for a third run to retain the bowling. Miller took the throw in and performed what he doubtless thought was a happy dispatch. When Chester declared Simpson not out Lindwall, near the wicket, threw up his hands to high heaven and spoke, or pronounced, volumes of expostulation. The scene was ripe with that comedy which is inspired whenever mortal man sees things with an indignation out of proportion and can do nothing about the circumstances which have provoked it. If looks could kill, Chester would have fallen dead on the field of play, killed by Miller's glare. Our Test match cricketers nowadays are becoming histrionic. They should form a dramatic company and produce, say, Macbeth.

The wicket was tolerably comfortable though not entirely above suspicion when Australia went in. Moreover Bailey was unable to bowl at full pressure. But Bedser at once tormented Morris again with the new ball. To a spacious length coming to him on the offside Morris drove as though towards cover, but the inside edge of the bat snicked grotesquely for two down to fine leg. Then he was nearly caught in the slips off Bedser, heart in his mouth. From Bedser's next over Hassett was definitely missed in Bedser's leg trap with his score 10, a stroke urged on him by a splendid inswinger. Compton could not hold the sharp, low, but by no means difficult, chance, a chance foretold both by the nature of the ball bowled and by Hassett's way of coping with it, the only way.

Quick compensation consoled Bedser in his next over. Morris, as plainly vulnerable as a condemned man who has recently eaten a more or less hearty breakfast, flicked another inswinger by sheer impulse and was well and rapaciously caught. The name of Bedser must by now be graven deep in Morris's heart.

A ball from Lock turned abruptly to Harvey as soon as he came to the crease and temporarily raised our hopes. But before lunch, by which time Australia had scored 51 for 1, Lock's five overs had cost some twenty runs. A cut from Lock by Hassett was the prettiest stroke of the match so far.

SPORT IN THE WICKET

After lunch Lock's spin was quick enough twice to baffle Harvey, and a ball from Bedser rose to the shoulder of Hassett's bat, speeding thence for four over the slips' heads. It was a wicket now fit for good sport, willing to conspire a little and equally with good batsmen and good bowlers alike. Justice was done to Bedser when Hassett turned a ball on his pads to short square leg's hands, a stroke he had no alternative but to make. So the match was becoming open and in the balance; Australia 70 for 2 and the time of day twenty minutes to three. The large crowd, naïve and expectant, made zoological noises whenever a ball struck a pad and a bat missed its aim, and Harvey missed his aim more times in a quarter of an hour than Warren Bardsley in half a day.

When his score was 24, Harvey was very lucky to edge Bedser through the slips, but though as hard pressed by the attack as

England were at any time yesterday Australia contrived to get runs, good strokes or fortuitous. Here is the main difference between the two teams.

Miller began with some pokes and prods which should have brought an apologetic blush to the face of a great player. Then against Bailey, who came on so that Bedser might rest a while, Harvey committed another mis-hit of no pedigree. There has been no constant standard of style or etiquette in the present rubber. The players are, so to say, always prone to drink out of the wrong glass or even eat peas off their knife.

Miller was adjudged caught first slip after his bat had seemed to come down on a semi-yorker from Bailey; this too was a stroke of cautious technique to produce against a ball as honest as well could be. Hole edged Lock crudely the moment he reached the wicket; next he totally missed an offside ball from Bailey. The critic who goes by results would have said the Australians hereabout were contending with a really unpleasant pitch. I hold to the view that it was of a kind that brings the best skill and all the resource out of truly great batsmen and bowlers alike. When Australia's total stood at 106 for three Laker had not bowled, so Hutton apparently considered the wicket was well-behaved enough. He even entrusted Bailey to try off-breaks until half past three, at which time Laker sent down his first over and Harvey cut a long hop for four.

The afternoon fluctuated from excellence to indifference, not to say professional incompetence. Seldom did the cricket appeal to the sense of art. Harvey in an hour and forty minutes made 50; again he mingled a few fine hits with miscalculations hard to account for in a player regarded truly great and finished. The connoisseur of the game found little constantly satisfying in the proceedings except the bowling of Bedser, who always answers to the requirements of technique considered in the absolute. Lock was a first-class bowler without suggesting that he was, as they say, 'class', and the England fielding seldom transcended levels of industry that is paid by the hour. The Australian batsmen, for all the dislocations in their rhythm, attended to loose stuff and as a consequence their innings was not sterile. It is their readiness to play strokes which does indeed give them the advantage over England. At tea Australia were 157 for three after roughly three hours' batting—ten runs behind England's 167, accumulated in time more than twice as long.

After tea Harvey yet again missed his aim, this time at a half volley to the off. The old-time cricket writers invariably agreed that a batsman was 'beaten' if he missed his aim. Harvey now missed a ball from Bailey fatally and was leg-before. With all respect to Bailey I say that a great batsman would not miss his aim against a Bailey armed only with an old ball after he had been at the wicket two and a half hours, which was the duration of Harvey's 71. De Courcy began superbly, pulling Bailey for two fours consecutively from the over in which Harvey got out. And Hole swept Lock round for four the next ball after one—definitely and surprisingly another sign of the Australians' quick opportunism. One unpleasant ball sends an English batsman into his shell for hours.

Hole, though frequently looking insecure, added usefully to the score but De Courcy's promising prelude came to a full close when he received a really nasty spinner quick off the pitch from Lock and, like Harvey, was leg before. So after passing England's 167 with only three wickets down Australia at the fall of their fifth batsman were no more than sixteen ahead. Hole here completed fifty in an hour and 54 minutes, including eight fours, some of them forward drives strong and elegant. He moved from the back foot with a frequency not common among contemporary Australian batsmen. Bedser with the new ball was the menace confronting Benaud, in fifth wicket down.

BAILEY'S BEST ROLE—BAILEY

The game was openly in the scales now. England desperately needed an Australian collapse before left too far behind. Quick to his cue Bailey bowled Benaud off the pads—his third victim in the innings so far, the others Harvey and Miller. He asserts himself by belief in himself as much as by any extraordinary talent; of all his histrionic achievements his best role is Bailey.

Benaud was no sooner back in the pavilion than England's perilous state was vastly retrieved by a remarkable catch by Lock in Bedser's leg trap backward and square. He held a clean hit by Hole one handed with an ease as deceptive as it was entertaining. The swinging round of the match roused the Headingley crowd to full and traditional vocalism. Untrustworthy middle batting had allowed a favourable situation for Australia to deteriorate into one of questionable shape; the fourth innings at Leeds in this summer's climate might well tax more skill than we have seen at the wicket in this match to date.

Bailey brought down the house in an attempt to catch and bowl Lindwall; the return drive was so violent that it brought Bailey down too, flat on the earth, his prize just eluding him—another moment of drama needing a quick curtain and thunder and lightning. Lindwall was clean bowled by Bedser driving with intent and eye on distant roofs, chimneys, and churches; he was ninth out at 218. Archer in the gallant last-wicket resistance let us see more than one really splendid stroke swift over the grass. Langley also played a good part to the accompaniment of advice to England's bowlers from the crowd. He was out almost at close of play; Archer rightly not out if not invincible.

ENGLAND
First Innings

L. Hutton, b Lindwall	0
W. J. Edrich, lbw, b Miller	10
T. W. Graveney, c Benaud, b Miller	55
D. C. S. Compton, c Davidson, b Lindwall	0
W. Watson, b Lindwall	24
R. T. Simpson, c Langley, b Lindwall	15
T. E. Bailey, run out	7
T. G. Evans, lbw, b Lindwall	25
J. C. Laker, c Lindwall, b Archer	10
G. A. R. Lock, b Davidson	9
A. V. Bedser, not out	0
Extras (b 8, lb 4)	12
Total	167

FALL OF WICKETS

1	2	3	4	5	6	7	8	9
0	33	36	98	108	110	133	149	167

BOWLING ANALYSIS

	O.	M.	R.	W.		O.	M.	R.	W.
Lindwall	35	10	54	5	Archer	18	4	27	1
Miller	28	13	39	2	Benaud	8	1	12	0
Davidson	20·4	7	23	1					

AUSTRALIA
First Innings

A. L. Hassett, c Lock, b Bedser	37
A. R. Morris, c Lock, b Bedser	10
R. N. Harvey, lbw, b Bailey	71
K. R. Miller, c Edrich, b Bailey	5
G. B. Hole, c Lock, b Bedser	53
J. de Courcy, lbw, b Lock	10
R. Benaud, b Bailey	7
A. K. Davidson, c Evans, b Bedser	2
R. G. Archer, not out	31
R. R. Lindwall, b Bedser	9
G. R. Langley, c Hutton, b Bedser	17
Extras (b 4, lb 8, w 2)	14
Total	266

FALL OF WICKETS

1	2	3	4	5	6	7	8	9
27	70	84	168	183	203	203	208	218

BOWLING ANALYSIS

	O.	M.	R.	W.		O.	M.	R.	W.
Bedser	28·5	2	95	6	Lock	23	9	53	1
Bailey	22	4	71	3	Laker	9	1	33	0

FOURTH TEST (THIRD DAY)

LEEDS, SATURDAY

After less than an hour and three-quarters of cricket rain set in shortly after one o'clock, and that was the end of the third day in this Test match at Leeds. England scored 62 for the loss of Hutton's wicket after he and Edrich had batted with more than a show of assurance.

The position of affairs now is slightly in Australia's favour, though the weather and the wicket on Monday are likely to play as influential a part in bringing about a decision as anything that may be done by the variable techniques of the cricketers themselves. The issue is still very much in the balance.

When the Australians came into the field at half-past eleven this morning and were taking up their positions Edrich was seen to be practising strokes near the wicket against an invisible ball, presumably to refresh his memory. Then Lindwall attacked, struck Hutton on the pad second ball, and from his third Hutton scored 2 from a square forcing thrust to the on, and from the fifth survived a hopeful or rather empirical appeal for leg before. Chester's dismissal of this appeal was vociferously supported by the crowd on the square leg boundary. The two teams, by the way, seemed to be in good health and progressing as well as could be expected in the circumstances. A magnificent drive to the off from Lindwall suggested that Edrich was out of danger; he now moved forward with some confidence to the fast bowling.

DAMPED HOPES

And Hutton, though obviously anxious and not at once sure of touch, brought all his concentration and intensive defensive technique to bear on the situation. Altogether the prelude to the innings was in a bright major key, promising a reasonably substantial score on the fairly comfortable pitch; in less than fifty minutes 36 runs were on the board with Lindwall and Miller out of action. Opportunity could almost be heard (by the physical ear) knocking at England's door. One or two edged strokes by Edrich were probably the consequence of his injured hand; all in all, though, he looked as though he were seeing the ball most times. He cut a short one from Miller with the savage swiftness of Johnny Tyldesley.

A drizzle of rain was falling towards one o'clock and apparently Hassett wanted to leave the field, so as to spare his bowlers the inconvenience which is caused by slippery leather. He spoke to Hutton about it, presumably, then the umpires consulted with each other and the game went on.

Ironically enough, Hutton was out immediately after this legal colloquy; he held his bat out almost absent-mindedly to a ball from Archer which rose amiably to the off, not calling for any act of self-preservation; and he was caught at the wicket. Maybe he lost concentration because of this enforced, if momentary, preoccupation with the English climate and the question of what amounts or consistency of moisture constitutes rain at Headingley, where doubtless different standards and definition regarding the problem are in vogue than at, say, Old Trafford. Whatever the reason the loss of his wicket at such a moment, England's score 57, was grievous.

Ten minutes later rain, authentic, visible, and drenching, descended, driving the cricketers into the pavilion and changing the congested crowd into a floating population of moist, disappointed, if not dejected, bodies.

AUSTRALIA

First Innings

A. L. Hassett, c Lock, b Bedser	37
A. R. Morris, c Lock, b Bedser	10
R. N. Harvey, lbw, b Bailey	71
K. R. Miller, c Edrich, b Bailey	5
G. B. Hole, c Lock, b Bedser	53
J. de Courcy, lbw, b Lock	10
R. Benaud, b Bailey	7
A. K. Davidson, c Evans, b Bedser	2
R. G. Archer, not out	31
R. R. Lindwall, b Bedser	9
G. R. Langley, c Hutton, b Bedser	17
Extras (b 4, lb 8, w 2)	14
Total	266

FALL OF WICKETS

1	2	3	4	5	6	7	8	9
27	70	84	168	183	203	203	208	218

BOWLING ANALYSIS

	O.	M.	R.	W.		O.	M.	R.	W.
Bedser	28·5	2	95	6	Lock	23	9	53	1
Bailey	22	4	71	3	Laker	9	1	33	0

ENGLAND

First Innings		Second Innings	
L. Hutton, b Lindwall	0	c Langley, b Archer	25
W. J. Edrich, lbw, b Miller	10	not out	33
T. W. Graveney, c Benaud, b Miller	55	not out	3
D. C. S. Compton, c Davidson, b Lindwall	0		
W. Watson, b Lindwall	24		
R. T. Simpson, c Langley, b Lindwall	15		
T. E. Bailey, run out	7		
T. G. Evans, lbw, b Lindwall	25		
J. C. Laker, c Lindwall, b Archer	10		
G. A. R. Lock, b Davidson	9		
A. V. Bedser, not out	0		
Extras (b 8, lb 4)	12	Extra (lb)	1
Total	167	Total (1 wkt)	62

FALL OF WICKETS

First Innings

1	2	3	4	5	6	7	8	9
0	33	36	98	108	110	133	149	167

BOWLING ANALYSIS

First Innings

	O.	M.	R.	W.		O.	M.	R.	W.
Lindwall	35	10	54	5	Archer	18	4	27	1
Miller	28	13	39	2	Benaud	8	1	12	0
Davidson	20·4	7	23	1					

FALL OF WICKET

Second Innings

1
57

BOWLING ANALYSIS

Second Innings

	O.	M.	R.	W.		O.	M.	R.	W.
Lindwall	7	0	25	0	Archer	9	5	7	1
Miller	10·3	2	20	0	Davidson	2	0	9	0

FOURTH TEST (FOURTH DAY)

LEEDS, MONDAY

Want of intelligent purpose endangered England's position today after Edrich and Compton had embarrassed Hassett in a stand of considerable resolution.

England took the lead with only two wickets down and at tea were 40 in front and seven wickets in reserve. Compton undefeated 47. The pitch was not at all uncomfortable after much rain and the ball was ageing and Lindwall had gone into his sweater. But Compton proceeded for nearly an hour to score no more than half a dozen runs. Watson, too, did nothing in particular, and not particularly well. And all the time the chance was running to waste of catching Australia tomorrow on possibly a wicket not after their heart's desire, facing a task of scoring a total beyond technical scope in the conditions.

Does the present England policy go to work on the assumption that the onus is on Hassett to attack to win the rubber? The question is not at all rhetorical.

Shortly before the match was resumed Edrich was seen in a distant part of the ground practising straight drives while Compton fielded, assisted by a small boy. It is heartening to think that somebody during the course of this match has had the enterprise to form a volunteer reserve for the England eleven.

WHY LEAVE MANCHESTER?

Once again an England innings ran into trouble immediately, for after Miller had completed the over interrupted by Saturday's weather, and after Archer had sent down an over from the other end, Lindwall clean-bowled Graveney first ball. Graveney made a sleepy lamish, half-forward push at a good length ball of ordinary pace through the air. Then the England innings went once more into the key of B minor and the sky became covered with cloud as threatening as Lindwall. The responsibility now on Edrich and Compton was so heavy that it might almost have been perceived visually; but all the same Edrich pulled a short one from Lindwall for four boldly enough. After fourteen runs had been scored in 35 minutes rain cleared the field and once more the huge unsheltered crowd gazed on vacancy and got wet while doing so. It occurred to me now that it might, after all, be a good idea to send this rubber back to Manchester.

The sudden downfall of Graveney was momentarily doubtless

depressing to the England innings; he has more than once faltered as a batsman at the beginning of a morning after having continued batting from overnight. He might do well to set his alarm clock an hour earlier. Lindwall's habit of taking a wicket without loss of time in his first few balls is extraordinary; and I cannot recollect that any other bowler has shared his ability to get fatally to work with such an avid rapidity.

The storm passed by and the game was proceeded with at a quarter past two; and Compton hooked Archer for four from a rising ball, a melodramatic stroke which provoked the crowd to roars of applause, but caused a quiver of apprehension in the bosom of the discerning onlooker. Much more assuring was a fine leg glance for four by Edrich—but this, too, was a little feverish of pulse. Not yet was the England innings finding a steady basic tempo. The accelerandos were not proportionately related to the diminuendos. A beautiful lifting ball left Edrich without a prompt answer but it flashed harmlessly by on the offside, then Compton was missed at square leg off Miller from a pulled stroke rather enforced on him, which went for three. A hard chance. Compton was here fifteen and England 92 for 2.

England reached 100 and wiped out the deficit by a truly brilliant square cut by Edrich for four off Miller. The match and maybe the rubber was in a fascinating balance, for the weather was promising to clear so that a fourth innings for Australia on a turning pitch tomorrow was an enthralling if spectral possibility. England needed to score prosperously now if ever; Hassett therefore recalled Lindwall at ten minutes to three. England 107 for two, Edrich 48, Compton 25. The crowd watched him in silence as he ran to attack. As the new ball would be available after another ten overs some of us thought that Hassett might have kept Lindwall a little longer on the leash; probably Hassett felt (as I felt) that the Australian situation was peremptorily calling for another wicket, Edrich's or Compton's, this instant minute. And twice did Edrich snick Lindwall perilously, but things were apparently going England's way as a reward for an improved attitude of mind by both batsmen. The loose ball was hit with alacrity as it should have been while the ground was still damp but drying.

Hassett's control of his bowling was here peculiar. Hole came on presumably to try off-breaks with a ball still more or less slippery. But it was, of course, right to give Lindwall a pause and breather five overs in advance of the change of ball from old to new.

The Australian attack we must not forget, has suffered a grievous handicap from the loss of Johnston, who would surely have provided the back-bone of the bowling in this afternoon's conditions; for he might have 'lifted' unpleasantly most times.

TURNING POINT

Edrich reached 50 in 190 minutes and in spite of occasional mistakes of timing looked resolute and ready to pull the short stuff or go forward with head down to the overpitched length. And Compton, though now dependent on the application of talent and not inspired by genius to that mastery which makes its own law, was reliant enough and clearly reasonably safeguarded by his experience. Just after half past three when England's total was 135 for two Lindwall took the new ball. The next half hour, I now believed, would settle whether Australia would win this match and the rubber; and whether maybe they would save it. The atmosphere tightened with expectancy and slight foreboding. The sun was shining in a way that could scarcely have gratified Hassett; his inexpressive face hinted of some concern.

It was yet again Lindwall who at the turning point eased Hassett's anxieties. Edrich sliced an outswinger as he endeavoured to drive towards cover and he mis-hit and was caught. His gallant, hard-fibred innings lasted four hours and he hit ten boundaries. He and Compton held England's third wicket two hours and a quarter and added 73.

So when Watson went to the wicket hailed by friends, relations, and small boys England were 40 in front with seven wickets standing. Neither side could afford to make a mistake at this point; the tightrope was taut, everybody pulling, nobody sure of his foothold. A great hook for four by Compton from Lindwall turned the years back to his wonderful summer of 1947: 'once a genius, always a genius'. An appeal for leg before by Lindwall against Watson when he was only two was dismissed by umpire Lee with proper impartial dignity and by the crowd with equally proper derision. At tea England's lead was 48, three wickets down, Compton not out 47. Each team had equal reason to hope for the best and to fear the worst. The value of the 48 runs plundered by Australia's last wicket on Friday has rocketed to a kind of stratosphere of currency.

After tea the problem confronting England was two-fold—not to lose quick wickets and to score with a shrewd political opportunism. Hassett's aim, of course, was to keep runs down or bring about a complete England collapse as would reinsure him, so to say, against the hazards of a fourth innings on a wicket likely to lend gentle aid to a spinning ball if there was no further rain. Watson immediately after tea pulled Archer hugely for four to long leg, hitting under a rising ball to a boundary unguarded.

Compton's innings arrived at 50 after just under three hours, a valuable performance I suppose, even if it reminded us of Dr Middleton's metaphor about Phoebus Apollo turned fasting friar. Yet again did England's batting drift into negation exactly when common sense and nothing more asked for competent stroke-play directed by a little enterprise. The new ball waned, Benaud bowled on a pitch of no use to him. But the rate of scoring dwindled; in some 45 minutes after tea eighteen runs were scored. England apparently decided that after all their main job was to save themselves, even though all the time they must have known they were playing to Hassett's secret, and perhaps not so secret, wishes. The Australian fieldsmen seemed to take a skittish view of England's tactics after tea. They chased the ball in twos and kicked it about to one another as though sharing a private joke. At any moment I expected Hassett to ask Chester to bowl.

INTENSE IMMOBILITY

At twenty past five the umpires decided to interrupt play because of bad light. At twenty minutes to six another effort to get on with the game was made and legally enforced. Compton submitted straightway to having a maiden over bowled at him by Benaud; indeed he definitely collaborated with it. Following Edrich's dismissal the virtue went deplorably out of the England innings. Watson was out to an agile running catch in the region of the gully from a stroke of no purpose or eyesight; he is apparently under the delusion that in every Test match he plays henceforth we expect him to give us an encore to his dour, patient, Spartan innings at Lord's.

Simpson was out first ball caught off his glove; England 72 ahead, five wickets lost. Bailey came forth to frustrate a hat trick by Miller, which he did by a defensive bat of intense immobility. Then, the same over, he drove as grand and stylish a four to the off as any seen in the match. After yet another interruption by rain Lindwall bowled again at a quarter past six and to avoid a bouncer Bailey leaped away and backward with so much of a contortionist's elasticity that he resembled for the time being a mark of interrogation. The cause is not lost while he is there—and intact.

ENGLAND

First Innings		Second Innings	
L. Hutton, b Lindwall	0	c Langley, b Archer	25
W. J. Edrich, lbw, b Miller	10	c de Courcy, b Lindwall	64
T. W. Graveney, c Benaud, b Miller	55	b Lindwall	3
D. C. S. Compton, c Davidson, b Lindwall	0	not out	60
W. Watson, b Lindwall	24	c Davidson, b Miller	15
R. T. Simpson, c Langley, b Lindwall	15	c de Courcy, b Miller	0
T. E. Bailey, run out	7	not out	4
T. G. Evans, lbw, b Lindwall	25		
J. C. Laker, c Lindwall, b Archer	10		
G. A. R. Lock, b Davidson	9		
A. V. Bedser, not out	0		
Extras (b 8, lb 4)	12	Extras (b 1, lb 5)	6
Total	167	Total (5 wkts)	177

FALL OF WICKETS
First Innings

1	2	3	4	5	6	7	8	9
0	33	36	98	108	110	133	149	167

BOWLING ANALYSIS
First Innings

	O.	M.	R.	W.		O.	M.	R.	W.
Lindwall	35	10	54	5	Archer	18	4	27	1
Miller	28	13	39	2	Benaud	8	1	12	0
Davidson	20.4	7	23	1					

FALL OF WICKETS
Second Innings

1	2	3	4	5
57	62	139	167	171

BOWLING ANALYSIS
Second Innings

	O.	M.	R.	W.		O.	M.	R.	W.
Lindwall	27	7	67	2	Davidson	7	2	17	0
Miller	30	11	42	2	Hole	3	1	6	0
Archer	25	12	31	1	Benaud	7	3	8	0

AUSTRALIA
First Innings

A. L. Hassett, c Lock, b Bedser		37
A. R. Morris, c Lock, b Bedser		10
R. N. Harvey, lbw, b Bailey		71
K. R. Miller, c Edrich, b Bailey		5
G. B. Hole, c Lock, b Bedser		53
J. de Courcy, lbw, b Lock		10
R. Benaud, b Bailey		7
A. K. Davidson, c Evans, b Bedser		2
R. G. Archer, not out		31
R. R. Lindwall, b Bedser		9
G. R. Langley, c Hutton, b Bedser		17
Extras (b 4, lb 8, w 2)		14
Total		266

FALL OF WICKETS

1	2	3	4	5	6	7	8	9
27	70	84	168	183	203	203	208	218

BOWLING ANALYSIS

	O.	M.	R.	W.		O.	M.	R.	W.
Bedser	28·5	2	95	6	Lock	23	9	53	1
Bailey	22	4	71	3	Laker	9	1	33	0

FOURTH TEST (FIFTH DAY) LEEDS, TUESDAY

The fourth Test match ended in another draw, with the Australians batting against time. To say the truth England scarcely deserved to escape a thrashing, for after Laker and Bailey had rallied a desperate situation, made next to hopeless by the injury to Compton who could bat only with a crippled hand, the England innings after lunch showed no spirit at all.

There was a time when some display of spirit might even have beaten Australia or at any rate pressed them hard. Quite apart from competitive values Test match cricketers owe something to the game as a challenge to character and the sportsman's readiness to take a risk in the cause. The onus to win the rubber, let us repeat, is on England. England at lunch no more than Australia were losing this match. They lacked vision and spirit alike—and both would work miracles, even in contemporary cricket.

The large crowd was very quiet when at half-past eleven Evans continued England's innings with Bailey, in Compton's absence. Silence deepened to mute anticipation of the worst when Evans gently propelled a slower ball from Miller straight to the hands of square mid-on. A more pleasing sight was the way spin jumped up when Benaud bowled instead of Lindwall at noon. He bowled it to

Laker, who no doubt was not at all depressed by signs that the wicket was developing a certain resilience. At the morning's outset Bailey hooked Miller with a flourish and against Lindwall resisted, with quite austere self-denial, the temptation offered by a sudden bouncer to suffer concussion. Benaud could not again root out the spot on the pitch that had caused us to raise our eyebrows, and on the whole the Australian attack once again seemed lacking in power to make a quick end with an old ball to an innings fairly far gone.

FRUSTRATING THE AUSTRALIANS

Laker, in spite of a narrow escape in the slips when 13 from a short ball by Lindwall suddenly and surprisingly fast, played with much confidence and tranquillity. Bailey was clearly not thinking of losing his wicket for hours, given a single sound limb or breath in his body. The stand of Laker and Bailey must have caused as much exasperation and frustration to the Australians as the stand of Bailey and Watson at Lord's. So easily, indeed, did Laker play that we could only deplore that Compton, or some other performer of positive strokes, was not in action at the other end.

Still, it was a truly gallant stand, considering the modest technical scope of the two batsmen who achieved it. Some of Laker's hits to the off had an assurance and style which might well have been envied by one or two of the young Australians who chased them as they sped to the off side with a speed that told of perfect timing. Bailey defended on principle, half volleys or good ones; he patted the pitch violently several times an over. Laker, who made nearly all the runs, hardly patted it at all. Lindwall with the new ball came on before lunch and he and Miller sought desperately to put an end to a piece of resistance which to them must have seemed so much anticlimax, offensive to their dignity. But Laker drove Lindwall for four with a calm, classic forward poise—comical considering the circumstances.

At lunch Laker and Bailey were still in possession and England 135 ahead with four wickets in reserve. It was a left-handed spinner from Davidson that ended the partnership just after the interval with Laker caught from it at slip. The seventh wicket fell at 239, and Laker and Bailey had scored 57 together in a few minutes under two hours. Laker played Lindwall admirably, moving forward to him. Frankly, Lindwall today was often far-removed from a great fast bowler. He seems very much dependent on the new ball. Lockwood and Richardson bowled fast and brilliantly with the same ball throughout the longest innings.

H   225

COMPTON BACK

Compton came in to the sound of heartening cheers; a doctor's injection had been given him to alleviate pain in his wounded hand. He was loudly appealed against for a catch in the slips off Lindwall before he had scored again, a low fast chance to Hole. But the umpires after consulting gave Compton in; maybe the ball hit the ground. The Australian appeal was rhetorical enough, almost like that of a losing side. It must have been a near thing.

Another spinner from Davidson lifted itself up vertically to Bailey, who withdrew from it as if stung. But he looked at it as though at an intruder on his devotions; for he was now batting with a ritualistic push, runs for him obviously mere vanity and earthly dross. Compton was totally leg before at ten minutes to three, and now England's position and Australia's were at the mercy of the pitch—England eight wickets down and 145 in front. And none of us could tell yet how the wicket would behave.

In three-quarters of an hour following lunch England scored 9 runs; I here got the impression that if England were hoping for victory it was in the way that a poor relation, himself not in the best health, hopes to inherit the goods of somebody who might somehow pass away sooner.

The policy of England's innings after lunch was inexplicable. In 75 minutes no more than eighteen runs were added. Such methods were not safeguarding England from defeat or leading to a win, for time was running out. Then Lock struck an unannounced four and, the same over, was well caught on the leg side from a really swash-buckling sweep of the bat. This cricket and Bailey's belonged to another dimension, in which possibly two and two make five. At ten minutes to four Bailey today had made 24 runs in rather more than three hours and a half. He was not so much patience on a monument as the monument.

But all the England batting after lunch was so deliberately protective, with no effort at runs, that we are obliged to conclude that it was done to orders, orders lacking the imagination to grasp at the far from outside chance looming England's way to get a grip on the rubber. Such negation is removed from sport; a dreary bore and a belittlement of cricket. Up to lunch England's tactics had been sensible, but the persistent stone-walling after lunch while the game hung in a nice balance potential of rare sport, is, I think, beneath discussion.

BETTER TO HAVE . . .

Needing 177 to win in 115 minutes the Australians began with a bravery and swift precision of strokes that quickly dispersed the gloomy atmosphere of England's innings, which had suggested that the spiritual brokers were taking possession. Morris attacked like a cultured and manly cricketer; 27 runs raced over the field in less than a quarter of an hour; then Hassett played a spinner from Lock into his stumps. Lock proceeded to bowl two really vicious balls at Hole, confirming the optimistic view that England could have thrown some hazard to fortune and batted like players of heart and faith. Though twice beaten as soon as he came in Hole pulled the first short ball he received from Lock for four.

I would sooner lose a match this way, playing as the Australians did now, than win a whole rubber by England's fearful protectiveness. When Laker bowled instead of Lock away from the stand end Morris pulled him high and beautifully for four and Bailey leapt like a harlequin trying to catch the ball as it soared above him. The same over Morris was stumped playing forward, an abrupt end to an innings which had burned with gem-like flame. It is because cricket was originally played in the manner of Morris this evening that poets have written about it. Played in England's way of batting during this match, cricket might have occupied the attention of Karl Marx and the like.

Hole pulled Bedser with panache; Harvey drove Laker to the off, then waited for one to pitch and reveal itself whereat he cut it deliciously. Runs were attempted with application of skill and freedom of style. Almost every ball Lock returned to Laker, and Harvey pulling against the spin 'foozled' his stroke dangerously. Always bat with the tide as George Gunn says and has always said. Hole risking his life in the cause skied Bedser to leg, but nobody could catch the ball. With an hour to go Australia wanted 99.

The spirited batting apparently brought out the sunshine. For the first time since Thursday the place and the scene appeared to have some connection with pleasure and animation in life. The first hour of Australia's second innings produced 88, whereupon Hole glanced Bedser twice for fours to leg from consecutive balls, strong rhythmical strokes on swiftly circling feet. A splendid on-drive, a snick, and a square drive plundered three fours from three balls from Lock all to Harvey. It was as if a bottle of champagne had been opened by the pressure inside, cork and vintage and all.

With 66 to get and 50 minutes left Harvey was leg before to

Bedser trying a quick turn to leg. Davidson, in next, was delivered a capacious wide by Bailey, a risky bowler to put on in the circumstances, except that he pitches often where he cannot be reached and does not get through an over too quickly. From Bailey Hole was caught easily and with excellent judgment on the leg boundary just as a grand hit was going for six. Sixty to make, four wickets taken, 35 minutes remaining.

At this point Hutton took the precaution to rearrange his field; not once, not twice, but several times. Why the left-handed Davidson should have been sent in instead of Miller must be counted amongst the various unaccountable doings in this game. De Courcy struck Bedser for a colossal six to leg at five minutes past six. But this was the last kick in the match.

At the finish Australia were only thirty runs from their goal, but they had won on points and by the value of the pleasure given. The last cheer though was for Bailey. The English usually take to heart those who thrive on vicissitude and come through the strait gate. A plucky cricketer.

ENGLAND

First Innings		Second Innings	
L. Hutton, b Lindwall	0	c Langley, b Archer	25
W. J. Edrich, lbw, b Miller	10	c de Courcy, b Lindwall	64
T. W. Graveney, c Benaud, b Miller	55	b Lindwall	3
D. C. S. Compton, c Davidson, b Lindwall	0	lbw, b Lindwall	61
W. Watson, b Lindwall	24	c Davidson, b Miller	15
R. T. Simpson, c Langley, b Lindwall	15	c de Courcy, b Miller	0
T. E. Bailey, run out	7	c Hole, b Davidson	38
T. G. Evans, lbw, b Lindwall	25	c Lindwall, b Miller	1
J. C. Laker, c Lindwall, b Archer	10	c Benaud, b Davidson	48
G. A. R. Lock, b Davidson	9	c Morris, b Miller	8
A. V. Bedser, not out	0	not out	3
Extras (b 8, lb 4)	12	Extras (b 1, lb 8)	9
	—		—
Total	167	Total	275

FALL OF WICKETS
First Innings

1	2	3	4	5	6	7	8	9
0	33	36	98	108	110	133	149	167

BOWLING ANALYSIS
First Innings

	O.	M.	R.	W.		O.	M.	R.	W.
Lindwall	35	10	54	5	Archer	18	4	27	1
Miller	28	13	39	2	Benaud	8	1	12	0
Davidson	20·4	7	23	1					

FALL OF WICKETS
Second Innings

1	2	3	4	5	6	7	8	9
57	62	139	167	171	182	239	244	258

BOWLING ANALYSIS
Second Innings

	O.	M.	R.	W.		O.	M.	R.	W.
Lindwall	54	19	104	3	Davidson	29·3	15	36	2
Miller	47	19	63	4	Hole	3	1	6	0
Archer	25	12	31	1	Benaud	19	8	26	0

AUSTRALIA

First Innings		Second Innings	
A. L. Hassett, c Lock, b Bedser	37	b Lock	4
A. R. Morris, c Lock, b Bedser	10	st Evans, b Laker	38
R. N. Harvey, lbw, b Bailey	71	lbw, b Bedser	34
K. R. Miller, c Edrich, b Bailey	5		
G. B. Hole, c Lock, b Bedser	53	c Graveney, b Bailey	33
J. de Courcy, lbw, b Lock	10	not out	13
R. Benaud, b Bailey	7		
A. K. Davidson, c Evans, b Bedser	2	not out	17
R. G. Archer, not out	31		
R. R. Lindwall, b Bedser	9		
G. R. Langley, c Hutton, b Bedser	17		
Extras (b 4, lb 8, w 2)	14	Extras (b 3, lb 4, w 1)	8
Total	266	Total (4 wkts)	147

FALL OF WICKETS
First Innings

1	2	3	4	5	6	7	8	9
27	70	84	168	183	203	203	208	218

BOWLING ANALYSIS
First Innings

	O.	M.	R.	W.		O.	M.	R.	W.
Bedser	28·5	2	95	6	Lock	23	9	53	1
Bailey	22	4	71	3	Laker	9	1	33	0

FALL OF WICKETS
Second Innings

1	2	3	4
27	54	111	117

BOWLING ANALYSIS
Second Innings

	O.	M.	R.	W.		O.	M.	R.	W.
Bedser	17	1	65	1	Laker	2	0	17	1
Lock	8	1	48	1	Bailey	6	1	9	1

Umpires: F. Chester and F. S. Lee.

PRELUDE TO FINAL TEST
AT THE OVAL

LITTLE need be said to prepare the mind and eye for the fifth Test match of the rubber, both teams have fairly revealed themselves squarely matched, with a modicum of exceptional talent handicapped by a monstrous amount of mediocrity. Maybe England have an advantage of all-round technical ability, but Australia are the tougher minded and the younger and more virile in outlook.

Since the game at Trent Bridge in June, England's cricket has more and more tended to act defensively and, as a consequence, a moral advantage has been lost. It will be as well if the match at Leeds is forgotten entirely in the England councils of war at Kennington Oval this morning. None of us wishes ever again to read of so-and-so's (or Bailey's) 'heroic efforts', denoting an innings of 50 in five hours, while the match is still anybody's.

With the issue precariously balanced, the victory in the end will most likely go to the side which enjoys the better share of whatever luck is at hand. But fortune likes to be pursued. England certainly won't win the rubber by waiting for Australia to lose it, or by dithering in policy in the hope that an ally will turn up in the shape of a 'sticky' wicket. England have lost more than one Test match in recent years because of lack of positive and flexible plan. Much will depend today on the toss for innings, but there could be a 'snag' here.

It is all very well for us to pray that Hutton might win it. But suppose there has been a storm in the night leaving the wicket softish and springy on top, and bone-hard below the surface? Which of us, were we Hutton, would cheerfully bat first and face Lindwall in such circumstances? On the other hand, wouldn't we want to 'slip' Bedser at them before the turf became reliable and full of runs?

DECEITFUL 'VOICES'

Our prayers, of course and if any, will have been for another glorious day of sunshine, a perfect pitch, and first innings on it by England. Here, though, temptation may come before Hutton in deceitful guise: 'A smooth lawn of Oval turf, the barometer set fair and a whole week before you! Make the most of your opportunity. Stay in as long as you can, build up a huge score—then, maybe, the rain will come, or the wicket crumble . . .' Frankly I believe defeat will come to England if such notions or 'voices' are attended to; only by playing good and sensible cricket—after the Australian manner—can England hope to win. The loose ball should be hit, the good ball respected—that is all, or nearly all, there is 'to it'.

England's Selection Committee have risked much in choosing Trueman as fast bowler. I saw him at Lord's in the match between the Royal Navy and the Royal Air Force: and though he took ten wickets in two innings for 112 runs, his bowling was frequently so bad in length and direction that I felt myself at times shivering with apprehension at the thought of what Morris, Harvey, Hassett, and de Cource could have done with it.

He might achieve transfiguration at the Oval, some such miracle will be necessary on his behalf, so let us add a codicil to the petition to Providence referred to above. Trueman may quite credibly 'crash his way' through an Australian eleven with batting very doubtful in the middle of an innings. Contemporary Test match standards of technique and character are so low that 'sensational' performances are within the reach of cricketers who are scarcely adornments to ordinary county company day by day.

The two great bowlers of the rubber are Lindwall and Bedser. Each, as I say, may wish to bowl at once this morning. Taking a six-day engagement by and large (and policy must go to work assuming the match will last six days, though charity and common decency would wish an earlier end), England's attack has a better all-round appearance than Australia's, which so far has leaned heavily on the new ball. The improvement in W. A. Johnston's form and soundness of limb must have come as a relief to Hassett. Most of us, in reviewing the rubber so far, have been inclined to underrate the grievous loss sustained by Australia by the injury to their finest all-round bowler. The Australians, I am told, are prepared to take the risk of going into action today with an almost wholly fast or quick attack. But Hassett hasn't much choice of spin material; Ring has ability to turn prodigiously from leg—and he missed a succulent chance at Lord's on the closing afternoon.

Hill 'rolls' the ball too much from outside the leg-stump, he has wasted himself not attacking the middle-to-off. One of the saddest aspects of Australian cricket today is the fact that the great school of spinners from leg, with the 'googly', from Hordern, through Mailey to Grimmett, Fleetwood-Smith, and O'Reilly, has apparently been allowed to wane.

England are in no happier state regarding the same beautiful art, the new lbw rule has encouraged the laziest, easiest, and most uninteresting of all kinds of bowling—in-swinging and off-breaks to the leg-trap—usually bowling of the negative order which dare not face the challenge of a player's best strokes, but bowls so as to avoid them and waits for the batsman to make a mistake.

WHAT WE DESERVE?

On the whole I would not risk a shilling on either team's chances. Moreover, a victory by England or Australia at the Oval won't get us much further towards deciding which of the two is definitely the better lot. Frankly, I have preferred watching the Australians, for with all their youthful brashnesses, they have looked and have actually given us cricket more handsome to watch, happier and more self-reliant, than England's. Winning or losing, Hutton and his men owe a gesture to the art of the game. But the imp of irony in me, to be frank, is gloating at the possibility of a six-day Test match and in the end—another draw! That would certainly 'serve us all right', as they say. For, really, whoever arranges a Test match with a time-limit extending beyond four days deserves all the tedious mediocrity in the world, in fact, probably enjoys it.

FIFTH TEST (FIRST DAY)

THE OVAL, SATURDAY

Today at the Oval was mainly disappointing to everybody. Hassett, though lucky winning the toss, yet again saw his team bat insecurely on a good wicket. Hutton also must have suffered frustration because his bowlers failed to finish off the Australian innings for a total of less than 200 after having removed the five most productive runmakers of the side for 118. The crowd plainly went home more than a little disillusioned. As for the student of the art of cricket and lover of the individual contribution of character which can elevate cricket beyond the scope of a game—well, he might just as well have stayed at home and listened to the radio.

The play on the whole was commonplace and anonymous, excepting the gusto of young Trueman, with his sturdy coltish action, and the liveliness of Evans, who in coping with Trueman behind the stumps was occasionally obliged to emulate in turn a man on a flying trapeze, an outnumbered goalkeeper, and a fish temporarily flipping about out of water.

An innings by Lindwall enchanted the eye for its rhythm of stroke play in front of the wicket; it was Lindwall who came in to bat at the fall of Australia's seventh wicket for 160 and strongly levered the match out of England's grip and scored 62 in 112 minutes, with eight boundaries. But he was dropped on the offside by Graveney when his score had not gone beyond 25. He mishit Laker in an aim at the senior gasometer. Graveney needed to turn to find his bearings to get beneath the ball, then with it in his hands he allowed it to escape. Perhaps at first he thought of leaving it to Bedser. The mishap occurred as though in slow motion; and it was one of those fielding blunders a cricketer experiences in a nightmare, with thousands of spectral spectators looming behind him as the ball hovers above him. And they are all saying, 'He'll miss it. He'll miss it.'

<h3 style="text-align:center">PITY HE DID</h3>

The runs made by Lindwall may well be seen to have gravely affected the course of the match before we have done with it. For in spite of all the faults and limitations of the Australian innings, the aggregate of 275 reached in the end places England under the obligation to head it by at least a hundred as insurance against any change in the weather and the never desirable ordeal of fourth innings in a Test match.

The England attack failed Hutton at the pinch. There would have been cause for many rejoicings had Australia's score fallen below 200. Hutton, as at Leeds, seemed disinclined to put Lock on to bowl against batsmen ready to drive in front of the wicket. Surely such strokes are more safely made from bowling that turns into the bat than against spin which like Lock's turns away from it? But there it is—the England attack could not sweep aside the Australian 'tail'.

Langley helped Lindwall add a priceless 38 for the ninth wicket and, to sharpen the edge and render more and more audible the general gnashing of teeth, another 30 runs were made by the last wicket, W. A. Johnston being once more invincible or at least immovable. Not only couldn't England's bowlers take wickets now; they couldn't even keep both ends of the wicket 'tight' in the encircling gloom. And here it must be stated that Australia's innings was played for long in a poor light, against which no appeal was lodged.

The ease of Lindwall's innings urges me to suspect that Hassett at least shares Hutton's chagrin at the course of events, for though the pitch was, as they say, on the 'green' side it was good enough for good batsmen. And when Australia passed the first 100 with Hassett and Harvey settling down many of us prepared for the worst—or, according to a point of view not necessarily partisan, the best. Harvey got out trying to hook, even as his innings was beginning to assume the lustre of menace; the ball was a long-hop bowled by Trueman, but a long-hop still rising sharply when Harvey struck across it.

Trueman more than realized expectations, though not yet is he more than a promising young fast bowler. Today he was really fast at times, though never invisible. Often his direction faltered or sprawled to the legside, in which direction he would have been bludgeoned temporarily out of Test cricket by Bradman or McCabe. When he attacked the offside, especially in a period after lunch with the pitch enlivened by brief, gentle rain, he began to look a fast bowler destined one day to succeed to a great tradition. More than this it would be foolish to say of him at present.

FOOTBALL IN THE AIR

The atmosphere of the morning, suggestive of autumn's ripe presence and the approach of football, encouraged the late swinging ball. Bedser bowled the first over and Hassett turned the second ball of the match to leg for four, whereat Hutton sent a man to guard the long-leg boundary, a clear case of setting your field a posteriori, to say. Trueman, attacking from the pavilion end, ran a long, square-shouldered, tight-bottomed course to the wicket, with the fast bowler's proper show of hostility. He walked back to his starting place slowly, dark and sullen of countenance. From the last ball of his first over, which rose hip-high, Morris made a spasmodic glance to leg, a swift chance to Compton standing very fine near Evans, and though he grasped the ball, could not hold it as he was falling sideways to the left. Hutton's field for Trueman was not exactly intimidating—two slips, a 'gully', two short legs, a long leg, and a third man, each of the latter in a profound perspective.

Morris, a beautiful batsman when he plays forward, again chose to remain on an uneasy back foot, pushing defensively across his pads; he scarcely suggested legitimate relationship to the Morris we saw and admired on the closing evening at Leeds. He was out leg-before to Bedser, standing erect and not making or envisaging a stroke, apparently deceived by late swing. Hassett, looking tinier than ever or the great plain of the Oval, made his usual neat runs, and now and again was interrupted in his studies while the pigeons were being dispersed; presumably they were getting in the way of the line of his vision towards the boundary. Trueman here bowled a no-ball so quick of pace that Hassett's stroke to it was as retrospective as unproductive. A few 'bouncers' by Trueman were excellent signs of temper in the young man, but let us hope he will restrain himself in the company of Lindwall. Maybe Hutton will see to that.

HASSETT PRECISE

Australia's first wicket fell at 38. Bailey, who had come on for Trueman, then defeated Miller, also leg before. Miller pushed forward at a vivacious inswinger 'off the seam', a stroke without eyesight or presence of mind. A feature of the morning's cricket, in fact of the Australian innings as a whole, was the number of times the batsmen missed aim, or the ball collided with legs or other parts of the anatomy. The bowling, though good and steady, was only of the class a batsman is expected to play day by day in first-class circles; it was not of abnormal excellence. I can only suppose the varying light handicapped eyesight peering down the wicket.

Until Lindwall and Langley got together and 'middled' the ball, Hassett was more precise of touch than the rest of his accredited batsmen, for the reason that he happens to be a product of the antique school in which the straight bat was put to the ball as a first principle, down the line and not drawn across the flight.

The Australian innings, as I have hinted, was emerging from the embryonic during the Hassett-Harvey partnership. Harvey, though guilty of a bad stroke to the slips off Bedser as soon as he reached the crease, struck Bailey to the off, a stroke quick and strong at the wrists, the back foot stabbing the earth. Hassett once or twice leaned his bat persuasively on half-volleys and sent them flowing to the on for threes. In less than an hour before lunch Hassett and Harvey scored 57 with the ease of long habit. Trueman from the Vauxhall end temporarily waned his fires and was not so fast that his slow ball could be detected by force of contrast. After lunch, though, he enjoyed immense satisfaction, which the crowd shared extravagantly. Here indeed we arrived at the period leading to our ultimate and ironic laugh on the wrong side of the face.

First, a superb ball from Bedser came up from the pitch, freshened by a shower of soft rain, found the edge of Hassett's bat and Evans held one-handed a born wicketkeeper's chance. Hassett's innings, already valuable, was taking deep root, so Bedser's blow at this juncture was brilliant and major.

Then with Australia's total still 107 Harvey committed his fatal error, pulling against Trueman with less than a great batsman's

235

power of selection. For, as I say, the ball was still rising. In making the hook stroke the eye should not be taken off the ball when it pitches; the important questions is its altitude and velocity, its rise or its fall, at the moment the bat is swung and applied. But this is a generalisation and a diversion (not, of course, addressed to Harvey). To dismiss Harvey, Hutton had to run after the mis-hit, under the skimming flight, and held a grand catch with the air of a man who was not prepared to let this prize go, no, not on his life. Harvey was brought down on a very dangerous and flashing wing; he is a beautiful stroke player rather than a batsman wearing the impregnable armour of the truly great and masterful.

After a slight pause for another shower a really fast ball by True-man pitched on the offside but close to the stumps, beat de Courcy by velocity and was edged to Evans's gloves. Now were we taken sardonically in and shown the riches of the world—Australia 118 for five in a match with the rubber at stake. Hole and Archer held on together and lifted the score to 160 by defence and counter-attack. Hole bats with style, if without enough of substance. He would have been happy in the Kent eleven in the heyday of C. H. B. Marsham. Trueman got rid of Hole at the right moment, much as he got rid of de Courcy—another swift, good length to the off; Trueman should certainly concentrate his attack mainly on or just outside the off stump.

Hole was scarcely back in the pavilion before Archer returned too, caught and bowled by Bedser from, I take it, a 'lifting' ball on a pitch not without resilience, though not at all malicious. By dis-missing Archer, Bedser excelled statistically Tate's record of 38 wickets in a rubber between England and Australia, and when Archer departed, Australia 160 for seven, England began to feel the sweets of the afternoon turning sour in the mouth.

After tea Edrich missed Davidson at first slip off Laker, then Davidson plundered a dozen in one over from Bailey, including two off-drives perfect in poise and forward thrust. The eighth Australian wicket put on 47 before Edrich retrieved himself by catching Davidson in his nimblest manner. Australia's last three wickets were permitted to help themselves to 115 runs.

TO CAP IT ALL

At the afternoon's decline, in a light dim enough for the bird of ill-omen, Lindwall bowled a terrific over at Hutton. One ball whizzed like the comet that announces deaths of princes; it streaked upward to a bat held in self-defence and, glancing from it, knocked Hutton's cap off his head, and the cap nearly fell on the stumps. Had it done so Hutton would have been out, and the Oval would have heard again, coming from somewhere not of this world, the devilish laughter heard at Kennington Oval 71 years ago this month when Peate was bowled trying to drive Boyle and Australia won by seven runs.

AUSTRALIA
First Innings

A. L. Hassett, c Evans, b Bedser	53
A. R. Morris, lbw, b Bedser	16
K. R. Miller, lbw, b Bailey	1
R. N. Harvey, c Hutton, b Trueman	36
G. B. Hole, c Evans, b Trueman	37
J. de Courcy, c Evans, b Trueman	5
R. G. Archer, c and b Bedser	10
A. K. Davidson, c Edrich, b Laker	22
R. R. Lindwall, c Evans, b Trueman	62
G. R. Langley, c Edrich, b Lock	18
W. A. Johnston, not out	9
Extras (b 4, nb 2)	6
Total	275

FALL OF WICKETS

1	2	3	4	5	6	7	8	9
38	41	107	107	118	160	160	207	245

BOWLING ANALYSIS

	O.	M.	R.	W.		O.	M.	R.	W.
Bedser	29	3	88	3	Lock	9	2	19	1
Trueman	24·3	3	86	4	Laker	5	0	34	1
Bailey	14	3	42	1					

ENGLAND
First Innings

Hutton, not out	0
W. J. Edrich, not out	1
Total (no wicket)	1

To bat: May, Compton, Graveney, Bailey, Evans, Laker, Lock, Bedser, Trueman.

BOWLING ANALYSIS

	O.	M.	R.	W.		O.	M.	R.	W.
Lindwall	1	1	0	0	Miller	1	0	1	0

FIFTH TEST (SECOND DAY)

THE OVAL, MONDAY

Yet again did England raise our hopes then depress them on this, the second day. At half-past two the score had gone beyond a hundred with only Edrich out and Hutton and May were playing commandingly, with brilliant strokes. All seemed set fair for a prosperous voyage along the sunny afternoon.

A peculiar mood came into England's innings when Johnston bowled at the Pavilion end and by actual and potential spin compelled the batsmen to alter gear. He certainly got enough out of the pitch to suggest that it was beginning to show willingness to respond to spin. The truth is that though Johnston's spin put the England innings out of joint, the wickets of importance fell to swing or pace; and not for the first time the passing of Hutton apparently elevated the spirits of the Australians as much as it lowered those of his colleagues. Compton and Graveney faltered sadly with much depending on them.

A QUICK START

The sun shone from a blue sky with white clouds in it when the match opened this morning. Against Lindwall and Miller in the fresh of this August morning Hutton and Edrich scored confidently, though both missed off-side balls from Lindwall, their forward lunges much too late for the speed: moreover, Hutton snicked fortuitously for two to leg in Lindwall's first over.

Edrich set a tempo of scoring which put more than thirty runs on the scoreboard in half an hour; he forced Lindwall to the on for three in Lindwall's third over, then hooked Miller contumaciously for four, and next ball swung him for four high over the leg trap. Lindwall by means of a Nijinsky leap got a finger to the ball, but the only chance presented was that of a contusion or a removed nail. The wicket so far was amiable to batsmen. So was the bowling.

Hutton played Miller to the leg boundary serenely, popped a ball from Lindwall which lifted a little, but the stroke was not in the field's danger zone, and drove the same bowler for two to the on so easily that the rhythm of the hit, easy as the pendulum of Big Ben, stole yards of pace from the ball.

Edrich's assurance dispersed mists of gloomy self-doubt which have hung over an England innings lately; possibly he was urged to go beyond the technical scope of any batsman facing a fast bowler in a Test match while the ball retained seam and polish, for he hit to

238

the on across the line of a potential yorker from Lindwall and succumbed leg before. Still, his little innings contributed a moral value beyond the scorers' powers of estimation.

May, in next, was a cricketer much blessed not to have his off stump knocked flying first ball, a very fast one from Miller which shaved the wicket while May's bat thudded down by reflex action very late in the day, so to speak. Curiously and inexplicably Hassett allowed Lindwall only two balls with which to exploit May's natural unease at the outset of an already disconcerted innings, then took him off. I have known fast bowlers who would have declined their sweater at such a moment. May drove Miller for a sumptuous four to the off, but was surely nearly leg before to Miller's well-tempered square-armed skimmer.

For a while May looked less than a young batsman born to greatness; he checked his strokes dubiously and played forward with a short front leg. When he was only nine he was fortunate to miss an off-side ball from Davidson because he reached to it at arm's length 'most. As May gradually modulated from a tentative chromatic key to one of a more diatonic resonance, Lindwall probably watched his progress with more than an academic interest. For the Australian attack waned to respectable industry every over that aged the ball.

Johnston was steady, more or less aiming at or outside the leg stump. Davidson's approximations to pace differed from Archer's mainly because Davidson is left-handed and Archer right. Some element of variety and surprise might have here been introduced into Australia's attack if Hassett had instructed Davidson to bowl right-handed and Archer left. On the easy wicket, Hassett was at a loss for real spin from the back of the hand. (If I had been told in Armstrong's and Mailey's and Grimmett's period that I would live to see the day when an Australian team would take the field at the Oval without a bowler commanding authentic finger spin, I could no more have believed the prophecy than I would one day have believed I would hear the Fifth Symphony of Beethoven played without 'cellos.) Johnston endeavoured to exploit his slower stuff, but all in all the batsmen were under no obligation to look for problems of flight or ask questions to the ball while it was in the air.

Lindwall bowled from the Pavilion end when England's score stood promisingly at 77 for one: his pace was now a shade quicker than E. A. Macdonald's, when that satanic prince of fast bowlers indulged his fancy to go on round the wicket with off-spin. These Australian bowlers of Coronation year put me in mind of remittance men I have known in their own country: they wait for the new ball to come periodically to relieve them from temporary embarrassments.

At lunch England were 89 for one, Hutton not out 46, May not out 21, and May had then been batting 85 minutes. Hutton looked safe as Threadneedle Street: so many runs has he scored at the Oval in Test matches that I am sure the Australians would support any move to award him the Chiltern Hundreds.

After lunch the England innings was kindled to a temporary and really brilliant and consuming fire. Hutton drove Miller through the covers gloriously, a hit of sculpturesque rhythm and substance, a stroke poised classically as though on a pedestal. In the same over he pulled to leg with a circling wing of the bat as lovely as the flight of the pigeons he disturbed in the long field. Then May drove Archer through the covers, another stroke handsome enough for the cricketer's Parthenon.

Two other quick fours by May, both off Johnston, one to the off, the other to the on, also thrilled the sense of speed and beauty. England passed the hundred mark at half past two, and no cloud of trouble, not one even as large as a man's hand, was to be seen in the English sky, excepting that Hutton would have been run out, sent back by May, if Hassett at the wicket, had gathered the ball.

SUDDEN CHANGE

Suddenly, as though some invisible agency had operated on the pitch, the atmosphere and technique of the batting changed. Johnston crossed over to the Pavilion end, and this time his slow medium bowling began to turn, though it was a ball that came with his arm that broke the splendid stand for England's second wicket after it had added one hundred runs in roughly two and a half hours.

Compton began in heavy weather and there was nearly a run out characteristic of Compton. The game's transformation became dramatic with England's total 154, for here the third wicket fell, and moreover it was Hutton's, clean bowled by Johnston, and he was not, I think, beaten by spin; for the ball travelled, again, with Johnston's arm and was well pitched up to the crease. Hutton's stroke seemed a little relaxed, even careless.

It is not generally realised how great is the strain this rubber has subjected him to, psychologically if not technically. Few England batsmen have been asked to carry his responsibility, and at one and the same time contribute both to the spinal column and the cerebellum of an England eleven. For the first time in the rubber, I believe, Hassett to-day did not at once claim the new ball, due when England were 154 for three; he continued to rely on the spinning potentiality of Johnston—which might appear to make nonsense of my remarks above about this Australian attack's dependability on the new ball; but I cannot withdraw them out of concern for the wit of them.

Compton scored only seven in 50 minutes and did nothing at all for nearly half an hour after Hutton departed. He could not trust Johnston out of his sight for the briefest moment and Johnston was not spinning all that much. This wicket is an angel at the moment compared with what it will be in England's second innings unless rain comes to bind it together. Now was it necessary for England to score runs from every ball the slightest loose.

After tea Compton was out to a culpably negligent half-glance at Lindwall swinging wide to leg; Langley caught him grandly as he fell to the left on the ground. England four out for 167 were thus once more and after all precariously placed when Bailey came in— Bailey born to trouble (which he enjoys) as the sparks fly upward.

The new ball was claimed and Graveney snicked Lindwall convulsively and Miller held a magnificent catch in the slips. This was a flashing ball doing its work like aconitum or rash gunpowder. England 170 for five—and oh! the vanity of our pleasure and expectation only some two hours ago.

EVANS'S FROLIC

But Evans came in here perky and indecorous as Till Eulenspiegel himself and with a bat as busy as a man swatting wasps from his head, not defensively but aggressively, snicked, drove, and pulled the fast bowling and also played Miller once with his bottom. A pull by him off Lindwall was a thump of sheer gusto. So Lindwall retired again into his sweater. Twenty-nine runs scampered over the field in 20 minutes because of Evans and his high-spirited distrust of science to cope with the crisis.

Meanwhile Bailey batted according to his Test match habit— blade to the ball which he met in the middle of it, statuesque in the manner of some monumental stonemason emulating Michelangelo. Bad luck ended a gallant sixth-wicket stand worth 40. Evans turned a ball to leg, dashed impetuously for a single, was sent back, slipped and fell, and was run out. Two stylish fours to the off reminded us of what Bailey can do when he is batting down at Southend-on-Sea. Both these strokes in the same over by Johnston urge me to correct a word in a sentence appearing above and exchange the name of Michelangelo for 'Phideas'. Laker flicked fatally at an unusually fast one from Miller who celebrated his success with a gesture as triumphant as if he had overthrown Jack Hobbs himself.

A blow on the body swayed Bailey backward, but only as a blow by a direct hit at an Aunt Sally at a fair sways it: it comes back again without going over and you lose your money. Bailey remained intact at the close, if not invincible, after two hours of calm obstinacy. I wonder he had not driven Miller mad by this time. He is not only an anchor for England; he barnacles the good ship to the floor of the ocean.

ENGLAND
First Innings

L. Hutton, b Johnston	82
W. J. Edrich, lbw, b Lindwall	21
P. B. H. May, c Archer, b Johnston	39
D. C. S. Compton, c Langley, b Lindwall	16
T. W. Graveney, c Miller, b Lindwall	4
T. E. Bailey, not out	35
T. G. Evans, run out	28
J. C. Laker, c Langley, b Miller	1
G. A. R. Lock, not out	4
Extras (b 4, w 1)	5

Total (7 wickets)   235

To bat: Bedser, Trueman.

FALL OF WICKETS

1	2	3	4	5	6	7
37	137	154	167	170	210	225

BOWLING ANALYSIS

	O.	M.	R.	W.		O.	M.	R.	W.
Lindwall	23	4	58	3	Davidson	9	1	20	0
Miller	27	8	60	1	Archer	8	1	23	0
Johnston	31	12	61	2	Hole	7	4	8	0

FIFTH TEST (THIRD DAY)

THE OVAL, TUESDAY

Victory for England in a rubber against Australia and in this country is surely at hand after 27 years of waiting, and we have seen its blessed approach on an afternoon at Kennington Oval, where in 1926 Chapman led England to a victory as desirable.

It was then an afternoon of fresh wind and sunshine such as to-day's, and at the end of the match the multitude gathered in front of the pavilion and to the tune of the chimes of 'Bow Bells' they sang 'We want Chapman, Hobbs, and Sutcliffe, we want Larwood, Rhodes, and Geary.' To-morrow, in the absence of evil witchery, the crowd here will call for, if they do not in these times sing, 'We want Hutton, Lock, and Laker, we want Bedser, Evans, and Bailey.'

This Oval wicket turned into a spinner's happy hunting-ground, especially a left-hander's. Lock missed no chance after one or two preliminary doubtful overs; and Laker, if not at his most spitefully angular, made his necessary contribution.

The Australians can scarcely be said to have collapsed or disgraced themselves, though one or two of their more renowned and experienced batsmen failed helplessly where young players, not yet steeled by an ordeal as scorching as to-day's, succeeded up to a point. Australia made 162 in three hours, thanks to superb stroke-play and bravery of Archer, Davidson, and Hole.

Our sympathy must go to Hassett in his bad luck at having run into so troublesome a pitch as this—but the match is not won or lost yet, so we had better remember Dr Johnson's advice on the question of what sort of Christian attitude we should adopt to any dangerous marauder—'We should knock him down first and pity him afterwards.'

Not until the last over before lunch did Australia capture England's last three wickets in the first innings to-day and then England enjoyed a useful advantage of thirty-one. Bailey was astonishingly bowled at twenty-eight minutes past one after he had frustrated the Australian attack yet again for hours—to be precise, for three and three-quarter hours.

Apart from a miscalculation against a spinner from Johnston, he not only seemed unlikely ever to get out but defended as though the idea never occurred to him that any way of removing him from the crease existed in law or custom. Now and again he performed a truly fine stroke, for example a square pull off Lindwall, a back cut off Johnston, a brilliant off drive from the same bowler, reminding us of the Bailey who tries to win matches for Essex in the spare time left over to him when he is not saving matches for England—and really it cannot amount to much time.

Yesterday I described his batting as monumental, but the term is unjust and inadequate. After all, to be monumental is to be, sooner or later, perishable, suggesting some object or substance made by mortal hands and subject to wear and tear in space and time as conceived in human consciousness. A Test match innings by Bailey is geological, and nothing less. So easily did he counter and reduce to nullity all efforts to remove him from the scene that we could only wonder why the Australian bowling had so often challenged the finest arts of Hutton, May, Compton, and Graveney.

Even Trueman was capable of staying in with Bailey nearly three quarters of an hour, and it needed Johnston's best spinner to get rid of him. Then Bedser supported Bailey to hold England's last wicket seventy minutes, adding 44. Bedser was in last with 14 wanted for a win on the first innings; if the occasion has been England's second innings, and the rubber now visibly at stake, would he have held the fort as tranquilly as he held it now. For surely we could have trusted Bailey.

Maybe such a question will put us on the rack of intolerable fact, asked in the tense of the immediate future before we are through with this match of swaying fortune. Not for the first time during this series of Test matches, and this summer, the Australian attack has failed rather dispiritedly to break a resistance of a rearguard action at the pinch.

Bailey at one period this morning scored only two runs in forty minutes; in the olden times it was a general supposition that when the eighth or ninth wicket had fallen any accredited batsman who happened to be in possession of the other end of the wicket would set to work and score as quickly and avidly as may be. Other times, other manners—besides, in Test matches Bailey is not as other men. He bats, if not for eternity, at least and at the earliest, for posterity.

Hassett and Morris began Australia's second innings at a quick and perhaps rather feverish tempo and temperature. But a superb pull square by Morris off Trueman, which sent a long hop to the boundary with a fearful crack, told us that bombardment had certainly been begun on the young Yorkshireman. But Trueman was taken off after hurling down two overs, and Hutton called his spinners into play.

At once a rasping breakback from Laker, round the wicket, trapped Hassett leg-before; he could do nothing at all about it. Hole joined Morris, Australia 23 for one. Morris, baffled by flight and spin from Lock, put the ball up in the air on the off side out of actual danger; thus Australia went statistically ahead, though both

Morris and Hole scarcely appeared in any happy or prosperous state.

Lock and Laker promised now to get a wicket any ball; and many of them whipped across or whipped in as though the pitch had suddenly gone half-way to the devil. Morris and Hole astutely chose their bowlers, Morris taking Lock, Hole taking Laker, each keeping away from spin leaving the bat. And for a brief agonising few overs both Laker and Lock threatened to lose grip, Lock especially, because he bowled just too quick and too short. Hole hit Laker for a swinging four square to the on, and next ball, which nipped again, Laker overwhelmed him, also leg before. A moment later Lock clean-bowled Harvey with a length on the airy side, moving with his arm. So, three wickets down, Australia were 29 only to the good; on the face of it a losing position, if only Laker and Lock remained steady.

Miller, once dangerous in moments such as these, is to-day a quiescent if not disused volcano and was easy game for Laker; he groped his way into the leg-trap of Laker, and before the roaring crowd had regained breath, Morris padded up without constructive ideas to Lock and died the modern hero's death, leg before. Four wickets had fallen in sixteen balls, and Australia's total was 61 for five when De Courcy and Archer came into partnership and a situation severely challenging to the quick eye and intrepid nerve of youth.

They showed fight and took risks. De Courcy pulled Laker vehemently and strongly for four, and Archer drove Lock to the off-boundary in style. Next ball he forced a good one away to the left of square and De Courcy, impetuously, was run out backing up with over-eagerness, unable to turn and desperately writhe his way back. Australia 85 for six, 54 in front, if in front they could here be said to be at all.

Defiant in vicissitude, no doubt sick at heart for De Courcy's misfortune, Archer drove Lock for a colossal and beautiful six into the seats under the press box. Next he got a four to leg from Laker, whereat Davidson hit Laker square, powerfully yet easefully, into the depths of the crowd on the square-leg boundary for another six. The cricket at this point was sparkling sport—a difficult attack, the match and the rubber half in England's grip, and two Australian youngsters, undismayed if desperate, hitting magnificently. But Davidson might have succumbed quickly to Lock if a solitary slip had stood adjacent to his left-handed bat.

Bedser bowled now, Laker crossing over to the Pavilion end in place of Lock: Laker usually bowls at the Oval with the Pavilion behind him and looks straight at it every time he begins his short placid run. Another brilliant hit past cover off the back foot by Archer, and yet another stroke of the highest and most mettlesome quality in the same over, brought us to tea-time, with Australia leading by 100 exactly. Archer, not out 44, had played with the lustrous gallantry which glorifies causes half lost; his strokes were of thrilling power, yet as precise as they were swift and brave. In 45 minutes, following the dismissal of Morris, Australia scored 70 runs—which is true cricket whether the match be lost or won.

ARCHER SATISFYING

Immediately after tea, Archer drove for four to the off from Bedser, who bowled for Laker, but Lock then defeated Davidson, who left the crease crestfallen, though he had played his part in a stand whose statistical value of 50 was much less than its true worth in terms of character.

Archer, too, was out five runs later, the eighth wicket to fall at 140. He got a perfectly vicious spinner from Lock, which rose to the top of Archer's blade as he was wincing away from it; Edrich held a remarkable tumbling slip catch. Archer deserved a fairer end—at least he deserved an end which gave him a technical chance: for his innings was, in its spirit and its quick, crisp, and quite passionate stroke-play, as quickening and satisfying to a born cricketer's sense and imagination as any witnessed in this rubber.

Another spinner by Lock, but reasonably unplayable, accounted for Langley; and so at five o'clock on a sunny August evening at Kennington, Johnston came in last, the score 144.

Lindwall, before getting ready to bat against Bedser, surveyed the scene with comprehensive eye, not so much looking to find out where the fieldsmen were stationed, but whether the pavilion or the gasholder remained in the old familiar places. He pulled Lock for six with a vengeance, then chose to run a single to deliver Johnston to the attack, and Johnston, as though enjoyably conscious that his batting average this summer is 60 and more an innings, lofted Lock high for three. Lindwall, missed in the slips off Lock when his score was ten, swung his bat ponderously at Laker in the next over and was caught delightfully next to the Pavilion gate by Compton, the hit just failing to achieve another sumptuous six. Johnston elevated his batting average to seventy, and it is certain that the contemplation of it brings much merriment to him, for he is much given to humour. He has surrendered his wicket only once in the season so far, and has visited the crease some thirteen or fourteen times.

FINGERS CROSSED

The crowd hailed Hutton and Edrich jubilantly to the wicket to begin England's task of getting 132, and Lindwall attacked furiously. Edrich edged him blindly over the slips but hooked Miller savagely for four, then Johnston bowled at Lindwall's end and Lock's. Obviously Hassett had concluded that nothing but spin could save Australia, so he persisted with Miller. The theory was all right, supposing that Australia possessed the bowlers suitable to the pitch, personally I would have encouraged Lindwall to do his damnedest a little longer.

Hutton off-drove Johnston classically and next ball stopped a nasty low one in the block-hole. Apart from one deplorable mistake England scored 38 with apparent comfort before the drawing of stumps. Hutton was thrown out running to his own call.

With nine wickets to fall England need 94. We may surely lay out the red carpet and get the bellringers ready without tempting providence. Hassett, let us argue, simply hasn't the right bowling at his command to exploit the wicket.

AUSTRALIA

First Innings		Second Innings	
A. L. Hassett, c Evans, b Bedser	53	lbw, b Laker	10
A. R. Morris, lbw, b Bedser	16	lbw, b Lock	26
K. R. Miller, lbw, b Bailey	1	c Trueman, b Laker	0
R. N. Harvey, c Hutton, b Trueman	36	b Lock	1
G. B. Hole, c Evans, b Trueman	37	lbw, b Laker	17
J. H. de Courcy, c Evans, b Trueman	5	run out	4
R. G. Archer, c and b Bedser	10	c Edrich, b Lock	49
A. K. Davidson, c Edrich, b Laker	22	b Lock	21
R. R. Lindwall, c Evans, b Trueman	62	c Compton, b Laker	12
G. R. Langley, c Edrich, b Lock	18	c Trueman, b Lock	2
W. A. Johnston, not out	9	not out	6
Extras (b 4, nb 2)	6	Extras (b 11, lb 3)	14
Total	275	Total	162

FALL OF WICKETS
First Innings

1	2	3	4	5	6	7	8	9
38	41	107	107	118	160	160	207	245

BOWLING ANALYSIS
First Innings

	O.	M.	R.	W.			O.	M.	R.	W.
Bedser	29	3	88	3	Lock		9	2	19	1
Trueman	24·3	3	86	4	Laker		5	0	34	1
Bailey	14	3	42	1						

FALL OF WICKETS
Second Innings

1	2	3	4	5	6	7	8	9
23	59	60	61	61	85	135	140	144

BOWLING ANALYSIS
Second Innings

	O.	M.	R.	W.			O.	M.	R.	W.
Bedser	11	2	24	0	Laker		16·5	2	75	4
Trueman	2	1	4	0	Lock		21	9	45	5

ENGLAND

First Innings		Second Innings	
L. Hutton, b Johnston	82	run out	17
W. J. Edrich, lbw, b Lindwall	21	not out	15
P. B. H. May, c Archer, b Johnston	39	not out	6
D. C. S. Compton, c Langley, b Lindwall	16		
T. W. Graveney, c Miller, b Lindwall	4		
T. E. Bailey, b Archer	64		
T. G. Evans, run out	28		
J. C. Laker, c Langley, b Miller	1		
G. A. R. Lock, c Davidson, b Lindwall	4		
F. S. Trueman, b Johnston	10		
A. V. Bedser, not out	22		
Extras (b 9, lb 5, w 1)	15		
Total	306	Total (one wkt)	38

FALL OF WICKETS
First Innings

1	2	3	4	5	6	7	8	9
37	137	154	167	170	210	225	237	262

BOWLING ANALYSIS
First Innings

	O.	M.	R.	W.			O.	M.	R.	W.
Lindwall	32	7	70	4	Davidson		10	1	26	0
Miller	34	12	65	1	Archer		10·3	2	25	1
Johnston	45	16	94	3	Hole		11	6	11	0

FALL OF WICKET

Second Innings

$$\frac{1}{24}$$

BOWLING ANALYSIS

Second Innings

	O.	M.	R.	W.		O.	M.	R.	W.
Lindwall	2	0	8	0	Johnston	6	2	16	0
Miller	6	2	14	0	Archer	1	1	0	0

FIFTH TEST (FOURTH DAY)

THE OVAL, WEDNESDAY

In sunshine which might have come to us from an August at Kennington Oval more than a quarter of a century ago, a victory for England over Australia was vociferously celebrated today.

The result on paper suggests that after all the prize came to us fairly comfortably, but as a fact every run to the end needed hard work and determination to get. The Australians fought vehemently until a boundary hit or two would settle the issue. Then Hassett bowled like a gallant captain and opponent who chivalrously chose to be the first to present the laurel wreath.

Had the gentlest wind of chance blown Australia's way the finish would have unsettled the nerves and, possibly, unseated judgment. W. A. Johnston, Australia's only spin bowler, missed taking important wickets by inches, for several mis-hits from him eluded a field which on the whole appeared as omnipresent as avid and brilliantly safe.

TOO MUCH FOR JOHNSTON

But though no patriotic spectator dared take events for granted, the die was all the time cast against Australia. Ably and manfully though Johnston worked away, over after over, the wicket called for spin at the other end of the pitch as well. England needed too few runs with no need for hurry. No single bowler not a genius in his class could have won the match by dint of his own arm in the circumstances which challenged and brought the best out of Johnston, as splendid and sterling-hearted a cricketer as Australia ever sent to us.

Hassett, in a humorous speech to the crowd, paid his generous tribute to England. He has the philosophy to ask himself, now the battle is done, if he did not make a mistake in going into action at the

249

Oval in so crucial an engagement with inadequate reserves of spin.

Edrich's unbeaten innings of 55 was worth framing in gold. He controlled the bridge on a voyage by no means sailed in smooth and entirely charted waters. Throughout my comments on these Test matches, I have taken the view that the collective ability of the two teams was so evenly balanced that the merest straw of chance would sway the scales. England have won today because they commanded in Lock and Laker the bowlers suitable to the wicket on which Australia had to bat when the issue was anybody's.

LESSON

One lesson of the rubber should already find the Australians at least receptive. So long as wickets are covered in Australia so long will England win matches against Australia in this country whenever rain and sun or wearing turf call for batsmen experienced against spin. It was England's turn, as they say, and every cricketer will be mightily pleased that all's well that ends well, for Hutton's sake. With heavy weight of responsibility on his shoulders he has done his job with unwavering patience and determination. England, and —as important—all Yorkshire, may be proud of him, more than ever.

In the hushed presence of a huge crowd Lindwall began the morning with a fairly amiable over to May, who played it with the middle of the bat. Then after another over by Johnston, also a maiden, thanks to brilliant fielding by Harvey who stopped a fine hit to the covers by Edrich, May drove Lindwall beautifully for three to the off with time to spare. For Johnston's efforts at spin Hassett optimistically placed three slips and a very close forward leg. May hit him past Harvey for four, a stroke so swift and perfectly timed that even Harvey was reduced to immobility. In the same over Johnston ominously struck the pads of both May and Edrich, appealing abortively and not with pronounced conviction in the first instance.

Lindwall bowled to a field with only one slip in it, two short legs, a third man, a long leg, a mid-on, a cover, and a mid-off; a defensive arrangement for him. Australia dared not risk to give a single run away. If by some miracle Australia could win even now, it would be only through the agency of Johnston that one could be worked. Had Ian Johnston been in action at the other end England might have stood only an even chance of winning.

An intended drive by May, which went over the slips hazardously, was evidence that Johnston could achieve the spin he urgently desired, given the right length and pace, though on the whole I fancied the pitch was far less sharp-tempered than it was yesterday afternoon. Johnston also turned one away quickly from the bat of Edrich when England were 60 for one, and thumped Edrich's glove the same over. Was the influence of the roller passing away, we tremulously asked ourselves, and thanked God that Grimmett was living in permanent retirement in Adelaide; and O'Reilly, though present now at the Oval, was safely occupied, and busily occupied, with a typewriter in the press box.

LINDWALL'S RESOURCE

Lindwall proved his command of an artistry and resource rare in fast bowlers. He placed a second slip and pitched an accurate length alternating from off to leg, thus keeping down the runs on a wicket not in his favour, and with an ageing ball. May received another quick away spinner from Johnston, his score 22 and England's 63, and was lucky indeed not to be caught high up in the slips. Then Edrich pulled Lindwall sweepingly for 4 and cut him, easing the tension; for the tight accuracy of the bowling had been getting on our, if not the batsmen's, nerves.

After an hour and a quarter's industrious accuracy Lindwall rested and Miller came on in his place with off-breaks. Lindwall, as honest servitor, put me in mind of shorn Samson at the millstone.

Yet again was May thrice blessed against a spinner from Johnston, only just escaping capture from an unpolicied slice over the slips. His score was 31 and England's 81 when we drew breath again. In Johnston's next over Edrich, too, came within an inch of falling to a slip catch; nothing of luck seemed to come Johnston's way. He was much more dangerous now than during his earlier overs, and with only the faintest of fortune's smiles he would have changed the quiet hopeful scene into pandemonium and the pleasant August high noon into a day of wrath.

May was guilty of another dreadful reflex action against Miller, then drove him for 4 to the off gloriously, and next ball swung round to leg and was caught there by Davidson, diving sideways graceful as could be. England 88 for two; only 44 needed now—and thank our stars the sum wasn't the 64 which might not have increased England's first-innings score if Bailey had failed at the pinch—if we may suppose without hurting his feelings that he could in any circumstances, and at any pinch, have failed England this Coronation year.

When Compton arrived at the crease, Lindwall returned to the attack for Miller, and by means of a clever steering stroke off him through the slips Edrich made England's total a hundred exactly. But Johnston yet again beat the bat, this time Edrich's, to no benefit of himself. He nonplussed Compton into the bargain and after two hours' splendid craft returned to the Pavilion at lunch without reward of a solitary wicket. It was after a similar unfair frustration that Cecil Parkin, when he had bowled magnificently two hours in vain, contemplated his analysis of fifteen overs and none for thirty and said, 'And they send missionaries to China!'

This morning Johnston's figures were eighteen overs, eleven maidens for 24 runs. He played a lone hand, and following a spell in which his pace was a shade too fast and his length a shade too short found the right rhythm. He technically defeated each of his opponents in turn, May thrice, Edrich twice at least, and Compton once in fact and more than once potentially.

In two hours England had made 63. We were not exactly riding to port triumphantly full sail, as severely baling out the boat to shore in a heavy sea. Thirty-one runs were all our hearts' desire when the match was resumed after the interval, Lindwall and Johnston in attack, and Edrich cut Johnston through Hole's legs at second slip for three, but he had again been hard pressed to cope with a spinner.

Edrich batted always with strong stern resolution. He turned Johnston sinuously to leg, where De Courcy writhed and spiralled as though for dear life to save the four, but in vain. He might well have been trying to stop the winning hit with only one wicket standing, so gallant was the despair of his effort.

Edrich, head over the ball, watchful and quick to hook or pull any short stuff on the leg stump or cut whenever the length and direction were suitable, continued to play experienced, assuring cricket, and the celebration of his fifty was exasperatingly delayed by truly beautiful fielding by De Courcy and Davidson. By a straight drive for two from Lindwall, Edrich reached the goal, to the full content of the crowd, after three hours twenty minutes' unrelaxed vigilance and skill. And a dozen runs more would bring in the consummation devoutly wished by thousands, and everybody hoped Edrich would still be there at the kill. Compton, a not altogether well-tuned second fiddle, contributed his portion.

At a quarter to three England wanted only nine, and Hassett went on to bowl in place of the heroically thwarted Johnston, whereat the police guarded the boundary and Hassett missed Edrich's leg stump, much to his amusement.

ENGLAND v. AUSTRALIA

Compton made the winning hit, a pull from Morris, at five minutes to three, Davidson having flung himself body's length and stopped a four the previous ball. Then the crowd ran over the field and congealed in a mass in front of the Pavilion, where the heroes were severally hailed, in vocally resonant, if not musical, numbers.

AUSTRALIA

First Innings		Second Innings	
A. L. Hassett, c Evans, b Bedser	53	lbw, b Laker	10
A. R. Morris, lbw, b Bedser	16	lbw, b Lock	26
K. R. Miller, lbw, b Bailey	1	c Trueman, b Laker	0
R. N. Harvey, c Hutton, b Trueman	36	b Lock	1
G. B. Hole, c Evans, b Trueman	37	lbw, b Laker	17
J. H. de Courcy, c Evans, b Trueman	5	run out	4
R. G. Archer, c and b Bedser	10	c Edrich, b Lock	49
A. K. Davidson, c Edrich, b Laker	22	b Lock	21
R. R. Lindwall, c Evans, b Trueman	62	c Compton, b Laker	12
G. R. Langley, c Edrich, b Lock	18	c Trueman, b Lock	2
W. A. Johnston, not out	9	not out	6
Extras (b 4, nb 2)	6	Extras (b 11, lb 3)	14
Total	275	Total	162

FALL OF WICKETS
First Innings

1	2	3	4	5	6	7	8	9
38	41	107	107	118	160	160	207	245

BOWLING ANALYSIS
First Innings

	O.	M.	R.	W.		O.	M.	R.	W.
Bedser	29	3	88	3	Lock	9	2	19	1
Trueman	24·3	3	86	4	Laker	5	0	34	1
Bailey	14	3	42	1					

FALL OF WICKETS
Second Innings

1	2	3	4	5	6	7	8	9
23	59	60	61	61	85	135	140	144

BOWLING ANALYSIS
Second Innings

	O.	M.	R.	W.		O.	M.	R.	W.
Bedser	11	2	24	0	Laker	16·5	2	75	4
Trueman	2	1	4	0	Lock	21	9	45	5

ENGLAND

First Innings		Second Innings	
L. Hutton, b Johnston	82	run out	17
W. J. Edrich, lbw, b Lindwall	21	not out	55
P. B. H. May, c Archer, b Johnston	39	c Davidson, b Miller	37
D. C. S. Compton, c Langley, b Lindwall	16	not out	22
T. W. Graveney, c Miller, b Lindwall	4		
T. E. Bailey, b Archer	64		
T. G. Evans, run out	28		
J. C. Laker, c Langley, b Miller	1		
G. A. R. Lock, c Davidson, b Lindwall	4		
F. S. Trueman, b Johnston	10		
A. V. Bedser, not out	22		
Extras (b 9, lb 5, w 1)	15	Extra (lb 1)	1
Total	306	Total (2 wkts)	132

FALL OF WICKETS
First Innings

1	2	3	4	5	6	7	8	9
37	137	154	167	170	210	225	237	262

BOWLING ANALYSIS
First Innings

	O.	M.	R.	W.		O.	M.	R.	W.
Lindwall	32	7	70	4	Davidson	10	1	26	0
Miller	34	12	65	1	Archer	10·3	2	25	1
Johnston	45	16	94	3	Hole	11	6	11	0

FALL OF WICKETS
Second Innings

1	2
24	88

BOWLING ANALYSIS
Second Innings

	O.	M.	R.	W.		O.	M.	R.	W.
Lindwall	21	5	46	0	Archer	1	1	0	0
Miller	11	3	24	1	Hassett	1	0	4	0
Johnston	29	14	52	0	Morris	0·5	0	5	0

Umpires: D. Davies, and F. S. Lee.